MW00824890

Principles
of Interpreting
the Revelation

Kevin J. Conner

Eric James Barrett

Principles of Interpreting the Revelation

*All scriptures taken from the King James
Version unless otherwise noted*

Published by City Bible Publishing
9200 NE Fremont
Portland, Oregon 97220

Printed in U.S.A.

City Bible Publishing is a ministry of City Bible Church, and is dedicated to serving the local church and its leaders through the production and distribution of quality materials.

It is our prayer that these materials, proven in the context of the local church, will equip leaders in exalting the Lord and extending His kingdom.

For a free catalog of additional resources from City Bible Publishing please call 1-800-777-6057 or visit our web site at www.citybiblepublishing.com.

Interpreting the Book of Revelation
© Copyright 1995 by Kevin J. Conner
All Rights Reserved

USA ISBN 0-914936-10-7
AUST. ISBN 0-949829-28-5

No portion of this book may be reproduced, stored in a retrieval system, or transmitted in any form or by any means electronic, mechanical photocopy, recording, or any other except for brief quotations in printed reviews, without the prior permission of the Publisher. Rights for publishing this book in other languages are contracted by City Bible Publishing.

ABOUT THE BOOK

"Principles of Interpreting The Revelation" has a twofold purpose: (1) It can be used on its own, or, (2) It can be used as a companion volume to **"Interpreting The Scriptures"** (Conner/Malmin).

In this latter text, the co-authors deal with the Science and Art of Hermeneutics. The text provides a condensed History of Hermeneutics, and the attendant problems which arose out of faulty principles of interpretation. The majority of the text deals with at least seventeen Principles of Interpretation that should be used in interpreting the Sacred Scriptures.

In the final chapter of that text, the chapter entitled, **"The Interpretation of Prophecy"**, a demonstration, by way of application, is given in the use of most of those principles, in brief, to the Book of Hosea.

This present text takes most of the same principles and applies them to the major eschatological book of the New Testament – The Book of Revelation.

Because of this, there is a certain and necessary amount of repetition from the previous text. It is recommended that the serious student acquire that text and use it as a foundation textbook for this companion volume.

However, this present text has been written in such a way that it is complete in itself apart from the other. This text deals with, what the author believes are, sound principles of interpretation that can and should be used in any exposition of The Revelation.

In a **Supplemental Chapter**, there are fifteen **Self-Study Guide Assignments** for the earnest student to do. These assignments take each of the fifteen Principles of Interpretation dealt with in this text, and, because hermeneutics is a science (knowing the rules), and an art (applying the rules), the student is challenged to apply these to some portion of Revelation.

The author has this assurance, that, whichever Eschatological School of Interpretation the readers identify with, and whatever difference of opinion or disagreement over the contents of this book, they will still find much that will be of help in the interpretation and understanding of this marvellous, amazing and miraculously inspired book – **The Book of Revelation.**

PRINCIPLES OF INTERPRETING THE REVELATION
TABLE OF CONTENTS

FOREWORD

Of all the expositions of the Book of Revelation the writer has read, very few writers really seem to set out the Hermeneutical Principles which have been used in their exposition. The more diligent student has to seek to discover them. This can only be done if the student has some knowledge and understanding of the science and art of hermeneutics - that is, the principles of Biblical interpretation.

It is this writer's strong conviction that a person's preaching, teaching and even counselling all rise out of two major platforms: sound theology and sound hermeneutics. These two may be likened to two sides of the same coin. Theology is one side and hermeneutics is the other side.

A person's hermeneutics determines a person's theology and a person's theology affects their hermeneutics. Proper application of the Word of God is dependent upon proper interpretation of the Word of God. Therefore, Biblical exposition, Biblical preaching and teaching must be founded on proper principles of hermeneutics, proper exegesis and sound Biblical theology.

It could also be said that sound hermeneutics, sound exegesis and sound theology are like a "threefold cord that cannot be quickly broken" (Ecclesiastes 4:12).

Of the number of text-books that this writer has written and published, the two most important text-books, in his mind, would be **"Interpreting the Scriptures"** (Conner/Malmin), and **"The Foundations of Christian Doctrine"** (Conner). The reason for this has already been stated. The first concerns sound hermeneutics, the latter concerns sound theology.

The student or reader of the writer's publications will see that, underlying and woven throughout all texts, the writer has sought to use Biblical principles of interpretation and follow Biblically sound theology.

Any time a text-book is written, the writer asks himself: Is sound theology woven throughout the text, and are there proper hermeneutical principles being used in expounding the Scriptures?

With reference to this present book, the writer believes that it cannot be over-emphasized or recommended strongly enough that the student obtain the text-book out of which this text arises; that is, **"Interpreting the Scriptures"** (Conner/Malmin). The reason for this will be obvious.

In **"Interpreting the Scriptures"**, the co-authors have done a fuller treatment of the subject of Hermeneutics, as to it's History, Foundation, and Principles. At the conclusion of that text, the authors provided an example, in brief, of the use and application of the listed hermeneutical principles to the writings of the prophet Hosea.

In this text, the writer has simply taken most of those hermeneutical principles and applied them to the Book of Revelation. Most of the principles spelled out in **"Interpreting the Scriptures"** have been used, adapted and applied to The Revelation. There has been a certain amount of repetition from that text into this text. This has been done for those students who do not have the afore-mentioned text, as well as preparation for the application of hermeneutical principles to the Book of Revelation.

The writer has completed, for his personal enjoyment, an unpublished verse by verse exposition of the Book of Revelation.

Because of this, and the numerous questions students ask about Revelation, the writer believes it would be helpful to provide a smaller text-book which sets forth the principles of interpretion that have been used in this exposition. This present text is the result. If the serious student uses these principles, he will be able to complete his own exposition or studies of this amazing book.

Each student should remind himself of the science and laws of the universe. A scientist does not **make** the laws of the universe. He simply **discovers** and **uses** them! So it is with hermeneutics. It is God who **made** certain laws of Biblical interpretation when He inspired, by His Spirit, the writers of Scripture. Man does not **make** these laws. The expositor's work is simply to **discover** and use these laws to do proper Biblical exegesis!

This is what the co-authors sought to accomplish in **"Interpreting the Scriptures"**. This is what the author has sought to accomplish in this text, **"Principles of Interpreting The Revelation"**.

In this text, the reader will be reminded of the hermeneutical principles of interpretation and then given examples of application. It is not meant to be, in any way, an exposition of The Revelation. It is simply to provide a demonstration of the application of hermeneutical principles and interpretative keys that should be applied in doing an exposition.

May the reader find as much joy and fulfilment in using and applying these hermeneutical principles to **"The Book of Ultimates"** - The Book of Revelation - as the writer himself has found over many years!

Kevin J.Conner
P.O. Box 300
Vermont
Victoria. 3133
AUSTRALIA

March 1995

CHAPTER ONE
HERMENEUTICAL PROBLEMS OF THE REVELATION

Undoubtedly one of the most difficult books in the Bible to interpret is **The Book of Revelation.**

As far as can be determined, it was the last book of the Bible to be written under inspiration of the Holy Spirit. Also, because of the nature of its contents, it is placed as the last book of the Bible, in the Sacred Canon of Scripture. The book was written about the close of the first century, although some expositors propose an earlier date.

Although the Bible, as a whole, has suffered much under the hands of unbelievers, and even believers, there are certain books of the Bible that have experienced greater attacks than the others. These books are the books of (1) Genesis, (2) Daniel and (3) Revelation. That is, the first, the twentyninth and the sixtysixth books of the Bible.

Any true believer, having some working knowledge of these books can see why there has been such an attack on the inspiration and contents of these books, being the first and the last books Genesis and Revelation, and Daniel, being nearer the middle of the Holy Library. Genesis is incomplete without Revelation. Revelation is incomplete without Daniel and Daniel is incomplete without Revelation. It is virtually impossible to interpret the book of Revelation without these other books, let alone the rest of the books of the Bible.

The author of this text has, over the years, read about forty different expositions of the Revelation. Most of them were contradictory. Some were extreme in their interpretation. Revelation is a book that has been the subject of ridicule and endless confusion. Because of the numerous, contradictory and extreme interpretations of this book and the confusion resultant from these things, many of God's people will not even read it. Even many preachers and teachers of the Gospel will not minister from this book because of other preachers and expositors who are in conflicting and contradictory mood.

Behind this, one has to perceive that the real author of confusion is Satan himself, exploiting, many times, the carnal minds of believers and the traditions of men. After all, the book of Revelation pronounces his final doom and eternal judgement in the lake of fire. However, the book does pronounce a distinct blessing on those that **"read, hear and keep"** the words of this book (Revelation 1:3).

As the second coming of the Lord approaches, the churches - to whom the book was sent - should seek the Lord for clear understanding of this book of ultimates, and be prepared for His coming.

The author has sought to discover WHY there is so much confusion about this book, and WHY there are so many conflicting interpretations among those who truly love the Lord and His appearing.

The answer presented here is applicable to the whole issue of Biblical interpretation. The answer may seem simplistic, but it is **an answer** and the author believes it is **THE ANSWER** to the whole question of **"WHY"** there are so many contradictory interpretations of this majestic book.

The root problem concerns the lack of use of proper principles of Biblical interpretation, or, in other words, Biblical Hermeneutics !

In the **Foreword** of the text, **"Interpreting the Scriptures"**, the authors (Conner/Malmin) say: "Generally speaking, Bible believing Christians are united in accepting the facts of **revelation and inspiration.** However, the major divisions and differences concern **interpretation and application.** Therefore we say, the problem is not over **"revelation and inspiration"** so much as it is over **"interpretation and application".**

The definition of these words becomes important to the understanding of the interpreter.

A. Revelation

Revelation is truth imparted which could not be discovered by natural reasoning. The Bible is the written revelation of God. All that man needs to know of God as to His nature, character and being, in this present earthly state, is founded in the holy and infallible Scriptures.

The Book of Revelation is such a revelation, revealing to man end-time events, from the establishment of the New Testament church to the coming of Christ, and then on into the eternal states. The events given to John could not be discovered by natural reasoning. All was given to John by revelation on the isle of Patmos (Revelation 1:9-10). All who would give themselves to expound this book must accept it as a revelation from God through man to man.

B. Inspiration

Inspiration describes the process by which revelation is recorded . The Scriptures are an infallible revelation recorded under inspiration of the Holy Spirit. As with all the other books of the Bible, so God brought forth infallible revelation through the apostle John, a fallible man, using his unique personality and giftings. Therefore the book of Revelation was written under inspiration of the blessed Holy Spirit. All who would expound this book must also accept it as revelation written under Divine inspiration (2Peter 1:20-21; 2Timothy 3: 16).

C. Interpretation

Interpretation has to do with hermeneutics. Webster's Dictionary defines hermeneutics as "the science of interpretation, or of finding the meaning of an author's words and phrases, and of explaining it to others; exegesis; particularly applied to the interpretation of the Scriptures." Hermeneutics has also been defined as both "the science and art of Biblical interpretation." As a science, it is concerned with proper principles of interpretation, and as an art, it is concerned with the proper application of those principles. Such is appropriate to all Biblical interpretation, but here we speak of the book of Revelation. What does the book of Revelation really mean? What principles can one use to properly expound this book? Improper principles certainly have produced improper and multiple interpretations of this book, which certainly must displease the Lord Jesus Christ, the head of the church.

The one who seeks to expound this book must seek and study to have proper Biblical principles of interpretation (2Timothy 2:15). Jesus Himself is the perfect and infallible interpreter of the Scriptures (Luke 24:27). He gave to the early apostles principles of interpretation by which His word can be expounded and understood. The purpose of this text is to set out Biblical principles of interpretation for use in, what can be, sound exposition.

D. Application

Application has to do more particularly with exegesis. The word "exegesis" means "to guide or lead out". It refers to bringing out the meaning of any writing which might otherwise be difficult to understand. Hermeneutics supplies the **principles** of interpretation, while exegesis describes the **process** of interpretation. Exegesis involves the **application** of the rules of hermeneutics. Proper **interpretation** of God's Word precedes proper **application** of God's Word!

Theologically speaking, application is taking truth revealed to one person or group and making it relate to another. The basis for this is the understanding that God's principles are timeless, that truth is truth in every generation. What is truth today was truth then. Truth is eternal. Scripture becomes the measuring rod of theology and theology becomes the measuring rod of personal application. Misapplication of the Scriptures arises out of misinterpretation of the Scriptures.

E. Illumination

One other word could be linked with the previous words, and that is the word **"illumination"**. **Illumination** has to do with the **perception** of truth brought about by the influence of the Holy Spirit. The believer should continually seek the Lord to give **illumination** on the **revelation** given by **inspiration.**

Sometimes teachers claim "revelation" as they expound the book of Revelation. Theologically this is not Scripturally sound. What they have received is simply some illumination on the revelation written under inspiration. Illumination is the Lord opening the eyes of one's understanding to receive that which is revealed in Scripture (Ephesians 1:17-18).

The Holy Spirit knows what He meant when He inspired John to write the Revelation. This necessitates the need for illumination, as it is the Holy Spirit's ministry to lead us into all truth and show us things to come (John 15:26; 16:12,13). The Holy Spirit as the Agent of revelation and inspiration also becomes the Agent of illumination, interpretation and application!

Thus:-   Revelation – Truth given

Inspiration – Truth recorded

Interpretation – Truth expounded

Application – Truth applied

Illumination – Truth understood

Solving the hermeneutical problems among expositors would certainly go a long way on the path to a more sure and sound exposition of the book of Revelation. Anyone who expounds the book of Revelation needs to have (1) Opened eyes, and (2) Opened Scriptures and (3) Opened understanding (Luke 24:31,32,44,45).

True Christians believe that the book of Revelation is indeed a revelation of God, from God. True Christians believe the book of Revelation was written under the inspiration of the Holy Spirit and that it is indeed a revelation given by inspiration of God, from God, to man, through man. There is unity over the matter of revelation and inspiration.

The differences, as already seen, have to do with interpretation and application. Each preacher or expositor has "their interpretation". Some even say that there are "many interpretations" of this book. So the interpretations may vary.

The same is true also, as already seen, of application. Application arises out of interpretation. Depending on the expositors principles of interpretation, the book has been applied to (1) The Church, or (2) The Jews or (3) The World, or to a combination of these. It has been applied to the past, the present and the future or to a combination of these.

In Summary: The author believes that if expositors of the book of Revelation had used proper Biblical hermeneutics - Biblical principles of interpretation - then there would not be the diverse interpretations that there are in our day. This is not to say all expositors are wrong, nor does this author in any way claim infallibility. However, this present text does endeavour to set forth Biblical principles of interpretation that should be used to interpret the book of Revelation.

One Final Word: The author very strongly recommends the reading and studying of the text already referred to; that is, **"Interpreting the Scriptures"** (Conner/Malmin). This present text is predominantly built on the hermeneutical principles set forth in that text. In reality, this text is simply an example or demonstration of the use and application of the principles of interpretation to the book of Revelation.

This text is in no way meant to be an exposition of Revelation, but a setting forth of principles that one should use in any exposition of this marvellous, amazing and majestic book. These are the principles which the writer himself has used in expounding this book.

CHAPTER TWO
SCHOOLS OF INTERPRETATION OF THE REVELATION

The expositor who puts his hand to this book will need to recognize the various Schools of Interpretation, for, undoubtedly, he will align predominantly with one of these Schools. Following are the major Schools of Interpretation. It will be seen that each have elements of truth, but, as a general rule, each have a large number of inconsistencies. It is these inconsistencies and contradictions that nullify their appeal as proper keys of interpretation of the book of Revelation. Other writers have dealt more fully with these various Schools of Interpretation, hence the brevity of definition and explanation given here (Refer Bibliography).

A. Preterist School - Time Past

The Preterist position, simply stated, is that the book of Revelation was intended to meet the needs of the threatened and suffering Christians of the churches of John's day. This view sees Revelation as symbolic of Roman persecution of the church, Emperor worship and the Divine judgments on Rome. Revelation relates only to those events, which are already fulfilled, and not to the future.

A Preterist is one whose chief concern is with the past. A Preterist maintains that the prophecies of the Revelation have been fulfilled in early Church History. The Preterist believes that the Revelation (Chapters 1-20) is simply a sketch of the history of conditions existing in the first century, under the Roman Empire. Revelation simply depicts the struggle of apostate Judaism, the paganism of political and ecclesiastical Rome against Christianity. The Preterist stresses the historical background of Revelation. Eternal destinies are predominantly taught in the final two chapters of the Revelation (Chapters 21-22).

Preterists see no predictive prophecy in the Revelation but do see much meaning for the churches mentioned in that early stage of history. Emperor worship would be judged, and the Rome/Babylon world would be judged, and eternity would bring blessings and great rewards for the saints.

Therefore the bulk of the book, according to this view, with the exception of those passages dealing with the day of judgment, was fulfilled in the early years of the Christian age.

The only real value for following generations of the church would be the lessons learnt from early Church History as depicted in so much of the symbolism in the Revelation. In a chronological time-line, the Preterist view would be:-

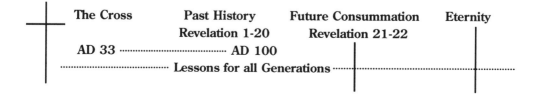

Undoubtedly, the early church saw application to their times, and received Divine strength and encouragement from the Revelation and its ultimate outcome of triumph in eternity. However, to say that Revelation was just the history of the first century and was fulfilled by the close thereof robs the book of what it really teaches concerning certain specifics pertaining to future events which are in the book, especially the events pertaining to the second coming of Christ.

B. Historicist School - Time Continuous

The Historicist position sees in the book of Revelation an unfolding of human history throughout the entire Gospel era. Various signs and symbols of the book are made to relate to various historical events.The Historicist is one who sees the Revelation giving a symbolic or allegorical panoramic presentation of the history of the church from the close of the first century and the apostle John to Christ's coming at the very end of time.

The Historical view is sometimes called the "continuous-historical" view, or a continuous-history application. The seven churches, the seven seals, the seven trumpets and the seven vials of wrath are all made to represent some particular part of history between John and the end of the present age.

The advocates of the Historicist School basically agree on the method of interpretation but there is not general agreement about the details. This method is often seen to be extreme in its interpretation. Extreme spiritualization (or allegorization) may be discovered in the various expositors in this School of Interpretation. One would have to be a profound student of history to even grasp the method applied in the Historicist School..

Irving L. Jensen in "Revelation" (p.19) says: "The continuous-historical view applies Revelation prophetically to all the centuries since the time of Christ. Only chapters 19-22 foretell events after Christ's coming."

In a chronological time-line, the Historicist view would be :-

The Cross

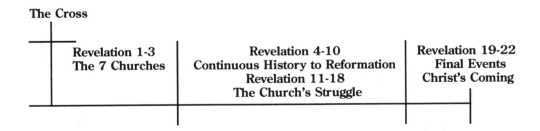

| Revelation 1-3 The 7 Churches | Revelation 4-10 Continuous History to Reformation Revelation 11-18 The Church's Struggle | Revelation 19-22 Final Events Christ's Coming |

Again, there would be some element of truth in the fact that Revelation does find its fulfilment in Church History. But the issue would be trying to force or slot the seals, the trumpets, and vials into certain periods of time without Scriptural warrant. The books this writer has read on the Historicist view are mostly extreme spiritualizations and allegorizations applied to events in church history.

Principles of Interpreting the Revelation

C. Presentist School - Time Unfolding

The Presentist view teaches that Revelation has an (a) Historical, (b) Present and a (c) Future significance.

The Presentist teaches that the Revelation showed to the early church that Christ was in control and He would triumph through all ages. The Revelation was written to encourage Christians in every age and each generation. The Presentist sees that Revelation contains visions of recapitulation covering the same period of time from a different point of view.

The seven churches, the seven seals, the seven trumpets and the seven vials are illustrations of this and are spoken of as "progressive parallelisms", as such unfold throughout church history, from the early church to Christ's advent. There are definate future events described in symbolic language.

The "Progressive Parallelism" view considers the book of Revelation as consisting of seven complete pictures of this Gospel age, presenting in symbolic language the principles of action which are characteristic of Divine, Satanic and human life. This means, that throughout the Revelation, you find the writer looking at the age from a different viewpoint in seven sections of the book, each section beginning with the start of the age and running through to the end of the age.

On a chronological time-line, the Presentist view, as a general method, would be :-

The Cross

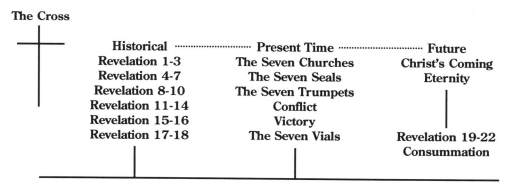

Historical	Present Time	Future
Revelation 1-3	The Seven Churches	Christ's Coming
Revelation 4-7	The Seven Seals	Eternity
Revelation 8-10	The Seven Trumpets	
Revelation 11-14	Conflict	
Revelation 15-16	Victory	
Revelation 17-18	The Seven Vials	Revelation 19-22
		Consummation

As with the previous view, there are elements of truth seen in much of this view. There is something in Revelation for every generation of believers. However, this view raises the question of hermeneutics again. What principles of interpretation can be rightly used to come up with the "progressive parallelistic" approach as in this general overview given here?

D. Idealist School - Time Principles

The Idealist view (sometimes referred to as the Symbolic or Spiritualist view) are those who lay great emphasis on the the spiritual elements, the spiritual truths, in this book. The Idealist does not attempt to interpret the meaning of the more mysterious visions. The Idealists believe that there are basically three classes of passages in the Revelation.

(a) Passages which are very clear in their spiritual teaching

(b) Passages that are more mysterious, yet contain instructive elements of truth

(c) Passages that have visions so veiled in symbolism that it is impossible to interpret them with any accuracy.

This view sees Revelation as a symbolic portrait of the cosmic conflict of spiritual principles. Revelation is not a predictive prophecy and is not to be identified with specific historical events. To the Idealist, the events of history are not so important as the spiritual lessons and the Divine principles underlying all. The timeless principles of Revelation reveal the conflict between good and evil in every age, to the very end. Revelation reveals the principle of Divine sovereignty and the final overthrow of all that is evil. Human history and destiny are not in the hands of men but in the hands of God and His Christ.

Revelation is but a symbolic portrait of the conflict of these spiritual principles rather than a predictive prophecy of specific historical events. Idealist expositors of the Revelation must look for spiritual truths and lessons in the series of visions given to John.

In a chronological time-line, the Idealist view would be:

The Cross

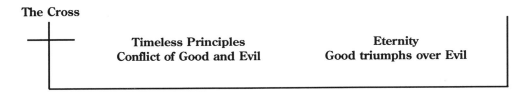

As with previous views, the Idealist method has some elements of truth. Truth is timeless. The principles of God's truth are indeed applicable in every generation. Any expositor of the Revelation should seek for spiritual truths and principles for his generation. However, application of truth must be founded upon proper interpretation of truth first.

The Idealist view leaves much to be desired in order to have a fuller and proper understanding and interpretation of the Revelation.

E. Futurist School - Time Future

The Futurist view holds the teaching that Revelation is a forecast of Church History, and that most of Revelation finds it's fulfilment in the "end-times", the final years before the second coming of Christ.

Though there are variations in this method and system of interpretation, generally speaking, the seven local churches in Asia represent seven eras of Church History. Chapters 1-3 are covered thereby.

Revelation chapters 4-18 have to do with a final period of tribulation in the earth, either seven years or three and one-half years, prior to Christ's coming.

Revelation 19 is Christ's actual second coming. Revelation 20 is spoken of as the future Millenniel Kingdom Age while Revelation 21-22 speak of the eternal states of the lost and the saved; unbelievers and believers.

Of the various schools, the Futurist sees most of Revelation from chapters 4-22 as prophetic of the "end-times", a short period of the time before Christ's return. As a general rule, the Futurist holds Revelation 1:19 as the key verse to the book. "Write the things which thou hast seen, and the things which are, and the things which shall be hereafter."

In a chronological time-line, generally speaking, the Futurist view would be:-

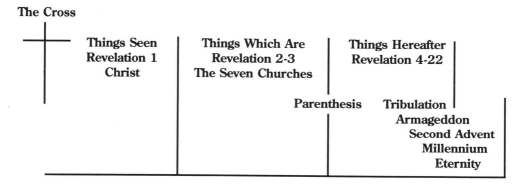

The Cross

Things Seen Revelation 1 Christ	Things Which Are Revelation 2-3 The Seven Churches	Things Hereafter Revelation 4-22
	Parenthesis	Tribulation Armageddon Second Advent Millennium Eternity

The Futurist method follows a more literal interpretation of the contents of Revelation than each of the other Schools. Also, the Futurist does not, generally speaking, tamper with the book as much as do the other Schools. The Futurist basically leaves the book to unfold in reasonable chronological order in which the chapters are written. It is certainly a much simpler approach in seeking to understand the book.

Though there are variations within the Futurist School, there is the basic view that the majority of the Revelation is in the future and finds fulfilment shortly before the Lord Jesus Christ returns the second time.

In summarizing the several Schools of Interpretation, it will be seen that the underlying major problem has to with the **"time element"** - the chronology of the Revelation. The issue is **WHEN** was the Revelation fulfilled? Or is it being fulfilled? Or has it yet to be fulfilled?

1. **For the Preterist,** all was fulfilled in John's day and early church history - Time Past!

2. **For the Historicist,** all is being fulfilled from John's day through to the second coming of Christ - Time Continuous!

3. **For the Presentist,** all is being unfolded during Church History and all will consummate at Christ's coming - Time Unfolding!

4. **For the Idealist,** all simply represents the conflict between good and evil over human and church history and the good wins out in the end - Time Principles!

5. **For the Futurist,** all will find fulfillment about the close of church history, and in the final years before Christ comes again - Time Future!

Is Revelation time past, time present or time future? Whether interpreted symbolically or literally, the issue of chronology is a major issue. Though John wrote of the things which must" **"shortly come to pass",** saying **"the time is at hand",** it is now over 1900 years since the Book of Revelation was written and the ultimate events of the book have not yet come to pass !

Christ has not yet returned. The final judgments have not taken place. The eternal city of God has not as yet been revealed.

The author of this text believes that **"the chronometrical principle"** is one of the important principles of interpretation that needs to be used for a proper understanding of this book. This will be considered in it's particular chapter.

So we may conclude this chapter by saying :-

Each of these systems of interpretation contain some elements of truth. No one system is the whole truth, as there is much of Revelation that has not been fulfilled. The final events of the final chapters of Revelation will find fulfilment in the end of the age and the generations that are alive to the coming of Christ. Revelation, if not tampered with, is, we believe, generally a most consecutive book and has enough of chronology within itself to interpret the book as a whole. This will be seen in the appropriate chapter of this text on The Chronometrical Principle.

CHAPTER THREE

THE HISTORICAL BACKGROUND OF THE REVELATION

As with any book of the Bible, be it Old Testament or New Testament, one of the important principles of understanding such is a consideration of the historical setting of that book. This is certainly so when it comes to the Book of Revelation.

A. The Divine Author

The Divine Author is none other than the blessed Holy Spirit. "All Scripture is given by inspiration of God", and Revelation is part of that "all Scripture" (2 Timothy 3:16). Peter tells us that the holy men of God spoke as they were moved and energized by the Spirit of God (2 Peter 1:21). John was one of those holy men of God who spoke and wrote as he was moved by the Spirit. John was "in the Spirit on the Lord's day" when he received the Revelation (Revelation 1:10). The Holy Spirit is the Divine Author, He is the Inspirer of the book.

B. The Human Writer

It is generally accepted that John, the beloved, the writer of the Gospel and three Epistles called by his name, was the writer of the Revelation. In contrast to the Gospel and these Epistles where John does not name himself, in the Revelation, several times, the writer says, "I, John...." (Revelation 1:4,9; 22:8,9). The book is given by the angel to the Lord's servant, John (Revelation 1:1). Some expositors do mention that this John lays no claim to apostleship and may not be the apostle John. Common reasoning of Scripture would point to some apostolic ministry writing such a climatic book which completes the New Testament canon of sacred Scripture.

The writer was in the Isle of Patmos for the word of God and the testimony of Jesus (Revelation 1:9). Whether exiled under a period of persecution or there on itinerant ministry is not stated. Tradition says that the apostle John was banished to the Isle of Patmos under the persecutions of Emperor Domitian to work in the mines. The internal evidence of the book does show that the writer was knowledgeable of the churches in Asia and had been a leader among them. He was also completely knowledgeable of the Old Testament Scriptures as well as being a follower of the Lord Jesus.

C. The Date Written

Two approximate dates have been put forth for the writing of the book of Revelation.

1. Early Date - AD 54-68

This date is during the reign of Nero. Certain expositors say that Revelation was written prior to the destruction of Jerusalem in AD 70 and is simply a prophecy of the coming destruction and desolation of the city, the temple, the land and Jewry.

2. Later Date - AD 81-96

This date is about the close of the reign of Domitian. There is more weight in the historical evidence for this later date than the former, as the following shows.

* Justin Martyr (AD 135) attributes the Book of Revelation to the apostle John.
* Theophilus of Antioch (AD 175) referred to Revelation in one of his writings.
* Irenaeus (AD 180) states it was written in the reign of Domitian, and quotes five passages from the writer as being John.
* Clement of Alexandria (AD 200) cited Revelation as authentic Scripture.
* Victorinus (AD 270) refers to Revelation.
* Eusebius (AD 325) agrees with Irenaeus.
* Jerome (AD 370) also agrees with Irenaeus in his comments.

The declining conditions of the seven churches in Asia would take time to develop from the birthday of the New Testament church (AD 35) and the founding of the various churches in Asia Minor. Most of them would have been planted in Paul's time, and on through to the time that John wrote the Revelation. The declining conditions of the churches would be seen developing in the eyes of the risen Christ. The later date certainly seems to be more preferable and acceptable in the light of these things.

D. Political Rome

Rome was the world kingdom in power at the time of the writing of the Revelation. The "iron rule of Rome" and her emperors was evident throughout the whole of the then-known world. All nations and all languages were under Rome's control.

Rome came into power over Palestine about BC 63 and since that time Jewry never had her independence. Herod the Great (Tetrarch of Galilee) was declared king of Judea about BC 40 and was the king in power during BC 4, at the approximate time of the birth of the Messiah (Matthew 2:1).

It was this Herod who took responsibility for the rebuilding and renovation of the Temple at Jerusalem, although it was never finished during his lifetime. The work began about BC 20, and while the main building was finished quickly, the outlying structures were not completed until about AD 64-66, only several years before the Temple's final destruction under Prince Titus and the Roman armies in AD 70. Herod died about BC 4 (Matthew 2:15,19).

Herod's three sons came into power in his realm after his death. Archaelaus ruled over Judea and Samaria. Antipas ruled over Galilee and Perea. Philip ruled over Trachonitis (Luke 3:1-2).

After reigning about 10 years, Archaelaus being disposed of, the Judeans asked for a Roman Governor to be appointed by Rome. They received a Procurator, whose duties were to collect taxes (sometimes through the Publicans who collected tax for Rome and anything extorted above that they kept!), command the military forces (Luke 3:14) and to act as Judge in special judiciary cases. The Procurator left minor cases to the local courts, or the Sanhedrin, which could try Jews and declare their guilt, but only Pilate could sanction the death penalty. Taxes collected went to Caesar.

Pontius Pilate was the fifth Governor of Judea (AD 25-35), under Tiberius Caesar, at the time of Christ, and it was under his hands the crucifixion of Jesus took place. He was recalled to Rome because of the cruel treatment of his subjects, and history tells us of his death by suicide.

Antipas was successful as a ruler, but married Herodias and was responsible for the death of John the Baptist (Mark 6:14-28).

When Claudius Caesar was emperor, Herod Agrippa I became king over Galillee, Perea, Judea, Idumea and Samaria. He favoured the Jews and was very popular until God struck him dead in AD 44 (Acts 12:1-23).

Palestine came under a period of the rule of the Roman Procurators from about AD 44-66. Palestine had seven Procurators during this time, among them being Felix and Festus (Acts 23,24,25 chapters). This period was a time of stress, upheaval and turmoil and, under the Zealots ended in open rebellion. The Jews were subdued with much cruelty. The Zealots continued in their agitation against Rome until a revolution broke out in AD 66, when one of the Roman Procurators endeavoured to plunder the Temple.

About this period, Vespasian came from Rome, but was recalled owing to the death of the Emperor Nero (AD 64). It was later, under Prince Titus, son of Vespasian, that the final and worst revolt took place. Here the horrible seige of Jerusalem took place, and the Temple was burnt, Jewry was scattered, taken captive and the land was desolated. Since that time, the national identity of Jewry and Judaism ceased. Palestine became desolate of temple, city and people, fulfilling the words of the Lord Jesus Christ (Luke 21:20-24; Matthew 24:1-2 with Leviticus 26).

Thus it is about twentysix years later that John writes to the seven churches in Asia. Rome is still in power. Palestine has been desolated. The Temple has been destroyed. Jewry is non-existent as a nation. Persecution is upon the church. Christianity was spreading and was heard of in the then-known world and was also numerically strong.

Following is a brief list of the Roman Emperors of the First Century unto the writing of the book of Revelation.

1. **Augustus Caesar- BC 31-AD 14.**
   Emperor when Jesus was born. He appointed Herod as king of Judea.
2. **Tiberius - AD 14-AD 37.**
   Appointed Pontius Pilate as Governor of Judea. Antipas was a friend of his.
3. **Caligula - AD 37-AD 41**
   He had an altar built in Judea for Emperor worship and ordered an image to be set up in the Temple at Jerusalem.
4. **Claudius - AD 41- AD 54.**
   Had a prosperous reign. He made Aggripa king of Palestine.
5. **Nero - AD 54 AD 68.**
   He was a cruel and despotic ruler. He burnt Rome, and accused the Christians as being the guilty ones. Christians were burnt at the stake under his rule.

Great persecutions came on the church. Tradition points to Peter and Paul being martyred under him.

6. **Galba, Otho, and Vitellius - AD 68-AD 69.**

   Each succeeded Nero, but each forfeited his life as the price of his ambition.

7. **Vespasian - AD 69-AD 79.**

   He was commander of the Roman legions in Syria and Judea and was proclaimed as Emperor by his army. He sent his son, Titus, to quell the rebellion in Jerusalem. Titus captured and then destroyed the city of Jerusalem and the Temple in AD 70.

8. **Titus - AD 79- AD 81.**

   Reigned peacefully over these years.

9. **Domitian - AD 81- AD 96.**

   He was one of the greatest persecutors of the Roman Emperors. During his time, the apostle John was exiled to the isle of Patmos and John wrote the Revelation. Just after the reign of Domitian, John died at Ephesus (according to tradition) and thus closed off the Apostolic Age.

It was in this First Century that the idea of Roman Emperor worship was promoted as part of Rome's political power. This idea encouraged the position of the emperors to that of 'deity'. Not all the emperors regarded themselves as divine. However, this Emperor-worship eventually became the cause of great persecution for the early church and the Christians throughout the Roman Empire. For the Christian, " Jesus is LORD", NOT any Roman Emperor. For this, both Judaistic Jews and Christians suffered persecutions and death ! The churches in Asia (Turkey) were faced with this constantly. Rome could tolerate each person worshipping their own gods or deities, but the uniting and binding tenet was "Caesar is LORD !". Social status mattered not. Rich or poor, bond or free, high or low class - all must recognize Caesar as LORD!

This then was the political backdrop for the writing of the book of Revelation !

E. Grecian Influence

The Grecian Kingdom, with its Greek culture and language, had left its impression on the world. Greek culture dominated the intellectual life of New Testament times. The Greek language was spoken universally. Greek thought, literature, philosophy and language had affected the then known world.

However, along with Grecian culture and intellectualism came Greek mythology. Greek mythology and symbology centered around the gods; demi-gods, semi-gods, both moral and immoral, most of which was characterized by a mixture of material from mystery religions of Oriental sources. Much was given over to gross sensuality, various rites which included fastings, sacrifices, ritualistic cleansings and ceremonies, along with mystic teachings about God, the gods, the half-god-half-man beings, along with teachings about immortality. But there was no Divine revelation in the wisdom of the Greeks. The city and altar at Athens summarized it when they wrote the inscription on that altar, **"An Altar To The Unknown God"**. Amidst the numerous gods at Athens, this epitomised their spiritual ignorance of the true God (Acts 17:22-23).

Paul also confirms this in 1 Corinthians Chapters one and two when he says that the Greeks with all their wisdom knew not God. Greek religion was both pantheistic and polytheistic.

All of this Grecian culture had its powerful influence on a world into which the Lord Jesus Christ came and into which Christianity was to propagate itself. It was into such a world that the Book of Revelation was to go, written in the Greek language. The affect of this Grecian culture, and mythology as well as the power of Rome was to be seen in the seven letters to the seven churches.

F. Apostate Judaism

The only religions which were of Divine origin were (1) Judaism or the Mosaic economy and (2) New Testament Christianity. All other religions were of Satanic or human origin, as seen in Rome, with its polytheistic religion, as also the Greeks.

Rome encouraged any and all religions, and the worship of national gods. Rome deified anything and everything that would bring health, success, protection or victory in war. Any religion was permitted as long as it encouraged these things and did not conflict with the Roman government or Empirical power, and, as long as the one binding "worship" was "Emperor worship". All other religions could be tolerated as long as this was the hub of the Empire's worship.

Judaism, however, was the only Divinely instituted religion. It was given to Moses by Divine revelation and maintained in a continuous revelation through the Law, the Psalms and the Prophets, until the close of inspiration under the prophet Malachi.

The main features of the Mosaic religion were as follows:-

1. Israel was the covenant nation, in covenantal relationship with the one and only true God.

2. The Law was given as the condition by which covenantal relationship could be maintained, along with the Lord's blessings. The law involved the moral, civil and the ceremonial laws.

3. The priesthood and the sacrificial system were the means of "typical grace" in ceremonial manifestation until the revelation of Prince Messiah who would take away sin by the sacrifice of Himself and His ministry as the eternal priest. The typical means of grace was revealed in the order of both Tabernacle and Temple.

No true prophet of God ever contradicted or violated the foundation principles given by revelation to Moses.

The tragic history of Israel shows how the nation lapsed continually into periods of idolatry and apostasy. For this reason, God permitted the house of Israel and the house of Judah to go into periods of captivity; the two major captivities being, the house of Israel taken into Assyrian Captivity (BC.721), and the house of Judah into Babylonian Captivity (BC.606), the latter being for a period of seventy years. At the close of the seventy years Babylonian Captivity, the house of Judah was restored to Palestine, and the city and the temple were rebuilt. After the ministry of the prophet Malachi, God ceased to speak to His people by the prophets, and Jewry entered into the period known as the "four hundred silent years" unto the ministry of John the Baptist.

During this period of time, Jewry was a subject nation under the Medo-Persian, Grecian and Roman kingdoms, and, at the time of Christ, Rome ruled. Jewry had experienced the ravaging of wars and troubles both within and without.

The religion of Judaism was permitted under Rome so long as it obeyed Roman government legislation. Judaism was legally recognized and protected under Rome. The Sanhedrin was allowed to exercise its powers in Civil affairs. By the time of Messiah's coming, Judaism was mainly corrupted. The important thing, however, was that the Scriptures had been preserved under Jewry (Romans 3.1-2), from which the New Testament writings would proceed, as the flower and fruit from the seed. God had, through this time, preserved unto Himself "a faithful remnant" awaiting the Messiah's coming.

At the time of John the Baptist and the Messiah's ministry, the religion of Judaism consisted of these major things.

1. The Temple

There was only ever one temple and this was the centre of all worship to Jehovah. The Temple became the binding power of Judaism. The high priest, the priests and the tribe of Levi were supported by the tithes and offerings of the people, and the temple itself kept in repair by the temple tax. The sacrifices, the offerings and oblations and the annual festival occassions all centered around the temple routine and services.

2. The Synagogues

The synagogues originated during the Babylonian exile when the Jews had no temple and they would gather together to read and discuss the sacred Scriptures. Under the period of the restoration from captivity, the temple was the place of worship, but the synagogues became the places where the scribes instructed and educated the Jews out of the Writings. Rabbis became the official teachers and interpreters of the Law, but they had corrupted the Law with numerous and burdensome interpretations (Matthew 23:4).

The synagogue service consisted of an opening prayer, a confession or recited prayer, a portion of the Law or the Prophets was read, and then an exhortation on the same, then a benediction. Offerings for the poor and needy were generally received also.

The officers of the synagogue were called elders. The services of the synagogue were in charge of an officer known as a ruler. The receivers collected and distributed the alms. The minister (deacon) acted as assistant ruler. The reciter of prayers served also as the secretary. Indications of this are seen in Acts 13:5,14-16,42; 14:1; 17:1-3.

References to Judaism are seen in Revelation 2:9,14; 3:9; 5:15; 7:4-8; 11:1,2; 21:2.

Many of the churches founded by Paul began with a nucleus of Jewish believers from the synagogues who received the gospel (Acts 18:7-10 is an example). Note also how John refers to "the synagogue" in Revelation 2:9 and 3:9.

3. The Feasts of the Lord

The Jews celebrated the Festival occassions; Passover, Pentecost and Tabernacles. They also celebrated post-Mosaic Festivals such as the Feast of Purim and the Feast of the Dedication.

4. The Jewish Sanhedrin

The Jewish Sanhedrin still had the power to handle Civil cases but could not execute the death penalty without Roman authority. The Jewish Sanhedrin consisted of the following: The High Priest (President), then 24 Scribes (Theologians), 24 Priests (Ecclesiastical), 22 Elders (Synagogues), making 71 in all.

5. Jewish Sects

There were a number of Jewish sects also at this time. These became the greatest opposers and enemies of Christ and were mainly responsible for His crucifixion. They were:-

* The Pharisees - the legalists and fundamentalists of Christ's day, but extremely hypocritical (Matthew 23),

* The Sadducees - the modernists of Christ's day, rejecting the resurrection of the body, unbelief in spirit or angelic beings (Acts 23 :1-8),

* The Herodians - a political party, desirous of maintaining the Herodian dynasty (Mark 3:6),

* The Zealots - a political party, endeavouring to usher in a Jewish-Messianic kingdom by force, who sought to overthrow Roman and Gentile power and rule.

The basic blessings of Judaism were the preservation of the infallible Scriptures, the preservation of the revelation of the one true God, and the preservation of Messianic promises and the seed line through the chosen nation and tribe.

However, it is important to remember that Judaism had basically become apostate and what did not become apostate has remained somewhat orthodox.

The Gospels reveal how the nation, as a whole, crucified their own Messiah, and thus acknowledged that Caesar was their king (John 19: 13-16). They rejected the fact of the rent veil, and the empty tomb.

In the Book of Acts, the apostle Paul fulfilled the principle of Romans 1:16, taking the Gospel "to the Jew first, and also to the Gentile". Paul generally went to the synagogues first, and then went to the Gentiles. In due time, and after continuous opposition and persecution, Paul turned from the Jew and became the great apostle to the Gentiles. Read carefully Acts 13:5,15; 14:1; 17:1,17; 18:5; 19:8;

1Thessalonians 2:14-17; Acts 28:8. The Jew judged himself unworthy of eternal life (Acts 13:46-48).

As a result, the natural branches were broken off because of unbelief, and now both the believing Jews and believing Gentiles become one in the olive tree (Romans 11:16-25). God was visiting the Gentiles to take out of them a people for His name (Acts 15:15-18).

These things need to be kept in mind when the Lord speaks in Revelation of those who say they are Jews and are not but belong to the synagogue of Satan (Revelation 2:9 and 3 :9); also in any consideration of the sealed ones of the twelve tribes of Israel (Revelation 7:4-8).

In AD 70 God used Titus and the Roman armies to destroy and desolate the temple, the city, the land and the people, thus fulfilling the prophetic words of the Old Testament prophets and the words of the Lord Jesus Himself.

Therefore, it should be remembered that, when John wrote the Revelation, Jerusalem had fallen, the temple had been destroyed, the land had been desolated and Jewry scattered to the four corners of the earth.

G. The Christian Church

It was virtually out of Judaism that Christianity was born. For a number of years, Rome simply looked on Christianity as a stem or branch of Judaism until the real issues became known. Judaism was "the seed", and Christianity was "the fruit".

With the rejection of the greatest manifestation of Divine power that the world has ever seen, and with the rejection of their own Messiah, Jesus Christ, Judaism entered into the final stages of apostasy. In AD 70, God permitted the whole system, with its temple, its priesthood, ordinances and religion to be judged and desolated. God forever sealed the fact that He was finished with Judaism and that Jesus Christ was greater than Moses. Moses received revelation from God. Jesus Christ was THE Revelation of God, and that, in human form. Jesus Christ is the head of the church, the head of Christianity. True Christianity cannot be interpreted apart from Him. There is no Christianity without Christ.

The Christian Church now becomes the election of grace, chosen out of Israel and Judah and Gentile nations. Judaism revealed its apostate heart when, as a nation, they rejected their Messiah, after such Divinely attested ministry. Then Judaism persecuted the church, the "ecclesia", and thus manifested antichristal attitudes. The Gospels reveal the attitude to Christ. The Acts reveals the same attitude to the Church, His Body.

The Christians at first, took the gospel to the synagogues, until, under persecutions from Jewry, they were forced to go to the Gentiles and the Jews of the Dispersion. The breach between Judaism and Christianity widened over the years. As noted, God brought Judaism to desolation in AD 70 and scattered the nation to the four corners of the earth.

The Lord Jesus, in Matthew 16:18-20 had promised to "build His church". In the book of Acts, we see the Lord building this church (Acts 2:47). Throughout the

Acts, and the Epistles, we see the full truth of the church both universal and local, composed of both believing Jews and Gentiles, baptized into one body. The church is the people of God in the earth.

About AD68-AD96, the persecution of Christianity began to take place in another form, and this, as already noted, under the Roman Emperors, especially under the emperors, Nero and Domitian. Religious persecution from Judaism, and political persecution from the Roman emperors was upon the church as a whole. Christianity came into conflict with Rome over emperor worship. Jesus alone was "LORD" - not Caesar! It was under the persecutions of Emperor Domitian that John was banished to the isle of Patmos and here received the Revelation.

Christianity had become world known and had attained much numerical strength. As such it was feared that it could imperil the Roman Empire. The refusal of the Christians to worship the emperor now became the basis of persecution for the Christians. Under such a period John wrote the Revelation.

Most of the New Testament books were in circulation among the young churches. The church is about sixty years from its birth. Decline and heresy is on the increase with the mixture of converts now coming into the church. The Lord tells John to write to the seven churches in Asia, and send it in a book to them. Christ, as head of the church, has much of commendation, condemnation, warnings, calls to repentance, and promises available for the overcomers. Each of the churches in these cities are challenged by the Lord, the risen head.

In the light of other New Testament Church Epistles written by Paul, it is evident that these seven local churches in Asia are both local example churches, and also representative churches with lessons to all the Lord's people through out the whole of the church era. There were far more than just seven churches in Asia.

Judaism clashed with the church, ecclesiastically; Rome clashed with the church, politically.

Any expositor will need to interpret Revelation with some understanding of the historical backdrop and setting and keep this constantly in mind for a proper and clearer exposition of this glorious book.

CHAPTER FOUR

METHODS OF INTERPRETING THE REVELATION

As with much of Scripture, so the Book of Revelation has suffered much at the hands of various methods of interpretation.

In **"Interpreting the Scriptures"** (Conner/Malmin, Chapter 3), the authors deal with the four methods of interpretation. The content of this chapter is taken and adapted from this text and its relevance is applied to the Book of Revelation. Any expositor must seek to discover what John meant when he wrote the Revelation.

Over the centuries, several methods of interpretation developed, along with their particular rules and their distinctive group of principles. This is certainly seen with the various methods and the resultant interpretations of Revelation. A brief consideration of these four methods is provided here, these being the Allegorical, Mystical, Rationalistic and Literal Methods of Interpretation.

A. The Allegorical Method

1. Origin:

The Allegorical Method originated through the union of Greek philosophy and religion. With the rise of philosophy, the Greeks began to realize that they could not interpret their religious writings literally and still hold to their philosophy. If both were taken literally, they would be contradictory. Because of their new found loyalty to philosophy, they had to conclude, in order to reconcile the two, that their religious writings meant something other than what they literally said. The method they created to do this was allegorism.

2. Definition:

The Allegorical Method presumes that beneath the plain and obvious sense of Scripture lies its true meaning. It believes that what the words of Scripture literally say are only the external "chaff" which hides the true spiritual "wheat" of the Word. In allegorization, a passage with obvious literal meaning is interpreted using a point by point comparison, which brings out a hidden spiritual meaning not evident in the plain language of the passage. This method has been applied to the whole of Scripture allegorists both ancient and modern.

This writer has read a number of expositions on the Book of Revelation and the following examples certainly show extreme allegorization of this book.

* The smiting of the sun, moon and stars is interpreted as the judgment on a king (the sun), a queen (the moon), and the government (the stars) - Revelation 6:12-13.

* The burning up of the earth, trees, grass, seas and so-forth is interpreted to be judgments on mankind, social rulers, the common people and the nations - Revelation 8:7-9.

* The drying up of the river Euphrates is interpreted as the desolation of the Turkish Empire - Revelation 16:2.

* The fire and brimstone from the army of horses in Revelation 9:17 speaks of the war-cannons drawn by horses into the battle.

* The two witnesses slain in Revelation 11:7 are spoken as of representing the Old and New Testaments being withheld from the people during the period of the Dark Ages.

* The songs of Moses and the Lamb are the songs of Revival under the Wesley brothers and Methodism - Revelation 15:3.

However, nothing in the language or context of Revelation even suggests such things. There is nothing in the language to convey such concepts. The abuse of symbolism is integrated with allegorism and leaves the book open to all sorts of contorted and distorted explanation and interpretation.

3. Evaluation:

Centuries have proven the Allegorical Method to be quite inadequate in the interpretation of Scripture. The error of this method, being at its foundational assumption, is that what God said in plain language is not really what He meant.

It is a dangerous method in that there are no Scriptural boundaries to guide its implementation. Undoubtedly, this is the reason for the great variety of contradictory theological positions among allegorists. Through the allegorical method, Scripture is interpreted apart from its grammatico-historical meaning. What the author was trying to plainly communicate is almost totally ignored, and what the interpreter desires to say is forced upon it. Allegorism obscures both the literal and the figurative elements in Scripture. By exalting the interpreter's intentions and ignoring the author's intended meaning, the allegorical method fails to reach the basic goal of interpretation, and therefore must be discarded. Allegorism is the search for secondary and hidden meanings underlying the primary and obvious meanings of a narrative. Allegorization makes the text say whatever the imaginations of the interpreter wishes it to say. This method must be rejected as we interpret Scripture, and more so in interpreting the Book of Revelation.

B. The Mystical Method

1. Origin:

Closely associated with the allegorical method is the Mystical Method of interpretation. Some scholars even view them as synonymous. However, here we will consider it on its own. In relation to the interpretation of Scripture, the origin of the Mystical Method can be traced to the Hagadic method of exegesis developed by the Palestinian Jews in the inter-testamental period. This method involved both **allegorical AND mystical** interpretations of the Old Testament. In being over-anxious to apply Scripture to the lives of people, interpreters mistook **application for interpretation** and read into Scripture depths of meaning not plainly there.

2. **Definition:**

The mystical method presumes that hidden beneath the surface of the words and their plain sense there lies a multiplicity of meanings. It goes beyond the allegorical method by opening the door wide into a variety of interpretations. Using the mystical method, a passage of Scripture with obvious literal meaning is interpreted to have a number of exalted spiritual meanings. Because of the professed desire to reach beyond the letter into the spirit of the Word, the function of this method has also been called "spiritualization".

As an example of mystical interpretation, Terry (p.165) refers to Swedenborg's interpretation of Exodus 20:13, "Thou shalt not kill." In applying a three-fold sense of Scripture to this commandment, he says that its **natural sense** is that murder, hatred and revenge are forbidden; its **spiritual sense** is that "to act the devil and destroy a man's soul" is forbidden; and its **heavenly sense** is that for the angels, hating the Lord and His Word is as murder.

3. **Evaluation:**

History has proven the mystical method to be misleading and of little value in the interpreting of Scripture. The error in its foundational assumption goes beyond that of the allegorical method in that it presumes that a Scripture may have any number of meanings. In other words, in authoring Scripture, God meant many things other than those He actually said. The objection to this is, that if God did not mean what He said, then how can the interpreter discover what He did mean? Instead of regarding Scripture as a sensible communication from God, mystics turn it into a riddle and make it say almost anything other than what God meant it to say. Differing from allegorizers, who tend to follow some system of comparison, spiritualizers are more erratic, not bound by any law. They each become a law of interpretation to themselves. By exalting the interpreter's intentions and ignoring the author's intended meaning, the mystical method fails to reach the basic goal of interpretation. This system must also be discarded.

C. The Devotional Method

1. **Origin:**

Like the mystical, the Devotional Method of interpretation originated with the Hagadic exegesis of the inter-testamental period. In seeking to apply Scripture to their own lives, Jewish scribes began to interpret them in the light of their own life situations. In their zeal for **application,** they produced **faulty interpretation.** In Church History, this method had its greatest emphasis among the Pietists of the Post-Reformation period. Thus it has also been known as the Pietistic method of interpretation.

2. **Definition:**

The devotional method believes that the Bible was written for the personal edification of every believer and that its personalized hidden meaning can only be revealed by the shining of a great inner spiritual light. The Scripture of 1 John 2:20,27 is often used as a proof-text of this. There John speaks of "the anointing that abides within" and "the anointing teaches us, and we need not that any man teach us." However, this is a faulty interpretation of this Scripture, for, other Scriptures show that God has set in the church, for the edifying of the Body of Christ, ... "teachers..." (Ephesians 4:11).

The devotional method searches the Scripture to discover meaning that will build up the spiritual life. In interpretation, that which is most important is not what God said to others, but what He is saying to the interpreter. Thus, to interpret the Scriptures devotionally is to search beyond their plain obvious meaning for spiritual meaning applicable to the believer's personal life.

An example of this has been seen in the way that **"The Song of Solomon"** has been interpreted. There "the bride" is "the believer" and his/her relationship with Jesus Christ in marriage. Extreme expositions have been produced on this book because the interpreter has not placed **interpretation before application!**

3. Evaluation:

Time has proven the devotional method to be quite dangerous as a system of interpretation. The chief danger of this method is that, in seeking to apply Scripture personally, the interpreter may ignore the plain literal sense of what God was saying to those in that particular historical setting, and thus apply Scripture self-centredly. Two other weaknesses, noted by Ramm (p.62,63), are that devotional interpretation falls prey to allegorization or excessive typology, and may become a substitute for the requisite exegetical and doctrinal studies of the Bible.

However, this does not rule out altogether the devotional, practical and edifying use of the Scriptures. Certainly this is a prominent part of the purpose of Scripture, and the Word of God is of no value to the believer unless it is applied to his life practically. The interpreter must recognize that Scripture is meant to be applied **devotionally,** but this can only be properly done after it has been interpreted **literally and historically.** Devotional interpretation must also be harmonized with doctrinal interpretation. The devotional method must in no way violate the theological. Sound theology precedes the devotional and is actually the safeguard from devotional extremes. The Book of Revelation provides much devotional thought, but the book must be interpreted on the foundation of sound theology.

D. The Rationalistic Method

1. Origin:

Having its seeds in ancient history, the Rationalistic Method blossomed during the Post-Reformation period and is still bearing fruit in this modern age. Through recent centuries, the seat of rationalism has been in Germany, where the Schools of Higher Criticism have attempted to undermine the authority of

Scripture. There are actually many different methods that are here being summed up under this title because of their common characteristics.

2. Definition:

The Rationalistic Method presumes that the Bible is not the authoritative inspired Word of God. It interprets Scripture as a human document in the light of human reason. With the Rationalist, "Nature is the standard and reason is the guide." If the Bible can be made to harmonize with the knowledge of the interpreter, then it is to be understood as meaning what it says; but if not, it is to be regarded as mythical, or used by way of accomodation. Thus, a sort of educated modern mentality is used to judge and interpret Scripture.

As examples of rationalistic interpretation, and to try and explain away the supernatural, Lazarus is said to have gone into a coma rather than having died, and Jesus is said to only have appeared to have walked on water. To undermine the authority and veracity of Scripture, historical events, such as crossing the Red Sea, and the transfiguration of Christ, are explained as either fanciful exaggerations or contrived myths.

The Book of Revelation suffers much at the hands of the rationalist! The supernatural elements woven throughout the Revelation have been rationalized away as being natural phenomena. The numerous symbols used in Revelation are explained to be mythical ramblings unintelligible to rational man, and are but the figment of Jewish allegorization!

3. Evaluation:

Several generations have proven this method to be little more than the method of unbelief. In fact, rationalistic exegesis could be better termed "exit-Jesus!" Though claiming the title, "rational", this method is actually irrational. It is virtually uninterested in what the writers literally said, but cares only for what the interpreter thinks they should have said. It exalts "the god of reason" above the authority of the Word of God. The Bible is not beyond reason, but it is not subject to reason. It is above reason but not contrary to reason. However, because of man's fallen state and sinful mind, imaginations and reason, reason should be subject to the Word of God and not the Word of God subjected to "the god of man's fallen reason". By it the interpreter sets himself up as the standard of truth and only sees value in Scripture as it confirms his conclusions. For the interpreter who views Scripture as the inspired Word of God, the rationalistic method in all of its various forms must be totally rejected. It is impossible to understand the Book of Revelation using the rationalistic method of interpretation.

E. The Literal Method

1. Origin:

In relation to Scripture, the Literal Method of interpretation is the oldest in existence. It is said to have originated with Ezra, the Father of Hermeneutics. The progress of its history can be traced to Christ, and the Apostles, the

School of Antioch, and the Reformers and to the fundamentalist Conservatives of the present day.

2. Definition:

The Literal Method assumes that the words of Scripture in their plain evident meaning are reliable; that God intended His revelation to be understood by all who believe; that the words of Scripture communicate what God wants man to know; and that God based the communication of truth on the regular laws governing written communication, thereby intending for it to be interpreted by those same laws. This is not to deny the Holy Spirit's involvement in both the production and the interpretation of the Bible.

The expression, **"literal sense"** may be defined as: **the usual, customary, and socially accepted meaning conveyed by words or expressions in their particular contexts. It involves that which a particular word meant to the original writers and readers.** It recognizes that a word may have different meanings in different contexts, and thus must be interpreted in the light of its contextual usage. It contends that, though a word may possibly have several meanings, in any one particular usage it generally will have but one intended meaning.

To interpret **"literally"** means to explain the original sense of the speaker or writer to the normal, customary, and proper usages of words and language. This method is also called the Grammatico-Historical method because, in order to determine the normal and customary usages of Bible language, the accepted rules of grammar and rhetoric must be considered and the historical and cultural aspects in Bible times must be taken into consideration.

Paul Lee Tan, in, **"The Interpretation of Prophecy"** provides some excellent thoughts on the literal method. Although the writers (Conner/Malmin) do not totally agree with the result of Tan's application of the literal method, they do endorse his expansion of it on pages 30-35 in the following four areas:

* The Literal Sense does not exclude the Figurative

Some interpreters have used the term "figurative" in opposition to the term "literal", as though the figurative meaning of words were opposed to their literal sense. However, in that figurative language is a part of normal communication, it also is encompassed by the literal system of interpretation. Thus, the literal includes the figurative.

* The Literal Sense does not exclude the Spiritual Meaning

Some interpreters have used the term "spiritual" in oppositon to the term "literal", as though the spiritual meaning of Scripture was opposed to its literal meaning. Under the title of "the spiritual method", some interpreters have spiritualized Scripture to mean something other than what it says. The literal method, though rejecting spiritualization, does admit the spiritual substance and nature of the Scriptures. The Bible is a spiritual book conveying spiritual truths and therefore must be spiritually interpreted. This can be done by accepting as sufficient the illuminated literal meaning of the words of Scripture.

* The Literal Interpretation does not exclude Application

Some interpreters confuse interpretation with application. John Calvin said, "The Word of God is inexhaustible and applicable at all times, but there is a difference between **explanation and application, and application must be consistent with explanation.**" The task of literal interpretation is first to discern the meaning of God's Word, and then, upon that basis, to apply God's Word. A general rule of the literal method is: **"There is ONE interpretation, but MANY applications!"**

* The Literal Method does not exclude Depth of Meaning

Some interpreters believe that the literal method greatly limits the believer in discovering the Divine depths of truth latent in Scripture. Indeed, some definitions of this do, but here it is defined to include depth of meaning within certain necessary limitations. In that God is the virtual Author of Scripture, some truths therein are patent, outward and obvious, while others are latent, inward and hidden. Historical events do have spiritual significance, and certain figures of speech, such as types, symbols, parables and allegories, do have hidden meaning. However, this meaning is solidly based on the earthly sense of the words used and necessitates that interpretation remain within the proper boundaries of truths plainly revealed in God's Word.

3. **Evaluation:**

In conclusion, the literal method stands out among the rest as the only sound, safe and sensible approach to the interpretation of Scripture. Each of the other methods have been proven inadequate in that they lack God-given and well-defined boundaries. It is upon the literal method that this text is built.

The writer believes that this method is indeed the safest and sanest approach in interpreting the Book of Revelation.

In studying Revelation, the expositor must recognize the truth of the old adage given by the Spanish Jew, Aben Ezra (AD. 1092), "If this principle of the plain interpretation of a passage be not opposed to reason, then why seek any other?"

So we may say, **"If the literal sense makes common sense, seek no other sense or we shall end up with non-sense!"**

There are verses and passages in Revelation that do not have literal or actual sense, but do have symbolic sense (Revelation 12:1-4; 13:1-2). However, the symbolic sense is founded on the literal or actual sense of the word or words used.

For example, in Revelation 12:1-4, John sees a vision of a woman clothed with the sun, standing on the moon and having a diadem of twelve stars on her head. In literal or actual sense, the sun, moon and stars simply mean the sun, moon and stars - not some other object or person in the passage. However, the sun, moon and stars are used in symbolic sense and are seen to be the "clothing" of the woman! But the symbolic sense is based on the literal or actual sense of those words. The literal method has been brought into reproach much because of some expositions on Revelation. "Blood to the horses bridles" (Revelation 15:20) has been taken to mean that horses will be swimming in rivers of blood from the slaughter of war. However, the literal/symbolical are so often inter-blended in Revelation that it takes the skill of the interpreter to discern and distinguish them.

"Blood" here, in the literal or actual sense of the word would mean "blood" - not "red paint!" "Blood to the horses bridles" would certainly be descriptive of the enormity of the slaughter and is used in symbolic sense!

As has been noted, hermeneutics is a science and an art, and it is one thing to know the rules of interpretation and another thing to apply them. In interpreting the Book of Revelation, the expositor needs both the science and the art to arrive at a balanced interpretation, and weaving the literal/symbolic as appropriate.

In concluding this chapter, Irving L. Jensen, in, **"A Self-Study Guide"** (p.16), speaks of "The Law of Plain Sense", saying, **"When the plain sense of Scripture makes common sense, seek no other sense; therefore, take every word at its primary, ordinary, usual, literary meaning unless the facts of the context indicates otherwise."**

This is what is meant in this text when we speak of the "literal method", or the literal/actual method of interpretation.

CHAPTER FIVE
PRINCIPLES OF RESEARCH IN THE REVELATION

The expositor of Revelation also needs to use proper principles of research along with proper principles of interpretation. Three basic principles of research may be likened to "a threefold cord which cannot quickly be broken" (Ecclesiastes 4:12).

A. Observation

Observation is simply asking: What does the Bible say? Observation is the collection or gathering of all the data in Scripture, or, in this case, Revelation, on any particular subject. In reading the Book of Revelation, What does it really say; not, What do I want it to say? For example, the first three chapters of Revelation have to do with the seven churches in Asia. What does each letter really say to each church?

To Ephesus He says, "You have left your first love." That's exactly what it says, along with other important things. So in observation, one simply gathers all the facts, all the details in the verse or passage under consideration. Revelation 2:1-7 is an example passage which gives the letter sent to the church at Ephesus.

B. Interpretation

Interpretation simply asks: What does the Bible mean? First of all, What did it mean to the receivers; not, What does it mean to me?

Myles Coverdale, A.D. 1535 says: "It shall greatly help you to understand Scripture, if you mark not only what is spoken or written, but of whom, and to whom, with what words, at what time, where, to what intent, with what circumstances; considering what goes before and what follows. To interpret Scripture then we must therefore investigate:

1. WHAT - What is actually being said (not "reading between the lines").

2. OF WHOM - Who is being talked about (Acts 8:30. "Of whom speaketh the prophet?)

3. TO WHOM - Who is being spoken to?

4. WITH WHAT WORDS - In what language? (Consider why such terms are used).

5. AT WHAT TIME - When was it written? (e.g., James was written before Romans; Revelation written about the close of the First Century).

6. WHERE - The writer's circumstances and perspective (e.g., Paul in jail when he writes Philippians; John on the isle of Patmos when he writes Revelation).

7. TO WHAT INTENT - The writer's purpose (e.g., Paul wrote to the Galatians to deal with Judaistic legalism; John wrote to the churches in times of persecution and apostasy).

8. WITH WHAT CIRCUMSTANCES - What circumstances were the recipients in? (e.g., Peter wrote his first epistle to believers in times of suffering; John wrote to the churches in times of distress).

9. WHAT GOETH BEFORE - The preceding context, what flows into the verse.

10. WHAT FOLLOWETH - The succeeding context, what flows out of the verse.

All of this belongs to the field of hermeneutics or principles of Biblical interpretation.

Using the example of the letter to the church of Ephesus, we note the procedure of the principles of research so far.

Observation - "You have left your first love". This is what it says.

Interpretation - What does "first love" mean and how does one leave their "first love"? The meaning of this would have to be researched throughout Scripture revelation. Therefore observation must precede interpretation.

C. Application

Application asks: How can this relate to me or to the believer in this day? Theologically speaking, "application is taking truth revealed or communicated to one person or group of persons, and making it relate to another."

The whole basis for this is the understanding that God's principles of truth are timeless. What was truth then is truth today. Truth is truth in every generation. Truth is eternal. Following are some general guidelines for the proper application of Scripture:

1. Application must be solidly based on sound interpretation, which must be built on proper observation.

2. We must know and understand what God was saying to them in Bible times before we can apply it to ourselves in our times. Misapplication of Scripture arises out of misinterpretation of Scripture. Many times teachers of the Word move directly to application before they have given proper interpretation.

3. Similarity of situation must exist in order for proper application to be made. The measure of authority and effectiveness of the application will depend on the degree of similarity of situation.

4. Application must not contradict sound theology. Scripture is the measuring rod of theology, and theology is the measuring rod of personal application. If application of Scripture contradicts sound theology, then it becomes invalid.

5. Information without application is insufficient. The purpose of information of Scripture is to bring one to application of Scripture. Application is making the meaning of Scripture relevant to one's life situations. The ultimate aim of Bible research is to be the best communicator of Scripture and it's life-changing and life-giving principles to the people of God.

In summary it may be said:

1. Observation is knowledge - the gathering of the facts.

2. Interpretation is understanding - explaining the facts.

3. Application is wisdom - applying the facts. It is important in the use of these principles that one realizes that each inter-relate and each depend on the other.

The following diagram briefly illustrates the principles of research with this "threefold cord", providing an example of what may be done in so much of the Scripture as well as in the Book of Revelation, using Revelation 2:1-7 for our example.

OBSERVATION	INTERPRETATION	APPLICATION
Gathering the Facts	Explaining the Faacts	Applying the Facts
Knowledge	Understanding	Wisdom
1. Church at Ephesus 2. Left first love 3. Repent 4. Do first works 5. Overcome and receive tree of life 6. Or remove lampstand unless repent	1. Local church in Asia 2. Original love for Christ 3. Change mind and heart 4. Original deeds of love 5. Tree of life forfeited in Eden restored 6. Local church removed unless repent	1. Churches or believers today 2. Maintain fresh love 3. Call to repentance 4. Do works of original love 5. Eternal life in Christ 6. Local church light extinguished unless repent

Truly **"a threefold cord "** is not quickly broken (Ecclesiastes 4:12).

CHAPTER SIX

THE REVELATION - THE BOOK OF ULTIMATES

In any exposition of the Book of Revelation, another important key is to recognize that this book is indeed **"The Book of Ultimates"**. It is the final book of the Bible and certainly belongs in this position as the contents show. All that begins in Genesis finds it's end in Revelation. Genesis is the book of beginnings and Revelation is the book of endings. It is the capstone of the pyramid of Divine revelation. In Revelation we see the purposes of God brought to their ultimate fulfillment. This is seen in several factors, which we consider in this chapter.

A. One Book of Many Books

It is impossible to read Revelation without immediately seeing the numerous quotations, references, allusions, in part or whole, directly from the Old Testament Scriptures, and even from the New Testament.

Characters and events of the Old Testament are mentioned throughout the Revelation. Revelation is actually one book made up of many books.

In contrast with the Gospels, the Acts and the Epistles, which often give the Old Testament book or prophet from which they quote, John in Revelation does not do this at all. For an example, Matthew often says, "That it might be fulfilled which was spoken by the prophet...", and then quotes from that prophet. Examples of this can be seen in these following references (Matthew 1:22-23; 2:15-17; 4:14-16; 5:18).

There are about 92 quotations or references in Matthew's Gospel from the Old Testament. There are about 102 references or quotations in the book of Hebrews from the Old Testament. However, Revelation has approximately 348 or more quotations, references or allusions in its chapters from the Old Testament. The number of Old Testament quotes, references or allusions vary among the different expositors and commentaries on Revelation, as the following shows.

* **H.B. Swete in "The Apocalypse of St John"** says that, out of the 404 verses in the book of Revelation, 278 allude or refer to the Old Testament.

* **Irving L. Jensen in "Revelation"** (p. 10) says, "Allusions to Old Testament imagery and prophecy appear throughout Revelation, though there are no direct quotations as such. Of its 404 verses, it has been observed that 265 contain lines which embrace approximately 550 Old Testament references. As one writer has said, "This book is the work of a Jew saturated with Old Testament prophecy, under the guidance of the word of Jesus and the inspiration of God."

* **Samuel Bagster in "Helps to Bible Study",** lists about 250 allusions in one way or the other to the Old Testament.

* **Merill C. Tenny in "Interpreting Revelation"** (p. 102-104) graphs a diagram of at least 348 quotations, references or allusions to the Old Testament.

B. Citations, Quotations, Allusions

Merrill C.Tenny in the above quoted text makes a distinction between a citation, quotation and allusion. With kind permission of the Publishers (Wm B.Eerdmans Publishing Company), the following material is adapted for the purpose of this text.

1. Citation

A citation is a fairly exact reproduction of the words of the original text, accompanied by a statement of the fact that they are being quoted and by an identification of the source. A comparison of Hebrews 4:7 with Psalm 95:7,8 is seen as a citation. Citations as defined here are not to be found in the Book of Revelation.

2. Quotation

A quotation is a general reproduction of the original text, sufficiently close to give the meaning of its thought, and to establish unquestionably the passage from which it is taken. The quotation may be loose, and still be a quotation.

3. Allusion

An allusion consists of one or more words, which, by their own peculiar character and general context are traceable to a known body of text, but which do not constitute a complete reproduction of any part of it. Allusions are numerous in Revelation. Revelation 11:3-6 would be an allusion. The two prophets or witnesses here who "shut up heaven that it rain not for three and one-half years" and "have power to smite the earth with plagues as often as they will", and "turn the waters to blood" would be an allusion to Elijah and Moses. They are not mentioned by name, nor is there any exact citation or quotation, but certainly fulfill the definition of an allusion. Tenny sets out the following chart showing the distribution of Old Testament quotations and allusions in the Book of Revelation. The chart is taken from page 104 of his text and used by kind permission of the publishers.

DISTRIBUTION OF OLD TESTAMENT QUOTATIONS & ALLUSIONS IN THE BOOK OF REVELATION

DISTRIBUTION BY SECTIONS		
Section	**Reference**	**Number**
Prologue	1:1-8	11
Vision I	1:9-3:22	38
Vision II	4:1-16:21	164
Vision III	17:1-21:8	95
Vision IV	21:9-22:5	24
Vision V	22:6-21	16
		Total 348

DISTRIBUTION BY BOOKS OF THE OLD TESTAMENT

Books	Number	Books	Number
Genesis	13	Psalms	43
Exodus	27	Proverbs	2
Leviticus	4	**Poetry**	**45**
Numbers	3		
Deuteronomy	10	Isaiah	79
Pentateuch	**57**	Jeremiah	22
		Ezekiel	43
		Daniel	53
		Major Prophets	**197**
Joshua	1	Hosea	2
Judges	I	Joel	8
II Samuel	I	Amos	9
II Kings	6	Habakkuk	1
I Chronicles	I	Zephaniah	2
Nehemiah	I	Zechariah	15
Historical	**11**	Malachi	1
		Minor Prophets	**38**

As can be seen, according to Tenny, at least 24 of the 39 Old Testament books have references, quotations or allusions found in the Book of Revelation. The books most quoted are the Psalms, Isaiah, Daniel, Ezekiel, Jeremiah and Zechariah. All are predominently prophetic books and certainly become a good foundation for the prophetic import of Revelation.

In this writer's mind and understanding, these things confirm the miracle of Divine inspiration. To try and describe this "miracle", it is as if the writer of Revelation gathered parts of practically all the other books of the Old Testament - as well as the New Testament books - and wove these fragments together into one book without contradicting any of them! That is indeed the miracle of inspiration!

Throughout Revelation, there is both **"fresh revelation context"** and **"woven context"**. "Fresh revelation context" is truth hitherto not known before by the writer, while "woven context" is the weaving together of previously known truth into the writing.

In Revelation, John receives fresh revelation of events pertaining to the time of the end, and the coming of the Lord. Things that were "sealed" to Daniel "to the time of the end" (Daniel 12) are now revealed ("fresh revelation context") to John, and things that were previously revealed in other books of the Bible are now woven together into one amazing book ("woven context").

Revelation 13 concerning the "mark of the beast" is really "fresh revelation context". Revelation 1:7 is an example of "woven context", for here John weaves together in one verse of his book a reference from Daniel 7:13 and references from Zechariah 12:10,12,14.

This is the miracle of Divine inspiration. Revelation has a language of its own, yet it weaves together many books into one book. This includes books of both Old and New Testaments. The language of this one book is made up of the language of all other books. In this one book, all other books meet and end. This one book completes all books. Old Testament and New Testament language is used here. The Lord has gathered up into this one book such a display of words taken from other books in Scripture, without any contradiction or violation of any revealed truth, and which would be humanly impossible, and put His seal on it for ever! This is the seal of God and the inspiration of the Holy Spirit and the amazing inter-flow of Old and New Testament language.

A worthy study for any expositor of Revelation (in fact, really compulsory!) would be to read and consider the total list of citations, quotations and allusions in Revelation from all previous books.

C. Old Testament Books in Revelation

As has already been seen, Revelation is "The Book of Ultimates". The book brings together so many "fragments" of previous Bible books in one complete book - complete in itself. It is the ultimate book of all Biblical revelation and inspiration.

Out of most of the books of the Old Testament, we select examples of "seed-thoughts" that find their ultimate fulfilment in Revelation. Of necessity these examples are brief, some books providing several and others just one example, giving the student some clues that point to the ultimate book. They show the infinite possibilities and joy of discovery of truth to any serious student and expositor if they would do the same on all the cross-references, citations, quotations and allusions in Revelation from other Bible books. For simplicity of approach, these citations, quotations or allusions are arranged in a three-column format, sometimes using reasonably exact verses, and other times chapters where such may be involved.

BOOK	SEED THOUGHT	REVELATION
1. Genesis		
1:1	Heaven and Earth	21:1
2:9	Tree of Life	22:2
3:1	Serpent and Woman	12:9
7:24	150 days Flood	9:5
9:13	Rainbow	4:3,10:1
10:10	Babel	14:8
10:19	Sodom and Gomorrah	11:8
19:24	Brimstone and Fire	14:10
22:7	My Son - A Lamb	5:6; 19:7
35:22	Twelve Sons of Jacob	7:5
37:9	Sun, Moon and Stars	12:1-2

37:7	Sheaves, Harvest	14:15
50:25	Bones/Resurrection	20:5

2. Exodus

2:10	Moses the Manchild	15:3
3:14-16	The Lord is His Name	1:8; 11:17
4:2	The Rod of God	11:1
4:14	Moses, Aaron, witnesses	11:3-6
13:18	Red Sea, Song of Moses	15:3
19:1	The Wilderness	12:6,14
16:15	The Manna	2:17
25-40 Chapters	The Tabernacle	11:19
	The Golden Lampstand	1:20
	Ark of God's Glory	11:19
	Table of Shewbread	2:17
	Altar of Incense	8:1-4
	Golden Censer	8:1-4
	Brazen Laver/Sea	15:1-6
	Brazen Altar	6:9-11
	Outer Court	11:1-2
	Holiest of All	11:19
28,29 Chapters	Garments of Glory	1:10-20
40	Glory of God	22:22-23

3. Leviticus

7:37-38	Sacrifice & Oblation	5:6
12:2	Birth of a Manchild	12:5
16:1-10	Day of Atonement	8:1-5
17:14	Blood of Atonement	12:11
23:1-44	Feast of Lord/Trumpets	8:1-6;1:10

4. Numbers

1,2 Chapters	Order of Twelve Tribes	21,22
3:12	First born of all	1:5
7:1-3	Twelve Princes	12:1
10:1-10	Silver Trumpets	1:10;4:1
11:1-4	Manna of God	2:17
18:12	Firstfruits to God	14:4
17: 1 -5	The Rod of God	11:1
21:4-9	The Serpent	20:9

| 22:5 | Balaam the Prophet | 2:14 |
| 35:9-13 | Cities of Refuge | 21-22 |

5. Deuteronomy		
13:1	False Prophet	19:20
17:6	Two Witnesses	11:3
17:18	Book in King's Throne	5:1-7
28:15	Curses of the Law	22:3
31:19	Song of Moses	15:3
33:1-2	Blessings on Israel	21:12

6. Joshua		
4:1-11	Twenty Four Stones	4:4
5:12	The Manna	2:17
6:8	Seven Trumpets	8:1-6
6:13	Seven Priests	8:1-6

| **7. Judges** | | |
| 4:27 | Trumpet of Victory | 11:15 |

| **8. Ruth** | | |
| 4:1-5 | Kinsman Redeemer | 5:9-10 |

| **9. I Samuel** | | |
| 16:13 | David the Anointed | 22:16 |

| **10. II Samuel** | | |
| 23:8 | Names -David's Mighty Men | 3:5 |

11. II Kings		
17:1	Elijah the Prophet	11:6
17:1	No rain-Three & Half Years	11:6

| **12. II Kings** | | |
| 2:11 | Translation of Elijah | 11:11-12 |

| **13. I Chronicles** | | |
| 24:1-19 | The 24 Temple Courses | 4:4 |

| **14. II Chronicles** | | |
| 4:1-13 | The Temple of God | 11:19; 5:5 |

4:12-13	Two Temple Pillars	3:12
4:4	Twelve Oxen	12:1; 21:14

15. Ezra		
3:1-13	Temple Priests	1:6; 5:9-10

16. Nehemiah		
3:1-32	Walls and Twelve Gates	21:10-21

17. Esther		
2:1-18	Bridal Purification	19:7-9

18. Job		
1:6,7	Satan, The Adversary	2:8-11

19. Psalms		
2:6	Mt Zion	14:1
2:9	Rod of Iron	2:7

20. Proverbs		
1:1-6	Wisdom	5:12; 13:18

21. Ecclesiastes		
4:1	Under the Sun	9:2

22. Song of Solomon		
6:10	Woman, Sun, Moon Clothing	12:1

23. Isaiah		
2:19	Rocks of Earth	6:15-16
6:3	Holy, Holy, Holy God	4:8
14:12	Fallen Star	9:1
26:9	Judgments in Earth	15:4
34:8	Vengeance	6:10
35:1	The Wilderness	12:6,14
47:1-13	Fall of Babylon	18:1-3
58:11	Trumpet to Mouth	1:10; 4:1
61:6	Priests to God	5:9-10
63:3	Winepress Trodden	14:17-20
66:7	Manchild Born	12:5

24. Jeremiah

1:11-12	The Rod of God's Word	11:1
3:16-17	The Ark of the Covenant	11:19
50:1-40	Fall of Babylon	18:1-3

25. Lamentations

1:12	Day of Fierce Anger	6:17

26. Ezekiel

1:1-10	Four Living Creatures	4:6-9
3:1-3	Eat the Scroll	10:1-11
8:5	The Image of Jealousy	13:11-18
9:1-11	Mark in the Forehead	14:1; 13:16
10:1-2	Fire over the City	8:5
14:21	God's Four Sore Judgments	6:1-17
21:26-27	The Crown to Him	19:16
33:7	Son of Man, Watchman	1:13
38:2	Gog and Magog	20:8
40:1-3	Measure the Temple and City	21:17
47:1-12	River and Trees of Life	22:1-2

27. Daniel

1-5	Fall of Babylon	17-18
2-3	Image Worship	13:11-18
4	The Man-Beast	13:1-18
7	Beast Kingdoms	13:1-18
	Ten Horns	
	Little Horn	
7:25	Time, Times, Half a Time	12:14;13:5
9:24-27	Seventy Week's Prophecy	11,12,13
10:1-21	Vision of Son of Man	1:10-20
11:16-28	The Wilful King	13:1-18
12:1-13	The Sealed Book	10:1-11
	The Time of the End	
	Time, Times, Half a Time	12:6,14 13:5

28. Hosea

2:8,22	Corn, Wine, Oil	6:5-6

29. Joel

2:10; 3:15	Sun, Moon, Stars	6:12-14
2:31	Moon as Blood	6:12-14

30. Amos		
3:6-8	Lion Roars	10:3
31. Obadiah		
1:15	Day of Lord	6:17
32. Jonah		
2:7	Prayer to Holy Temple	8:1-5
33. Micah		
1:2	Lord in His Temple	6:15
34. Nahum		
1:1-3	The Lord Revenges	6:9-10
35. Habakkuk		
3:9-11	Bow and Arrows	6:1-2
3:11	Sun and Moon	6:12-14
36. Zephaniah		
1:3	Man, Beasts, Fowls, Fish	19:17-18
37. Haggai		
2:6	Everything Shaken	6:13
38. Zechariah		
1:7-11	Four Horses	6:1-8
2:1-2	Measure Jerusalem	21:17
4:1-14	Golden Lampstand	1:20
	Two Olive Trees	11:4
5:5-11	Woman to Babylon	17:1-18
6:1-8	Four Horses	6:1-8
6:9-15	The King Priest	1:6; 5:9-10
39. Malachi		
3:16	Book of Remembrance	3:5; 13:8
4:4-6	Moses and Elijah	11:1-6
	Day of the Lord	

Any student who considers these "seed thoughts" will certainly see that the Book of Revelation is indeed an amazing "miracle book", the consummation of all books that preceded it. It would be humanly impossible to make up such a book, in the natural, without contradicting or violating the law of Divine inspiration. The same is true also of the New Testament books.

D. New Testament Books in Revelation

As already seen, Revelation is the book of ultimates of all Old Testament books, so the same is true of the New Testament books. From the books of the New Testament, we note "seed thoughts" as they find their ultimate in Revelation. Some provide more "seed thoughts" than others, but at least one will be seen from each book.

Revelation is the consummation of the teaching of Christ in the Gospels concerning His second coming and the end of the age events mentioned in each. The same is true of the Book of Acts as well as that found in the Epistles. Practically all of the books of the New Testament mention the second coming of Jesus, and, of course this is seen to take place in the Book of Revelation. This confirms indeed that Revelation is the book of consummation, the book of ultimates, as far as the purposes of God in Christ are concerned. Let us see the truth of this as we consider brief thoughts from the New Testament books.

BOOK	SEED THOUGHTS	REVELATION
1. Matthew		
4:8	Kingdoms of this world	11:15
5:23	Hell fire	14:10; 19:20
7:15	False prophets	16:13
17:3	Moses and Elijah	11:1-6
19:28	Twelve Apostles	21:14
24:1-31	False Christs	13:1-9
	False Prophets	13:10-18
	Rumours of Wars	6:3-4
	Famines	6:5-6
	Pestilences	6:7-8
	Earthquakes	6: 12
	Sun, Moon and Stars	6:13-17
	Second Coming of Christ	1:7
2. Mark		
13:3-37	False Christs	13:1-9
	False Prophets	13:10-18
	Wars	6:3-4
	Famines	6:5-6
	Pestilences	6:7-8
	Sun, Moon and Stars	6:12-17
	Fig Tree	6:13
	Coming of Christ	19:11-16

3. Luke		
21:5-36	Repeat all Above Truths	As Above References

4. John		
1:29,36	Lamb of God	5:6
2:19-21	Temple of God	21:22
5:29	Resurrection to Life	20:1-10
5:29	Resurrection to Damnation	20:1-10
6:31,49	The Manna	2:17
15:1	The True or False Vine	14:18-19
16:21	The Woman and Manchild	12:15

5. Acts		
1:10-11	He shall come again	19-16
17:7	King Jesus	17:14

6. Romans		
2:1-6	Day of Judgment	20:11-15

7. I Corinthians		
15:20-57	Resurrections/Last Trump	20:1-10

8. II Corinthians		
3:7-18	Glory of Moses	15:3-4

9. Galatians		
6:16	The Israel of God	21:12

10. Ephesians		
6:10-16	Heavenly Warfare	12:7-12

11. Philippians		
3:20	Christ from Heaven	19:11-16

12. Colossians		
3:1-4	Christ at God's Right Hand	5:8-10

13. 1 Thessalonians		
4:13-18	Trump of God	11:15
5:1-8	Thief in the Night	3:3; 16:15

14. II Thessalonians

2:1-12	The Man of Sin	13:1-10
	Great Apostasy	12:4

15. I Timothy

4:1	Doctrine of Demons	2:20-24
6:15	King of Kings, Lord of Lords	19:16

16. II Timothy

2:18	The Resurrection	20:1-10
3:8-9	Moses and Magicians	15:1-3

17. Titus

1:12	Prophets/Beasts	13:1-18

18. Philemon

1:25	Grace of Lord Jesus Christ	22:21

19. Hebrews

7:1	Melchisedek, King-Priest	1 :6; 5:9-10

20. James

5:7-8	Coming of the Lord	19:11-16

21. I Peter

5:13	Church at Babylon	18:1-5

22. II Peter

2.1	False Prophets/Teachers	13-1 8
2 4	Angels cast Down	12:7-12
2:6	Sodom and Gomorrah	11:8
2:15-16	Balaam	2:14
3:8	Thousand Years	20:1-6
3:4-13	New Heavens, New Earth	21:1

23. I John

2:18-23	The Antichrists	13:1-10

24. II John

1:7	Antichrist, Deceiver	13:1-18

25. III John

1:7	For His Name's Sake	2:3

26. Jude

1:6	Falling Angels	12:7-12
1:7	Sodom and Gomorrah	11:8
1:9	Michael the Archangel	12:7-9
	The Devil	12:7-9
	Body of Moses	15:3
1:14	Enoch's Prophecy	19:11-16
	Christ's Coming	
1:15	Judgment on All	

Such an array of "seed thoughts" from all the New Testament books, and so many of them used also in the Book of Revelation, show the magnitude of this final book, the book of ultimates! It will be noticed that some New Testament books have more seed thoughts than others, but that all do find their fulfilment in the Revelation, in the end of this age and consummating at the second coming of the Lord Jesus Christ.

E. Bagster's "Helps To Bible Study"

From Samuel Bagster's **"Comprehensive Helps To Bible Study"** (Old Undated Edition published by Samuel Bagster & Sons Ltd, London, p.174–175), we list all the passages in the Old Testament quoted or alluded to in the Book of Revelation. Samuel Bagster does this for each of the books of the New Testament, but, for the purpose of this text, we adapt his list of references or allusions quoted from the Old Testament as in the Revelation. The student would do well for himself to check these to see whether they are citations, quotations or allusions, as this becomes a vast field of study for the diligent student. It will be noted that Bagster does place a question mark (?) on a certain number of references but we have left them as they are from his **"Helps"**. The question mark is designated by the sign (?) as a possible allusion. Many times Bagster has both the question mark (?) and the letter "a" (a.?) together. Hence the following references have the question mark (?) or (a.?) signifying Bagster's notations.

REVELATION	OLD TESTAMENT BOOKS	REVELATION	OLD TESTAMENT BOOKS
1:4	a. Exodus 3:14	1:8	a.? Isaiah 44:6
1:6	a.? Exodus 19:6	1:12	a.? Zechariah 4:2
1:7	a.? Daniel 7:13	1:14,15	a.? Daniel 7:9
1:7	a.? Isaiah 40:5	1:14,15	a.? Daniel 10:5,6
1:7	a.? Zechariah 12:10-14	1:14,15	a.? Ezekiel 1:27
1:8	a.? Isaiah 41:4	1:14,15	a.? Ezekiel 8:2

REVELATION	OLD TESTAMENT BOOKS	REVELATION	OLD TESTAMENT BOOKS
1:14,15	a.? Ezekiel 43:2	6:14	a. Isaiah 34:4
1:16	a.? Isaiah 49:2	6:15,16	a.? Isaiah 2:9 and on
1:17	a.? Daniel 8:17	6:15,16	a.? Isaiah 2:19 on
1:17	a.? Daniel 10:8 and on	6:15,16	a. Hosea 10:8
1:17	a.? Isaiah 44:6	6:15,16	a. Isaiah 13:13
2:1	a.? Deuteronomy 23:14	6:15,16	a. Psalm 110:5
2:7	a.? Genesis 2:9	6:15,16	a. Joel 2:11
2:14	a.? Numbers 25:1	7:2 on	a.? Ezekiel 9:2 on
2:14	a.? Numbers 31:16	7:16	Isaiah 49:10
2:20	a.? l Kings 16:31	7:17	Isaiah 25:8
2:20	a.? l Kings 21:23	8:3	a. Leviticus 16:12 on
2:20	a.? 2 Kings 9:23	8:3	a.? Exodus 30:8
2:23	a.? Jeremiah 17:10	8:3	a. Psalm 141:2
2:27	a.? Psalm 2:9	8:5	a.? Ezekiel 10:2
3:7	a.? Isaiah 22:22	8:7	a. Joel 2:30
3:7	a.? Job 12:14	8:7	a. Exodus 9:23
3:9	a.? Isaiah 60:14	8:8	a.? Exodus 7:20
3:17	a.? Hosea 12:8	8:11	a. Jeremiah 9:15
3:19	a.? Proverbs 3:11,12	8:12	a. Ezekiel 32:7
3:21	a.? Psalm 110:1	9:4	a. Ezekiel 9:6
4:2,8	a.? Ezekiel 1:26,28	9:6	a. Jeremiah 8:3
4:5	a.? Exodus 19:16	9:7,8,9	a. Joel 2:4
4:5	a.? Ezekiel 1:13	9:7,8,9	a. Joel 1:6
4:5	a.? Isaiah 6	9:7,8,9	a. Joel 2:5
4:5	a.? Zechariah 4:2	9:20	a. Psalm 115:4
4:6	a.? Ezekiel 1:22	9:20	a. Psalm 135:15
4:6	a.? Exodus 24:10	10:2	a. Ezekiel 2:9
4:6	a.? Ezekiel 1:5	10:3	a. Jeremiah 25:30
4:6	a.? Ezekiel 10:12	10:4	a. Daniel 8:26
4:7	a.? Ezekiel 1:10	10:5	a. Daniel 12:7
4:8	a.? Isaiah 6:2	10:8 on	a. Ezekiel 2:8
5:1	a.? Ezekiel 2:9	10:11	a.? Jeremiah 1:9,10
5:6	a.? Isaiah 53:7	11:1	a.? Ezekiel 40:3,5
5:6	a.? Zechariah 4:10	11:1	a.? Ezekiel 41:13
5:6	a.? 2 Chronicles 16:9	11:1	a.? Ezekiel 40:47
5:8	a.? Psalm 141:2	11:2	a.? Daniel 7:25
5:10	a.? Exodus 19:6	11:4	a. Zechariah 4:3,11
5:11	a.? Daniel 7:10	11:5	a.? 2 Kings 1:9-12
6:8	a.? Ezekiel 14:21	11:6	a. 1 Kings 17:1
6:12,13	a.? Isaiah 24:18,23	11:6	a. Exodus 7:20
6:12,13	a.? Isaiah 13:13	11:7	a. Daniel 7:21
6:12,13	a.? Haggai 2:6	11:10	a. Esther 9:22
6:12,13	a.? Joel 2:31	11:15	a.? Daniel 2:44
6:12,13	a. Isaiah 34:4	11:15	a. Daniel 7:14
6:14	a. Psalm 102:26	11:18	a. Psalm 2:1-5

REVELATION	OLD TESTAMENT BOOKS	REVELATION	OLD TESTAMENT BOOKS
11:18	a. Psalm 46:6	15:8	a. Ezekiel 10:4
11:18	a.? Daniel 7:10,22	15:8	a. Isaiah 6:4
11:18	a. Psalm 115:13	15:8	a. 1Kings 8:11
11:18	a.? Daniel 11:44	16:2	a.? Exodus 9:10
12:1,2	a.? Micah 4:9,10	16:3 on	a.? Exodus 7:19,20
12:1,2	a.? Isaiah 66:7	16:6	a.? Exodus 7:21
12:3	a. Daniel 7:7	16:6	a.? Ezekiel 16:38
12:4	a.? Daniel 8:10	16:10	a.? Exodus 10:22
12:5	a. Isaiah 66:7	16:12	a.? Isaiah 1l:15,16
12:5	a.? Psalm 2:10	16:12	a.? Jeremiah 50:38
12:6	a.? Daniel 7:25	16:14,16	a.? Zephaniah 3:8
12:7	a.? Daniel 10:13,21	16:14,16	a.? Joel 3:2
12:7	a.? Daniel 12:1	16:14,16	a.? Zechariah 14:2
12:14	a.? Daniel 7:25	16:21	a.? Exodus 9:24,34
12:14	a.? Daniel 12:7	17:1	a. Jeremiah 51:13
13:1	a.? Daniel 7:3,7	17:2	a. Jeremiah 51:7
13:2	a. Daniel 7:5,6	17:3	a.? Daniel 7:7,8
13:5,6	a. Daniel 7:8	17:4	a.? Jeremiah 51:7
13:5,6	a. Daniel 7:25	17:8	a.? Daniel 7:11
13:7	a.? Daniel 8:10,24	17:12	a. Daniel 7:20,24
13:7	a. Daniel 5:19	17:14	a. Daniel 8:25
13:7	a. Daniel 2:37	17:15	a. Isaiah 8:7
13:10	a. Isaiah 14:2	17:15	a. Jeremiah 47:2
13:10	a. Genesis 9:6	18:2	a. Isaiah 21:9
13:14	a.? Daniel 3	18:2	a. Jeremiah 51:8
14:1	a. Psalm 2:6	18:2	a. Isaiah 13:21
14:1	a. Isaiah 59:20	18:3	a. Jeremiah 51:7
14:5	a. Psalm 32:2	18:3	a. Nahum 3:4
14:8	a. Isaiah 21:9	18:4	a. Isaiah 52:11
14:8	a. Jeremiah 51:8	18:4	a. Jeremiah 50:8
14:8	a.? Daniel 4:31	18:4	a. Jeremiah 51:6,9,45
14:10	a.? Psalm75:8	18:6	a. Jeremiah 50:15,29
14:10	a. Isaiah 51:22	18:6	a. Psalm 137:8
14:10	a. Jermiah 25:15	18:7,8	a. Isaiah 47:7 on
14:11	a. Isaiah 34:10	18:7,8	a. Jeremiah 50:31
14:14	a.? Daniel 7:13	18:11	a. Ezekiel 27:27
14:14	a. Isaiah 19:1	18:11	a. Isaiah23
14:15	a. Joel 3:13	18:18	a. Isaiah 34:10
14:19,20	a. Joel 3:13	18:20	a. Isaiah 44:23
14:19,20	a. Isaiah 63:3	18:20	a. Jeremiah 51:48
14:19,20	a. Lamentations 1:15	18:21	a. Jeremiah 51:63,64
15:3	a. Exodus 15:11	18:22	a. Isaiah 24:8
15:4	a. Jeremiah 10:7	18:22	a. Jeremiah 7:34
15:4	a. Psalm 86:9	18:22	a. Jeremiah 25:10
15:7	a. Ezekiel 10:7	18:23	a. Isaiah 23:8

REVELATION	OLD TESTAMENT BOOKS	REVELATION	OLD TESTAMENT BOOKS
18:24	a. Jeremiah 51:49	21:10	a. Ezekiel 40:2
19:2	a. Deuteronomy 32:4,41	21:12	a. Ezekiel 48:31
19:3	a. Isaiah 34:10	21:15	a. Zechariah 2:1
19:5	a. Psalm 135:1,20	21:15	a. Ezekiel 40:3
19:5	a. Psalm 115:13	21:19	a. Isaiah 54:11,12
19:8	a. Psalm 45:14	21:23	a. Isaiah 60:19
19:8	a. Isaiah 61:10	21:23	a.? Ezekiel 48:35
19:11	a.? Psalm 72:2 on	21:24,25	a. Isaiah 60:3,11,20
19:12	a. Daniel 10:6	21:27	a. Isaiah 52:1
19:13	a. Isaiah 63:1	21:27	a. Ezekiel 44:9
19:15	a. Psalm 2:9	22:1,2	a. Zechariah 14:8
19:15	a. Lamentations 1:15	22:1,2	a. Ezekiel 47:1,7,12
19:15	a. Isaiah 63:3	22:3	a.? Zechariah 14:11
19:17,18	a.? Isaiah 34:6	22:5	a. Isaiah 24:23
19:17,18	a. Ezekiel 39:17-20	22:5	a. Isaiah 60:19
19:19	a. Psalm 2:2	22:5	a. Ezekiel 48:35
19:20	a.? Isaiah 30:33	22:10	a.? Daniel 8:26
19:20	a.? Daniel 1:7-11	22:10	a.? Daniel 12:4
20:4	a.? Daniel 9:22,27	22:12	a. Isaiah 40:10
21:1	a. Isaiah 65:17	22:13	a. Isaiah 41:4
21:2	a.? Ezekiel 40 & 48	22:13	a. Isaiah 44:6
21:3	a. Ezekiel 37:27	22:16	a. Isaiah 11:1,10
21:4	a. Isaiah 25:8	22:17	a. Isaiah 55:1
21:4	a Isaiah 65:19	22:18	a. Deuteronomy 4:2
21:5	a. Isaiah 43:19	22:18	a. Deuteronomy 12:32
21:6	a. Isaiah 51:1		

While the student may not totally agree with Bagster's list of references to citations, quotations or allusions from the Old Testament in Revelation, at least there are numerous correspondences which confirm the miracle of inspiration in this book. It confirms the truth that Revelation is indeed the book of ultimates, combining in itself all truths that have gone before, from Genesis to Revelation.

F. Genesis and Revelation

There could be no better conclusion to the contents of this chapter than a brief comparison of the first and the last books of the Bible; the book of beginnings and the book of endings, Genesis and Revelation. All that began in Genesis, in seed form, finds its total fruitition in the Revelation.

Without Revelation, Genesis is incomplete. Without Genesis, Revelation is incomplete. The two books link **creation** and **redemption** together. All the books between Genesis and Revelation are a complete chain of Divine links in God's plan and purpose in creation and redemption. This is especially so in the opening chapters of Genesis and the closing chapters of Revelation. The following brief examples remarkably confirm the truth of these things.

GENESIS	REVELATION
1. The Earthly Paradise	The Heavenly Paradise
2. Entrance of Sin and Death	End of Sin and Death
3. The Beginning of the Curse	No more Curse
4. Entrance of the Serpent Satan	Serpent eternally Judged
5. Image of God in Man Marred	Image of God in Man Restored
6. The Rivers of Eden's Garden	The River in the City of God
7. The Tree of Life Forfeited	The Tree of Life Restored
8. The Alpha, First, Beginning	The Omega, Last, Ending
9. Beginning of Time	Time shall be no More

This writer believes that this chapter is one of the great "keys" to understanding the Book of Revelation. The context of the quotations, allusions or citations will surely provide much help in the understanding and interpretation of Revelation.

John, the beloved, the apostle of Jesus, was a Hebrew believer and then a Christian believer. As such, his mind was saturated with the language and understanding of the Hebrew Scriptures, the Mosaic Covenant economy, as well as the teaching of Jesus, the Messiah, and the truth of New Covenant realities. For John, all had passed to the cross. Ceremonials had been fulfilled and abolished, and now John uses Old Covenant language to describe New Covenant realities, but all pass through the cross.

Truly the words of the Preacher in Ecclesiastes is applicable to Genesis and Revelation: "Better is the END of a thing than the BEGINNING!" (Ecclesiastes 7:8).

CHAPTER SEVEN
THE STRUCTURE OF THE REVELATION

There are many different structures given by various expositors of the Book of Revelation. Some of them have good commendation; others are not worth too much consideration. Of course, an expositor's view and school of interpretation will determine his structure of the book, as does this present author's view.

Structure has to do with manner of building, construction, framework, the arrangements of parts, or how things are organized. For the purpose of this chapter, we will note briefly several differering structures of the book as presented by the varying Schools of Interpretation.

A. The Progressive Parallel Structure

Though there may be slight variations in this structure, the basic arrangement remains the same.

This view holds that there are seven sections in Revelation and that these seven sections run parallel. From the first coming of Christ to His second coming, these seven sections reveal the different aspects of events in the earth and the universe. The following is the framework of that school which expounds the Revelation accordingly.

FIRST COMING **SECOND COMING**
JUDGEMENTS

1. The 7 Churches with Christ in the midst - Rev 1-3

2. The 7 Sealed book & the Church in the midst of Persecutions - Rev 4-7

3. The 7 Trumpets of Divine Judgments - Rev 8-11

4. The Christ in conflict with the Dragon - Rev 12-14

5. The 7 Vials (Bowls) of the Wrath of God - Rev 15-16

6. The Judgment of Babylon, The Woman, The City & The Beast - Rev 17-19

7. The Judgements on Satan & His Hosts & then the New Heavens & New Earth - Rev 20-22

Another arrangement of the book, as related to the above view, is for the book to be divided into two major sections, each having three and four sections respectively, as the following diagram illustrates.

REVELATION 1 – 11

FIRST COMING		SECOND COMING
Revelation 1-3	Revelation 4-7	Revelation 8-11

REVELATION 12 – 22

FIRST COMING			SECOND COMING
Revelation 12-14	Revelation 15-16	Revelation 17-19	Revelation 20-22 Judgements Eternity

B. The Futurist Structure

Those who hold the futurist view set out the structure of Revelation in the following manner using Revelation 1:19 as the key verse for this structure.

Things which are	The Things which Shall be Hereafter	Eternal states
Christ in His church Rev 1-3 Seven Sealed book Rev 4-7 Seven Trumpets Rev 8-11 Great Tribulation Rev 12-14 Seven Vials Rev 15-16	Babylon Woman & City Rev 17-18 Armageddon Second Advent Rev 19 Millennium Rev 20	New Earth Rev 21-22
Past Future	Time of the End	Eternity

Though there are slight variations in the Futurist view, the above is the basic structure that those who hold to the Futurist position hold.

C. The "Heaven and Earth" Vision Structure

The following structure is taken from **"The Companion Bible"** (Structure on Revelation). The originator of this structure (E.W.Bullinger) shows that there are seven visions "in heaven" and seven visions "on earth", making fourteen visions in all, as seen in the following:-

Introduction	Revelation	
The People of the Earth – Revelation 2-3		
1. Vision in Heaven	Revelation 4-5	The Throne, The Book & The Lamb
Vision on Earth	Revelation 6:1 -7:8	The 6 seals & The Sealing Angel
2. Vision in Heaven	Revelation 7:9-8:6	The Great Multitude & the 7th Seal
Vision on Earth	Revelation 8:7-11:14	The 6 Trumpets, Little Open book, Two Witnesses.
3. Vision in Heaven	Revelation 11:15-11:19	The 7th Trumpet
Vision on Earth	Revelation 11:19	The lightnings, voices, thunders, earthquake
4. Vision in Heaven	Revelation 12:1-12	The Woman, The Child, The Dragon & 3rd Woe
Vision on Earth	Revelation 12:13-13:18	The Dragon, The Two Beasts
5. Vision in Heaven	Revelation 14:1-5	The Lamb & The 144,000 Sealed Ones
Vision on Earth	Revelation 14:6-20	The 6 Angels
6. Vision on Heaven	Revelation 15:1-8	The 7 Angels with the 7 Vials of Wrath
Vision in Earth	Revelation 16:1-18:24	The 7 Vials, Babylon, The Harlot Woman & City
7. Vision in Heaven	Revelation 19:1-16	Marriage of the Lamb & Second coming of Christ
Vision on Earth	Revelation 19:17-20:15	The Final Judgments
The Peoples of the New		
Heaven & New Earth	Revelation 21:1-22.5	The Bride City
Conclusion	Revelation 22:6-21	

The structure is worthy of much consideration. Heaven and earth are brought together in final things.

In the beginning God created the heavens and the earth (Genesis 1:1). Melchisedek blessed Abraham as priest of the Most High God, the possessor of heaven and earth (Genesis 14:19-22). Jacob saw the angels of God ascending and descending on the ladder connecting heaven and earth (Genesis 28:12). Jesus said, All power is given to Me both in heaven and in earth (Matthew 28:18). On that basis, His followers were told to go and make disciples of all nations.

Jesus Himself came from heaven to earth and after finishing the work of the Father on the earth returned to heaven (John 16:27-28). And here in Revelation, the book of ultimates, we see the connection between heaven and earth in the final purposes of God in creation and redemption.

The visions John sees are things in heaven, yet they pertain to earth. The temple or the sanctuary in heaven is the place of Divine purpose and plan, and the action takes place in earth.

As one proceeds through the Book of Revelation, it is seen that John generally sees things first in heaven, and then sees the resultant action of God in the earth. The place of the visions are in God's dwelling place, heaven, and then the fulfilment of the visions takes place in man's dwelling place, earth! Thus heaven and earth are brought together in the final ministrations of the Lord Jesus Christ.

The expositor of Revelation must consider each section and see how John is viewing everything either **"in heaven"** or **"on earth"**. This writer believes that this is a great key to the understanding and interpretation of this book.

The reader is referred to Chapter Two for the various Schools of Interpretation generally fall into similar structures, though the interpretation of events may vary. The general structure of the Preterist, Historicist, Presentist, Idealist and Futurist are brieflly outlined there and do not need to be repeated here.

D. The "Christian Millennialist" Structure

This writer has coined the designation, **"Christian Millennialist"** in order to classify his beliefs as to a millennium. By this is meant, briefly, that the writer does not hold to any **"Jewish Millennium"**, wherein the Mosaic economy is restored. Also, the writer is not an **"A-Millennialist"**, who believes the church is in a millennium now. Out of this position, the writer has come to hold that there is a structure to Revelation, and, for the purposes of this text, he has designated it as **"The Christian Millennialist Structure"**.

After considering the various structures upon which various expositor's interpretations of Revelation are built, this writer believes that there are some elements of truth in the several presented in this chapter. This is seen in the following.

1. The Progressive Parallelism Structure

There certainly seem to be **some chapters** of Revelation that do fulfill the **Progressive Parallelism** point of view, but **not all chapters!**

The chapters which would fulfill progressive parallelism would be Revelation chapters 11,12,13,14,15,16,17,18 and consummate with Revelation chapter 19. The writer sees two major reasons for this conclusion.

(a) Time Period

The first reason for this conclusion is that which pertains to the **"time period"** mentioned in several chapters. Revelation chapters 11, 12, and 13 each mention a period of time of three and one half years. It should be seen that this is not three and a half, plus three and a half, plus three and a half years, making it ten and one half years. Of course, this again depends on one's interpretation of this time-period. If this is indeed one and the same period of time, then the structure would be:-

Three & One Half Years
Revelation 11-1260 days
Revelation 11-42 months
Revelation 12 - Time, Times, Half a Time
Revelation 13 - Time, Times, Half a Time

Progressive Parallelism

(b) The Beast

The second key to these and other chapters mentioned as fulfilling progressive parallelism would be the term **"the beast",** whatever one's interpretation of **"the beast"** may be.

The first mention of "the beast" is found in Revelation 11:7. The final mention of "the beast" is in Revelation 19:19-20 where "the beast " is judged by the Lord Jesus Christ Himself. Then the eternal judgment of "the beast" is to be found in it's absolute final mention in Revelation 20:10, where "the beast" is thrown into the lake of fire along with the false prophet. "The beast" is mentioned from Revelation 11:7 to Revelation 20:10 at least 37 times! Surely this is a key to the understanding of these chapters grouped together in progressive parallelism!

When one uses **"The Comparative Mention Principle"** and compares Daniel 7 with Revelation 13, it will be seen that **"the little horn"** and **"the beast"** both make war with the saints for three and one half years, or time, times and half a time. One is therefore brought to the conclusion that "the little horn" of Daniel 7 and "the beast" of Revelation of which John speaks is one and the same, and that the period of time is also one and the same. Daniel and John are incomplete without each other.

Together "the beast" and "the time, times and half a time" would fulfill progressive parallelism and therefore the structure would be:

The Beast / Three & One Half Years
Revelation 11
Revelation 12
Revelation 13
Revelation 14
Revelation 15
Revelation 16
Revelation 17
Revelation 18

Progressive Parallel Chapters
Revelation 19
Christ's Second Coming

2. The Futurist Structure

The Futurist Structure has some elements of truth that, to this writer, are more consistent than the Progressive Parallelism point of view. This is seen in the following comments.

The seven churches are local churches, yet they do have a message for all churches of all times; that is, for all churches of this "church age". The vision of Revelation chapters 1, 2, 3 certainly would fulfill "the things that you have seen, and the things which are" (Revelation 1:19). It is a scene on earth with the risen heavenly Christ in the midst of His people.

The throne and the seven-sealed book certainly fulfills "the things which are hereafter" (Revelation 1:19 with 4:1), for John is now given the vision in heaven. In Revelation chapters 4,5,6,7 John sees the seven-sealed book being opened by the Lamb. It is not until the seventh seal is opened that there is any sign of the seven trumpets!

This makes the progressive parallelism structure weak in this area. The seven trumpets come out of the opening of the seventh seal, and NOT at the opening of the first seal !

Therefore we would have :-

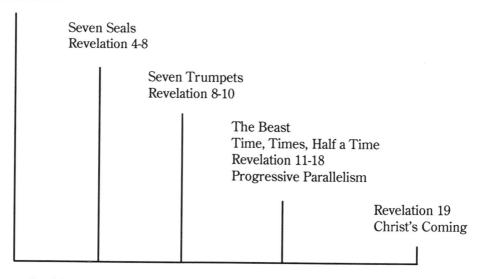

Seven Churches
Revelation 1-3

Seven Seals
Revelation 4-8

Seven Trumpets
Revelation 8-10

The Beast
Time, Times, Half a Time
Revelation 11-18
Progressive Parallelism

Revelation 19
Christ's Coming

By this structure, the Book of Revelation is not being forced into any one structure, but just unfolds in the order that John is given, and the order in which he wrote it.

If this structure does justice to the book (which the writer believes it does), we have Revelation chapters 20,21,22 to position. Revelation 20 speaks of a period of time and is certainly a chapter of controversy among the "Millennial Schools" of thought.

Again, the writer finds great difficulty in the progressive parallelism point of view. Such place the "thousand year" period, beginning at the first coming of Christ and use it to symbolize time over church history through to the second coming of Christ, as this simple diagram shows.

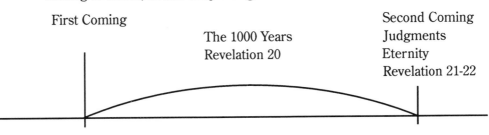

First Coming   The 1000 Years   Second Coming
               Revelation 20   Judgments
                   Eternity
                   Revelation 21-22

However, when it comes to the final chapters, Revelation 21 and 22, most expositors, regardless of their School of Interpretation, do see these chapters as depicting the eternal states.

Placing this structure together, the writer presents this as a sound structure on which an exposition of Revelation could be built.

THE BOOK OF REVELATION

Church History

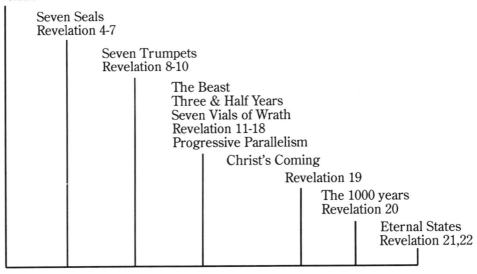

Seven churches
Revelation 1-3

    Seven Seals
    Revelation 4-7

       Seven Trumpets
       Revelation 8-10

          The Beast
          Three & Half Years
          Seven Vials of Wrath
          Revelation 11-18
          Progressive Parallelism

            Christ's Coming
               Revelation 19

                 The 1000 years
                 Revelation 20

                    Eternal States
                    Revelation 21,22

It is significant that the seventh seal, the seventh trumpet and the seventh vial all end alike with voices, thunderings, lightings and an earthquake. It is also significant that each of the sevens come out of their sevenths! Read carefully

Revelation 8:5; 11:19; 16:18. Undoubtedly this significance brings us to the second coming of Christ. If a **"time element"** were to be super-imposed on the above structure, the author would place it in the following manner.

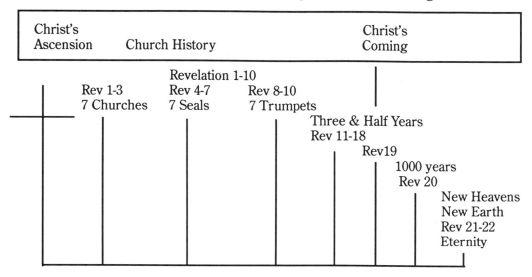

This structure is simple, and does not "force" chapters here and there, but lets the book unfold as we believe it was given to John in vision, and in the order that John wrote it.

The progressive parallel chapters have two major "keys" in them, these being: (1) The time-element of "time, times and half a time" (or three and half years), and "the beast" who reigns for that same period of time. Such confirm the thought that these chapters do run parallel; or, in other words, they progress together.

In Summary:-

1. The expositor of Revelation should have a sound structure, discerning what is unfolding and what is progressive and what runs parallel.

2. The expositor should understand the "time element" in Revelation as this is a great key to a proper exposition of the book.

3. The expositor should understand whether the vision concerns things in heaven or things on earth.

CHAPTER EIGHT

THE BOOK OF REVELATION - HISTORY OR PROPHECY?

In order to understand a writing, and here we speak particularly about Biblical writings, it's literary kind or style must first be determined. The book's literature must be determined whether it is Historical, Poetical, Apocalyptical or Prophetical. Within any literary style there can occur passages that use other literary expressions, such as symbols, parables, songs, psalms, riddles, allegories and so forth. However, the major literary style must be determined first. This is certainly true when it comes to the Book of Revelation.

Is the Book of Revelation historical, prophetical, symbolical, allegorical, poetical or spiritual? Various expositions of Revelation have arisen out of the particular writer's answer to this question. The various Schools of Interpretation confirm this matter.

* The Preterist, Historicist and Presentist Schools see Revelation primarily as HISTORY.

* The Idealist sees the book as predominantly SPIRITUAL and symbolical.

* The Futurist School sees the Revelation mainly as a PROPHECY.

The writer of this text would see that Revelation deals with both HISTORY and PROPHECY. The Historical section would be those chapters that deal with the conditions of the seven churches in Asia. The Prophetical section would be the larger part of the book. However, this needs further clarification and amplification, and also an understanding of Messianic prophecy as Revelation consummates with Christ's second coming.

A. Messianic Prophecy

Messianic prophecy has to do with the utterances of the Old Testament prophets whenever they speak of Christ and His church. The apostle Peter tells us that the prophets spoke of "the sufferings of Christ and the glory that was to follow" (1 Peter 1:10-12). Messianic prophecy may be divided into three groupings, based on the three stages of fulfillment.

1. The First Coming of Christ

These prophecies deal mainly with the birth, ministry, sufferings and exaltation of the Lord Jesus Christ.

Most of the Old Testament Messianic prophecies pertain to the FIRST coming of Christ and its related events. The student should read these Scriptures for examples of these things (Genesis 3:15; Deuteronomy 18:15-18; Psalm 2; 8; 22; 40; Isaiah 7:14; 9:6; 40:1-18; 52:14; 53:1-12; 61:1-4; Jeremiah 31:31-34; Micah 5:1-2; Zechariah 11; 12; 13).

The Synoptic Gospels show the fulfilment of these prophecies. John, the beloved, also wrote his Gospel. When John wrote the Book of Revelation, the Lord Jesus Christ's first coming was past history.

2. The Church

The next group of Messianic prophecies have to do with the church. After the sufferings of Christ, there would be the glory to follow (1 Peter 1:10-12 with Ephesians 3:21).

The Old Testament has numerous prophecies which speak of the Gentiles coming into the kingdom of God and of Christ. The New Testament clearly shows that these prophecies predicted the grafting in of the Gentiles into the faith-olive-tree. In this faith-olive-tree, believing Jews and believing Gentiles would be one body in Christ. In other words, Jew and Gentile would be born again into the kingdom of God and added to the church (John 3:1-5; Romans 9-10-11).

A comparative reading of these Scripture references confirm the truth of these things.

> Psalm 18:49 with Romans 15:9
>
> Deuteronomy 32:43 with Romans 15:10
>
> Psalm 117:11 with Romans 15:11
>
> Isaiah 11:10 with Romans 15:12 and Romans 11:13-25
>
> Ephesians 3: 1-6 with 1 Corinthians 12:13.

Other examples of Messianic prophecies concerning the New Covenant church can be seen by a careful and thoughtful reading of these further Scriptures (Isaiah 9:6-9; 26:1-4; 35:1-10; 54:1-17; Jeremiah 31:31-34; Joel 2:28-32; Zechariah 2:10-11 and Malachi 1:11).

When John wrote the Book of Revelation, the Holy Spirit had already been poured out some 60 years before at Pentecost. The church had been formed of repentant and believing Jews (Acts 2), and repentant and believing Gentiles (Acts 10-11). The "church epistles" had been completed.

The churches to whom John writes are in Asia Minor, and no doubt had been founded out of the great church of Ephesus. The church is God's new ethnic grouping.

John himself is one of the Twelve foundation apostles of the Lamb. He sees himself possibly as one of the 24 elders around the throne (Revelation 4:4). Undoubtedly he sees his name in the foundations of the bride city, New Jerusalem (Revelation 21:14).

The seven local churches of Asia are part of church history. However, because truth is truth in every generation, the word to these churches is applicable to all churches, at all times and in all places!

3. The Second Coming of Christ

The next group of prophetic utterances, which are Messianic, have to do with the second coming of Christ. The second coming actually consummates all that which He initated in His first coming.

The Old Testament has but a relatively few specific prophecies about Christ's second coming compared to the numerous prophecies which deal with His first coming. However, there are many second coming prophecies which deal with related events. Many of these prophecies speak of "the day of the Lord", and its climatic judgments.

While the burden of the Old Testament was, more especially, the first coming of Christ, the burden of the New Testament is, more especially, the second coming of Christ.

Some examples of second coming prophecies from both Old and New Testaments are seen in these references.

(a) Old Testament

Genesis 49:10; Isaiah 2:10-22; 13:6-16; 24:1-23; 30:26-33; 34:1-17; Daniel 2; Joel 3; Zechariah 14; Daniel 7; Malachi 4:1-4.

(b) New Testament

Matthew 24; Mark 13; Luke 21; 1 Corinthians 15:20-28, 50-57; 1 Thessalonians 4:14-18; 2 Thessalonians 2; 2 Peter 3:1-13.

(The student should take the time to read these Scriptures as they are too full to be quoted here).

However, the predominant message of the Book of Revelation is the second coming of Christ. The burden of the book is PROPHETIC! Christ has not yet come! He was to come again in like manner as He went to heaven. That is, visibly, bodily and gloriously (Acts 1:9-1 1).

The following references from the Book of Revelation itself all speak of His second coming, the ultimate burden of ALL prophecy, whether Old Testament or New Testament. Revelation is the book of Christ's second coming and events which lead up to it.

"Behold, He **cometh** with clouds ..." (Revelation 1:7)

"Hold fast till I **come** ..." (Revelation 2:25-26)

"If you do not watch, I will **come** on you as a thief in the night" (Revelation 3:3)

"The great day of His wrath is **come** ... "(Revelation 6:17)

"Behold, I **come** as a thief ..." (Revelation 16:15)

"Behold, I **come** quickly ..." (Revelation 22:7,12,20)

"Even so, **come,** Lord Jesus ..." (Revelation 22:20)

It is in Revelation 19:11-21 that one sees heaven opened and the Lord Jesus Christ coming the second time as "King of Kings and Lord of Lords".

It is here that the kingdoms of this world become the kingdoms of our God and His Christ (Revelation 11:15).

It is over 1900 years since John wrote the Revelation and many things in the book have not been fulfilled.

The Historical Schools of Interpretation fall far short of the prophetic content of the book. The Futurist School, in spite of varying interpretations, presents a more sound view for consideration, as to the book's prophetic import.

Is Revelation history or prophecy? The author of this text sees that it involves both. Revelation chapters 1, 2, 3 are history - past history of the seven local churches in Asia. Revelation chapters 4 through 19 are prophecy, unfolding through time, but more especially to the final years of this church age, consummating at the second coming of Christ. Revelation chapters 20, 21, 22 bring us to events at Christ's coming and on into the eternal states.

Whatever view one has of the Book of Revelation, understanding the **literary style** of this wonderful book will help the expositor and interpreter towards a proper and more sane interpretation.

CHAPTER NINE

THE THEOLOGY OF THE REVELATION

It has already been seen that sound hermeneutics and sound theology may be likened to two sides of the same coin. Theology arises out of hermeneutics and hermeneutics determines sound theology.

In the Book of Revelation is seen ample evidence of theology that flows through and undergirds the Bible as a whole. Sound Biblical theology is absolutely necessary in order to provide sound Biblical exposition of the Book of Revelation. An example of unsound theology may be seen in those who deny the reality and eternality of hell and the lake of fire and brimstone spoken of in Revelation 14:9-11. If an expositor does not believe in the Biblical doctrine of eternal punishment, then they certainly will not interpret the Book of Revelation properly. Other examples could be given.

This chapter is not meant to provide an exhaustive treatise on the theology of Revelation, but enough of an outline for the earnest student, upon which to build a sound expositon of the book. Enough will be given to show how theology underlines the whole of Revelation and how one cannot do a proper exegesis if there is not sound theology undergirding their exposition. The theology of Revelation is set out under the major designations of Biblical Doctrine.

A. The Doctrine of Revelation

The Doctrine of Revelation is woven throughout the Book of Revelation. Things are here revealed to John by the Spirit that he could not have found out by human ingenuity.

Jesus had told the disciples at the Last Supper that He would send the Holy Spirit to them. He had many things to say to them, at that time, but they were not able to receive them. However, Jesus said that when the Spirit of truth would come, He would show them things to come. He would take of the things of Jesus and show it unto them (John 16:7-15 with 1 Corinthians 2:10).

John is experiencing such in this book. He is "in the spirit" on the Lord's day and revelation is given to him concerning the Lord's second coming and many of the details involved. It is indeed "the revelation (the unveiling) of Jesus Christ" (Revelation 1:1).

Deuteronomy 29:29 tells us, "The secret things belong unto the Lord our God, but the things that are revealed belong unto us and to our children for ever, that we may do all the works of the law".

The Greek word **"Apokalupsis"** translated as **"revelation"**, means "an uncovering, to uncover or unveil". Here in this book, the Lord reveals Himself to John, as well as revealing the events that lead to His second advent and on through into the eternal states.

Revelation is the unveiling of Jesus Christ, the unveiling of the events flowing through the church age, the events of the end-times, and Christ's glorious coming, as King of Kings and Lord of Lords (Revelation 19:16).

The Doctrine of Revelation is indeed woven throughout the Book of Revelation . It is indeed **"The Revelation"**.

B. The Doctrine of Inspiration

Closely linked with the Doctrine of Revelation is the Doctrine of Inspiration. The Bible was written under the inspiration of the Holy Spirit. The Book of Revelation closes off the canon of inspiration. It is the final book. John is not the author, in true sense. He is the writer. God, by the power of the Holy Spirit is the Divine Author. John, by the inspiration of the Spirit is the human writer.

The Lord told him, **"Write it in a book..."** (Revelation 1:10-11; 21:5). On a number of occasions, John was told simply "to write". On one occasion, he was told "not to write" (Read Revelation 19:9, 21:5, 10:4).

Revelation is indeed a "miracle book", made up, as previously seen, of all books that have gone before. It is indeed the result of Divine inspiration. Any expositor must believe in the total inspiration of the Book of Revelation as given to John. Otherwise the expositor is on 'dangerous ground' when it comes to providing a true interpretation of this book.

Revelation is also like "a book of books". There is:-

1 . The Book of Revelation itself (Revelation 1:10-11 , 22:7,9,10,18)

2. The Seven Sealed Book (Revelation 5:1-10)

3. The Little Open Book (Revelation 10:5-10)

4. The Book of Life (Revelation 3:5, 13:8; 20:12)

5. The Books of Works for judgment (Revelation 20:1 2).

Paul tells us in 2 Timothy 3:16-17, "All Scripture is given by inspiration (Lit. God-breathed) of God, and is profitable for doctrine, for reproof, for correction, for instruction in righteousness, that the man of God may be perfect (complete), and thoroughly equipped unto all good works."

As one studies the Book of Revelation, one must accept the truth of inspiration and also the infallibility of the Scriptures as originally given. Revelation is part of "all Scripture". Revelation has doctrine, reproof, correction and instruction for believers of all ages . It should not be put aside as being impossible to understand.

The Bible is the Divine Library, consisting of 66 separate yet related books. It is worthy to remember that there are three major passages giving warning to any who would dare to "add to" or "take away" from the Divinely inspired writings (Deuteronomy 4:2; 12:32 with Proverbs 30:6). The final warning is found in the Book of Revelation (Revelation 22:18-19).

C. The Doctrine of God

The Doctrine of God is also woven throughout the structure and texture of Revelation.

God is revealed in His eternal Godhead; Father, Son and Holy Spirit. The Divine persons are seen in activity throughout the book, in things pertaining to both creation and redemption. The thrice-holy God is worshipped by the four living creatures (Revelation 4:8). The Father is in the throne. The Lamb is standing in the midst. The Holy Spirit is seen as seven lamps of fire before the throne. Such symbolizes the eternal Godhead (Revelation 1:4-5; 4:2-5; 5:1-6).

1. The Father God

In Revelation 1:4. the Father is seen as "Him which is, and which was, and which is to come".

In Revelation 4:1-3; 5:1, the Father is the One who is in the throne and who gives to the Lamb the seven sealed book.

In Revelation 7:2,10,12, the Father is seen as the living God.

In Revelation 11:15, the Father is the Lord, with His Christ, who possesses the kingdoms of this world.

In Revelation 19:1-6, the Father is the Lord God omnipotent.

In Revelation 20:11-15, all the dead are brought before the judgment throne of God.

And in Revelation 22:1 there is seen the throne of God and the Lamb.

God the Father is seen throughout the Book of Revelation, in all His power, glory and majesty, dealing with all things as pertaining to creation and redemption.

2. The Attributes of God

Both the essential attributes and the moral attributes of God are also alluded to throughout the Revelation. God is the unchanging One and His attributes remain the same throughout time and eternity.

Essential attributes of God are those attributes that are God's apart from any relationship to His creation or creatures. Such are seen and alluded to in the following.

* The Eternal God - Revelation 1:4; 4:8

* The Self-Existent God - Revelation 4:8-11

* The Immutable God - Revelation 15:3-4

* The God who is omnipotent, the Almighty - Revelation 15:3; 19:6

* The God who is omniscient, all knowing, all seeing - Revelation 13:8; 20:11-15

* The God who is omnipresent, everywhere present, at all times, the One which is (time present), which was (time past), which is to come (time future). In other words, the eternal - Revelation 1:8.

* The God who is sovereign over all - Revelation 11:15, 17:17.

Moral attributes are those attributes of God which are manifested in His relationship to His creatures, whether angelic or human.

* Perfect Holiness of the thrice-holy God - Revelation 4:8

* Perfect Righteousness - Revelation 16:5-7

* Perfect Love - Revelation 1:5; 4:19

* Perfect Faithfulness - Revelation 1:5, 17:14.

These attributes are appropriate to God as Father, Son and Holy Spirit. As God deals with angelic hosts, mankind and the earth, His essential and moral attributes are manifest.

D. The Doctrine of Christ

The Christological Principle sets out more fully the revelation of the Son of God as seen in the Book of Revelation. Sufficient for here is to see the major visions and revelation of the blessed Son of God.

In Revelation chapters 1,2,3, He is seen as the Son of Man, the great High Priest standing in the midst of the seven churches, to judge and cleanse His church.

In Revelation chapters 4,5, He is seen as the Lamb of God opening the seven sealed book.

In Revelation 10:1-3, He is seen as the "mighty angel", clothed with a cloud, a rainbow on His head, His face shining as the sun, His feet as pillars of fire, crying with the loud voice of the lion. He has in His hand the little open book.

In Revelation 14:14-16, He is seen as the Son of Man reaping the harvest of the earth for Divine judgment.

In Revelation 19:11-16, He is seen as King of Kings and Lord of Lords, the rider on the white horse, with the armies of heaven following Him. The Book of Revelation is ultimately "the revelation of Jesus Christ".

(**Note:-** For a fuller treatment on the Doctrine of Christ, the student is referred to the chapter in the text on **"The Christo-centric Principle"**).

E. The Doctrine of the Holy Spirit

The ministry of the Holy Spirit is one of the great themes flowing through Revelation and constitutes a study in itself as the following references clearly show. It is the Holy Spirit who came to complete the ministry of Jesus in the earth and in the church. Jesus spoke much of the Spirit's ministry in the upper room, at the Last Supper (John chapters 14,15,16).

John was "in the Spirit" when he received the Book of Revelation (Revelation 1:10). John also was "in the Spirit" when he saw the heaven opened and saw the seven sealed book (Revelation 4:2).

There are the seven Spirits before the throne of God (Revelation 1:4; 3:2; 4:5).

The seven churches are each called to "hear what the Spirit is saying to the churches" (Revelation 2:7,11,17,29; 3:6,13,22).

In Revelation 11:11 John sees the Spirit of life raise the two witnesses from death.

In Revelation 17:3, John is carried away "in the Spirit" to see the great harlot church; while in Revelation 21:10, John is carried "in the Spirit" to a great high mountain to see the holy city, New Jerusalem, the bride of Christ.

The final mention of the Holy Spirit is in Revelation 22:17, when "the Spirit and the bride say, Come".

The Holy Spirit is active in the final days, as He has been through church history. John was "in the Spirit" to receive this book. Surely, those who would seek to understand and interpret the book need also to be "in the Spirit". There is coming a time when the Spirit ceases to strive with men. The day of conviction and salvation will then be over (Read Genesis 6:3 with John 16:8-11).

F. The Doctrine of Angels

The Book of Revelation especially abounds with the ministry of angels. The Scriptures clearly teach that the angels are ministering spirits, doing the will of God, being sent forth to those who are heirs of salvation (Hebrews 1:13-14; Psalm 148:2,5; Colossians 1:16). The Book of Revelation shows that there is much activity of the angels in the last days before and up to the coming of Christ.

The word "angel" (Grk. "angelos"), simply means "messenger" and may refer to (1) The Lord Jesus Christ, as the Jehovah Angel, or (2) Ministers of the Gospel or leaders of the local church, or (3) Angelic spirit beings doing the Father's will, or else fallen and evil angels.

Generally the contextual language provides the clue as to which of these "angelic" groups is being referred to. In Revelation the Greek word "angelos" is used at least 76 times, showing the importance of angelic ministry in the end-times before and up to the coming of Christ. We group these "angelic" groupings in what we believe are their rightful classifications.

1. The Lord Jesus, The Jehovah Angel

The following passages in Revelation seem to indicate that the "angel-messenger" speaks of the Lord Jesus Christ Himself. The ministry executed seems to point more to Christ's ministry than ordinary angelic spirit being's ministry. It should be remembered that Christ was revealed in the Old Testament many times as "the Angel of the Lord". These appearances are spoken of theologically as " Christophanies", or pre-cross manifestations and revelations of the Lord Jesus Christ before His incarnation.

(a) The Angel-Sealer who comes with the seal of the living God points to the Lord Jesus Christ. No ordinary angel can perform such a sealing of the Spirit and write the name of God upon God's people (Revelation 7:2 with 14:1-2).

(b) The Angel-Priest with the golden censer, who offers the prayers of the saints on the golden altar before God points to the Lord Jesus Christ. No ordinary angel takes the prayers of the saints and offers them to God. There is one mediator between God and man, the Man, Christ Jesus. Prayer and worship to the angels is strictly forbidden (Revelation 8: 1-3).

(c) The Angel-Redeemer, clothed with a cloud, His face shining as the sun, having a rainbow about His head, whose voice is as the voice of a lion, speaks of the Lord Jesus Christ. He is the One who has the little open book in His hand and speaks of "My two witnesses". Such language is inapplicable to any servant angelic being (Revelation 10:5 ,8-10, 11:1).

(d) The Angel-Messenger who lights the earth with His glory points to Christ also (Revelation 18:1). Angels have glory but none have the glory of the risen Christ.

(e) The Angel-Binder, who binds Satan and casts him into the bottomless pit for 1000 years also points to the Lord Jesus Christ. He is the "stronger man who binds the strong man" and then spoils his house. This binding was judicially accomplished at Calvary (Revelation 20:1-3 with Matthew 12:28-29). It was the Lord Jesus Himself who conquered Satan personally, for Himself, and then representatively, for us. No ordinary angel was given this ministry.

In Scripture, the Son of God is seen as the God-Man, the Messenger of the Covenant or the Messenger of Jehovah (Malachi 3:1-2).

He who was the Creator of angels (Colossians 1:16), is better than angels (Hebrews 1:4-5), and is worshipped by angels (Hebrews 1:6), as the eternal Son of God, was made a little lower than the angels for the redemption of mankind (Hebrews 2:6-9).

As mentioned, in the Old Testament He appeared as an angel, and as a man. In the New Testament, He was born as a Man, yet seen in vision as an angel. He did not become an angel to redeem fallen angels, but He did become a Man to redeem fallen man who had been corrupted by a fallen angel, Satan.

In the Old Testament, He was particularly seen as the Jehovah-Angel. In the New Testament, He is seen as the Jehovah-Man, in the incarnation.

The Book of Revelation is a revelation of HIM in deed and in truth. Again the student is referred to the chapter on **"The Christo-centric Principle"**

2. Ministers of Churches as Angels

Ministers of the churches, or God's prophets and preachers are also spoken of as being "angels", or God's messengers.

(a) Israel, as a nation, was God's messenger (Isaiah 42:19).

(b) Haggai the prophet, was also God's messenger (Haggai 1:13).

(c) John the Baptist was spoken of as the messenger of the Lord (Malachi 2:7).

(d) Christ is called the messenger of the covenant (Malachi 3:1).

(e) The ministers of the seven churches of Asia are called "the angel of the church" (Revelation 1:1,20; 2:1,8,12).

(f) Angelic spirit beings are also God's messengers (Psalm 68:17; 104:4).

The language used in Revelation concerning the angels of the seven churches is inapplicable to angelic spirit beings unless they are fallen angels! Only the language of the context will provide clues of identification as to which "angel-messenger" is being spoken to.

3. Angelic Spirit Beings

The Book of Revelation reveals an active involvement of angelic spirit beings prior to the second coming of Christ, as well as at His coming. Again, the language of the passage context shows which grouping of "angel-messengers" is being referred to.

(a) Innumerable angels worship God and the Lamb (Revelation 5:14).

(b) Four angels restrain the winds of judgment blowing on the earth until the servants of God are sealed in their forehead (Revelation 7: 1).

(c) Seven angels sound the seven trumpets of judgments on the earth (Revelation 8:2,7,8,10,12; 9:1,13; 11:15).

(d) Michael and his angels engage in war with Satan and his angels and they are cast out of heaven to earth (Revelation 12:7-10).

(e) Angelic ministry is evidenced in the judgments of the earth (Revelation 14:6,8,9,15,17,18,19).

(f) An angel announces the fall of Babylon (Revelation 14: 8).

(g) An angel announces the everlasting gospel of judgment, warning the earth-dwellers not to take the mark of the beast (Revelation 14:6,9).

(h) The wicked will be tormented in the presence of the Lamb and the holy angels, whose ministry of grace they have spurned (Revelation 14:9-10).

(i) Angels are used as harvesters in the time of the end, both of the good and the evil. These harvests are symbolized under wheat and tares, good and evil fish, wheat and wine harvests (Revelation 14:17-19 with Matthew 13:24-30, 36-43, 49-50).

(j) Angels pour out from the heavenly temple the seven vials of judgments on unrepentant mankind (Revelation 15-16).

(k) An angel reveals to John the harlot and the bride (Revelation 17:1-7; 21:9).

(l) John saw an angel standing in the sun, calling the birds and beasts to the supper of the wicked in God's judgment (Revelation 19:17).

(m) The angels will be associated with Christ and the gathering of the redeemed of earth at His second advent (Matthew 16:27; 24:31-36; 25: 31; Mark 8:38; 13:27; 2 Thessalonians 1:7).

As there was much activity of angels in the Old Testament times, as well as New Testament times, Scripture indicates that the church can expect more in these last days, leading up to Christ's coming. The Book of Revelation certainly confirms this in a very great way.

Eternity alone will reveal how much ministry the angels have rendered to the redeemed over all ages, in the purpose and will of God, and the history of mankind!

G. The Doctrine of Satan and Demonology

The Book of Revelation also gives us details of Satanic and demonic activity in the last days. It also provides the ultimate fulfilment of Divine judgments on the old serpent, Satan, as pronounced in Genesis 3:15. "The seed of the woman shall bruise the serpent's head".

Let us consider the Revelation as to the major references concerning Satan and demonic activity to his final and eternal doom. Satan is revealed as the great opposer and counterfeiter of all that God does. For the purpose of this text, the references mainly come from Revelation itself.

1. Satan has a throne (Revelation 2:13).

2. Satan has great depths of false doctrine (Revelation 2:24).

3. Satan has a synagogue (Revelation 2:9; 3:9).

4. Satan has a kingdom of darkness (Revelation 16:10).

5. Satan influences the rulers of the kingdoms of this world (Revelation 11:15; 12:3,7-12).

6. Satan is the accuser of the people of God (Revelation 12:10).

7. Satan is the old serpent, the devil and the dragon (Revelation 12:3-17; 13:2,4,11; 16:13; 20:2).

8. Satan is the destroyer, called Abaddon or Apollyon (Revelation 9:11).

9. Satan is the deceiver of the nations of earth (Revelation 12:9; 13:14; 20:2-10).

10. Satan performs counterfeit miracles, signs and wonders (Revelation 16:4).

11. Satan controls the demonic spirits in his kingdom (Revelation 9:20).

12. Satan counterfeits the Godhead with his Satanic trinity of the beast (anti-Father), the anti-Christ (anti-Son), and the false prophet (anti-Holy Spirit). Read Revelation 16:13-14)

13. Satan is the angel of the bottomless pit (Revelation 9:1).

14. Satan seals his followers with a name, mark or number in their forehead or hand as his worshippers (Revelation 13:16).

15. Satan persecutes the woman who brings forth the manchild (Revelation 12:3-6, 13-17).

16. Satan and his angels are to be cast out of heaven to the earth in the time of wrath at the close of this age. This casting out is the result of angelic war in heaven (Revelation 12:4-13).

Revelation is also a book of war: Warfare that goes on in the spirit realm, between God and Satan; Michael and his angels at war with Satan and his angels.

* The beast makes war with the two witnesses (Revelation 11:7).

* There is war in heaven (Revelation 12:4-13).

* The antichrist and the ten kings make war with the Lamb and the Lamb overcomes them (Revelation 13:4,7; 17:14; 19:11,17). The age-long battle between the kingdom of light and the kingdom of darkness will come to an end.

17. Satan will be cast out from the earth into the bottomless pit for 1000 years at the second coming of Christ (Revelation 20:2-3).

18. Satan will be loosed out of the bottomless pit for a little season, after which he will be cast into the lake of fire and brimstone. This is eternal judgment upon Satan, the author of sin, and this same judgment will be on his angelic and demonic hosts, and all those of mankind who chose to serve him in this temporal life (Revelation 20:10-14).

The Book of Revelation gives the final account of Satan's activities and the eternal judgment that befalls him, and fallen angels and demon spirits who served him. It is indeed the ultimate judgment on Satan and his seed as promised back thousands of years ago in the Garden of Eden (Genesis 3:15).

The student should be able to see that that which pertains to the Doctrine of Satan and Demonology, in Revelation alone, provides much food for holy thought and food for teaching.

H. The Doctrine of Sin

The Book of Revelation also confirms the whole Biblical Doctrine of Sin. In this book, sin comes to its climax. Here sin is finally and eternally judged with the sinners who cling to their sin – unrepentant!

Here in the fullest sense of the words, Daniel 9:24 is fulfilled. Messiah will "finish the transgression, make an end of sins, make reconciliation for iniquity, and bring in everlasting righteousness, sealing up vision and prophecy".

There are a number of lists of sin given in both Old and New Testaments, all of which bring unrepentant mankind to the great white throne judgment. All sins are recorded in the books of works of every man's life, and all are judged accordingly. Eternal destinies are settled here in time (Revelation 20:11-15).

Revelation shows the holy God and His holy Christ dealing with sin and sinners. His desire is to "wash us from our sins in His own blood" (Revelation 1:5).

In Revelation chapters 2,3, Jesus, as head of the church, is lovingly exposing and seeking to deal with sin in the churches. Judgment begins at the house of God (1 Peter 4:7).

The sins of leaving first love (Ephesus); the doctrine of Balaam, idolatry and immorality, along with the doctrine of the Nicolaitanes (Pergamos); the idolatry and immorality of Jezebelism (Thyatira); the spiritual deadness and defilements of death (Sardis); the lukewarmness and religious self-satisfaction (Laodicea) — all have to be repented of in order for the Christ to remain in the midst of His church!

Revelation 9:20-21 shows mankind unrepentant of the sins of demon-worship, idolatry, murders, sorceries (drugs) and thefts.

Blasphemy is another great sin in the end-times in the Book of Revelation. Blasphemy against God, His name, His tabernacle and those that dwell in heaven, are seen throughout the book (Revelation 13:1,5,6).

The worship of the image of the beast is a sin that is unpardonable. To receive his mark, number or name brings the eternal punishment of the lake of fire and brimstone (Revelation 13:17; 14:9-11).

The sins of Sodom and Egypt are repeated and judged by plagues and fire and brimstone also (Revelation 11:8; 14:9-11; 20:10).

Abominations and filth are evident and also come up for judgment (Revelation 17:4,5).

The slaughter of the saints and the innocents comes up for judgment, filling up the number of the martyrs of the Lord (Revelation 6:9-11; 12:17; 13:7; 14:12,13; 15:2; 17:6; 20:4). In our times untold millions have been martyred for Jesus and entered into their reward.

The final listings of sins are found in Revelation 21:8 and 22:15. Among these lists are found the fearful (cowardly), the unbelieving, the abominable (dogs), the murderers, the whoremongers (sexually immoral), the sorcerers, the idolaters, and all liars. All find their part in the lake of fire and brimstone, which is the second death.

However, once the great white throne judgment takes place, then Satan, his evil angelic and demonic hosts, and all sinful, unrepentant and unredeemed mankind, are banished eternally to the lake of fire. Sin and sinners are eternally judged. This is what Revelation teaches us about the doctrine of sin. This theme alone is worthy of much consideration, providing teaching and preaching as a challenge to all, both believers and unbelievers !

I. The Doctrine of Salvation

Woven throughout Revelation are the final strands of redemptive truths pertaining to God and His Christ, and the people of God !

The Doctrine of Salvation includes in itself God's provision, and man's acceptance and application of it unto full salvation. Following are some of the particular words that belong to the whole plan of salvation. The references are brief but are basically confined to Revelation for the purposes of this text, but they should be read by the student.

1. Grace (Revelation 1:4; 22:21). Salvation is by grace through faith.

2. Redemption (Revelation 1:6; 5:9; 7:14; 12:11; 14:3-4). Redemption is available only through the blood of the slain Lamb of God (John 1:29,36).

3. Repentance (Revelation 2:5,16,21,22; 3:3,19). Repentance is the issue which divides all mankind into two classes; the saved and the unsaved, the found and the lost. The Lord calls His church to maintain repentance in order to maintain relationship with Him. Revelation also shows that there are those who

"repented not", and come up for judgment in due time (Revelation 2:21; 9:20,21; 16:9,11).

4. Prayer and Praise (Revelation 5:8; 8:3-4; 19:5). The prayers and praises of the saints have much to do in the purposes of God.

5. Kings and Priests (Revelation 1:6; 5:9-10; 20:6). Believers are called to be a kingdom of priests unto God and His Christ, and all that is involved in that twofold ministry.

6. Worship - there are seven worship scenes in Revelation, all of them together providing a wealth of spiritual food. The Lord tells John to "measure the worshippers" (Revelation 11:1). Following, in outline form, is a list of the seven worship scenes in Revelation.

   * Revelation 4:8-12 - Worship in relation to the throne of God.

   * Revelation 5:11-14 - Worship in relation to the sealed book.

   * Revelation 7:11-12 - Worship in relation to the tribulation saints.

   * Revelation 11:16-17 - Worship in relation to the seventh trumpet at His coming.

   * Revelation 14:1-5 - Worship on Mt Zion with the Lamb.

   * Revelation 15:1-4 - Worship in relation to the seven vials of wrath.

   * Revelation 19:1-5 - Worship in relation to the marriage of the Lamb.

The redeemed of the earth are called to be a repentant, praying, praising, worshipping kingdom of priests, and all is by the grace of our God and His Christ. This is redemption. This is eternal salvation!

J. The Doctrine of Eternal States

The Book of Revelation brings us to the finality of things pertaining to Time and to the Doctrine of Eternal States.

The Doctrines of **"resurrection from the dead"** and **"eternal judgment"** belong to each other. Resurrection precedes judgment. Judgment precedes eternal states (Hebrews 6:1-2).

1. Resurrection

Revelation speaks of the truth of resurrection. Christ was dead for three days and three nights, but now is alive for evermore (Revelation 1:18).

Revelation brings our attention to the truth of two resurrections; the first resurrection and the second resurrection. Those in the first resurrection are blessed, holy, and they reign as kings and priests with Christ. Those in the second resurrection are judged by the second death, which is the lake of fire (Revelation 20:1-6 with John 5:28-29 and Acts 24:15).

2. Judgment

Revelation is also a book of judgment. Christ is the High Priest Judge in the midst of His church. Judgment always begins at the house of God (Revelation 1,2,3 with 1 Peter 4:17).

* The seven sealed book lets the judgments of God loose in the earth (Revelation 4,5).

* The seven trumpets are also judgments of God in the earth (Revelation 8,9,10).

* The seven vials of God's wrath are the full judgments of God in the earth and on mankind (Revelation 15,16).

* Revelation 17 and 18 show the judgments of God on the Babylonian Harlot and the Babylonian City .

* The great white throne is the ultimate judgment and all whose names are not found written in the Lamb's book of life are cast into the lake of fire and brimstone (Revelation 20).

* Revelation chapters 21, 22 set out the eternal states of the lost and found, the saved and the unsaved, the redeemed and the unredeemed. The eternal destinies are either heaven or hell. People will live in eternity with the one they served in time; either Satan or the Lord! This is eternal judgment from which there is no escape! Revelation is indeed a book of judgment!

As mentioned at the beginning of this chapter, this chapter is not in any way meant to be, nor can it be, a full treatise on any of the major doctrines here. Such can only be done within the context of the whole Bible.

However, enough has been covered in this chapter to show the importance of **sound theology** along with **sound hermeneutics** for any exposition of Revelation. It must always be remembered that, flowing through and undergirding all books of the Bible are major doctrines, or, sound theology. No one book has the complete theology of the Bible. Only the total Bible provides that.

The Doctrines of Revelation, Inspiration, God, Christ, the Holy Spirit, Angels, Satan and Demonology, Sin, Salvation, Worship, Resurrection and the Eternal States - all find their consummation in the Book of Revelation.

The references to these doctrines have predominantly been limited to Revelation itself (although some from other books are given), in order to emphasize the fact that one must have sound theology in order to properly interpret the Book of Revelation.

Apart from any eschatological import of Revelation, each of these doctrines constitute great Bible themes and wonderful messages for exposition in themselves!

(For a full treatment of each of these doctrines, the reader is referred to the text-book, **"The Foundations of Christian Doctrine"**, by the author).

CHAPTER TEN

HERMENEUTICAL PRINCIPLES OF THE REVELATION

In previous chapters, it was seen that one of the major problems among Biblical expositors was not over inspiration and revelation so much as over interpretation and application. The reader is encouraged to refer back to those chapters as a reminder of these things.

Any preacher, teacher or author, who sets out to expound the sacred Scriptures must needs be governed, guided and controlled by certain basic principles of interpretation. This is especially so when it comes to interpreting and expounding those portions of Scripture that have to do with Historical and Prophetical things. If these principles are not followed and used properly, then the Scriptures, and here we speak more particularly of the Book of Revelation, can be made to say anything that the expositor wants it to say.

Many times, when expositions of things in Revelation are given, the hearer will ask, "How does the writer or speaker arrive at that conclusion?" Because of these honest enquiries, and this writer's conviction of the need for sound hermeneutics, in the following chapters are set forth some of the basic principles of interpretation. These are the principles that are used throughout an exposition of Revelation, and by which certain conclusions are drawn. We believe that all sound expositors of Revelation will use these principles.

Because each of the chapters that follow provide a Definition, Amplification and Demonstration of these hermeneutical principles, they are simply listed here in the order that these chapters follow.

A. The Context Group of Principles

Following is the first group of principles that should be used in exposition of any book of the Bible, but more especially are used to help one interpret Revelation.

1. The Context Principle
2. The First Mention Principle
3. The Comparative Mention Principle
4. The Progressive Mention Principle
5. The Complete Mention Principle.

These principles are grouped together because of their inter-relatedness. The First Mention, the Comparative Mention, the Progressive Mention and the Complete Mention Principles are actually specialized extensions of the Context Principle. When an interpreter uses these four principles, he will realize that these together constitute the Context Principle, the most important of all hermeneutical principles.

B. The Theological Group of Principles

The next group of principles here are referred to as the Theological Group. They are as follows.

1. The Election Principle
2. The Covenantal Principle

3. The Ethnic-Division Principle

4. The Chronometrical Principle

5. The Breach Principle

6. The Christo-Centric Principle

7. The Moral Principle

These principles are grouped together because they each arise out of the interpretation of the purposes of God as revealed in Scripture. The principles all assume the practice of allowing the whole of God's revealed purpose to affect the interpretation of the parts of His revelation. In using these principles, the interpreter will be causing the interpreted whole to affect the interpretation of it's individual parts.

Sound theology is a result of sound hermeneutics, as already noted. Both are like two sides of the one and same coin. To deface one side is to deface the coin. If one does not have sound hermeneutics, one does not have sound theology. The converse is true also. If one does not have sound theology, one does not have sound hermeneutics.

The Book of Revelation has as its undergirding foundation Biblical theology, and therefore needs Biblical hermeneutics to be properly interpreted.

C. The Figures of Speech Group of Principles

The third group of principles is spoken of as the Figures of Speech Group. They are as follows.

1. The Symbolic Principle

2. The Numerical Principle

3. The Typical Principle

4. The Parabolic Principle

5. The Allegorical Principle

Any reader of Revelation will soon discover that it has numerous symbols woven throughout its chapters. Symbolic objects, creatures, actions, numbers, names, colours, directions and place are part of the language of Revelation. It is impossible to interpret Revelation without a proper understanding of that which is symbolic in the book.

This specialized group of principles may be grouped together because they deal with figures of speech or extensions of them. Of course, these do not comprise all the figures of speech group used in Scripture. These are included as principles due to their prominence in Scripture, and the difficulties they present in interpretation. Also, the interpreter realizes that he cannot interpret the Book of Revelation without using some of these principles.

In this group, each of them use symbols. There are symbols used in types, parables and allegories. These symbolic elements have to be interpreted first in order to properly interpret the literary style of the passage of Scripture in which they may be used.

Although there are no specific types, parables or allegories referred to in Revelation, there are symbols there, and some of the symbols used in Old Testament types are referred to, hence their inclusion in this list.

We deal specifically with fifteen of the hermeneutical principles listed in this chapter in the chapters which follow. It is believed that all of them working together will help in the interpretation of the Book of Revelation. These principles are dealt with more fully in the published text-book, **"Interpreting the Scriptures"**, (Conner/Malmin).

CHAPTER ELEVEN
THE CONTEXT PRINCIPLE

A. Definition

The Context Principle is defined as that principle by which the interpretation of any verse is determined upon a consideration of its context.

B. Amplification

The word "context" is composed of two Latin words: "con", meaning "together"; and "textus", meaning "woven". It denotes something that is woven together. In literature it refers to the connection of thought running through a portion or the whole of a writing. In relation to Scripture, it signifies the connection of thought running through either the whole of Scripture, a Testament, a book of the Bible, or a particular passage.

In being used of God to weave Biblical contexts, the writers of Scripture utilized two methods; writing fresh revelation, and weaving together previous revelation.

1. Fresh Revelation Context

The writers of Scripture were inspired by the Holy Spirit to write thoughts previously unknown to them. Some examples of this are: Jeremiah's revelation concerning the New Covenant (Jeremiah 31:31-34), and Paul's revelation of the mystery of the Body of Christ (Ephesians 2:11-3:21). This method of writing context substantiates the need for illumination of the Holy Spirit in interpreting Scripture. That which the Holy Spirit inspires, the Holy Spirit must also interpret.

Undoubtedly John in Revelation receives fresh revelation and writes things previously unknown to him. This was especially so with regards to the second coming of Christ. The Lord Jesus told His disciples that, when the Holy Spirit came, He would take of the things of Christ and show it to them. The Holy Spirit would glorify Christ. The Holy Spirit would show them things to come (John 16:5-15).

An example of this would be the things that, to Daniel were to be "shut up and sealed to the time of the end" (Daniel 12), were certainly given to John in Revelation. Such would be "fresh revelation", which John was inspired to write (Revelation 1:3; 22:8-10).

2. Woven Revelation Context

Under inspiration, the writers of Scripture, at times, wove together thoughts already known to them. For example, to establish the universality of guilt in Romans 3:9-18, Paul weaves together five quotations from the Old Testament. Another example would be found in Hebrews 1:4-14. Here the writer weaves together seven quotations basically from the Psalms. He does this to prove the superiority of Christ above the angels. This method of writing context substantiates the need for a context principle of interpreting Scripture. If the

Spirit used Scripture to write Scripture, then He will also be able to use Scripture to interpret Scripture.

In Chapter Six we saw how Revelation is indeed "the book of ultimates". As a reminder to the reader, the Book of Revelation is, as it were, a composite book. It is made up, so to speak, of the language of all books that preceded it, without any contradictions.

Revelation would be more **"woven revelation"** than **"fresh revelation context"**. John, under the inspiration of the Holy Spirit, weaves together numerous things from previous books of the Bible, whether Old or New Testament books.

Examples of "woven revelation context" can be seen by a consideration of these verses.

1. Revelation 2:12-16

In this passage, being the letter to the church at Pergamos, the Lord mentions "the doctrine of Balaam", and "the sharp two-edged sword".

By a reading of Numbers Chapters 22,23,24 with Numbers 31:16, one sees what "the doctrine of Balaam" was in his causing the Israelites to fall into idolatry and immorality, and how, in due time, he was "slain with the sword".

This is not "fresh revelation context" but "woven revelation context".

2. Revelation 2:17

In this verse, we see how the Lord mentions "the hidden manna", and "the white stone with a new name written in it" which is to be given to the overcomer.

By reading Exodus 16 with Hebrews 9:4 we see the account of the manna that came from heaven and how a portion of it was "hidden manna", hidden in the ark of God.

And again, by a reading of Exodus 28:5-30, we see the two onyx stones on the shoulders of Aaron, the high priest, and in these two stones the names of the twelve tribes of Israel.

One cannot fail to see the "woven revelation context" in these examples. Balaam, the sword, the manna, the stone with a name in it — these thoughts are woven together in the letter to the church at Pergamos. Such is not really "fresh revelation" but "woven revelation"; thoughts already known to John.

The evaluations of the two methods above ("fresh" and "woven") lead us to the conclusion that the **method** by which the context was **written** gives rise to the **principle** by which the context may be interpreted. The involvement of inspiration in the writing of Scripture necessitates the interpreter receiving revelation. The weaving together of context necessitates the interpreter using the context principle.

These two principles are somewhat implied in 1 Corinthians 2:13 where Paul states that "we speak, not in the words which man's wisdom teaches, but that which the Holy Spirit teaches; comparing spiritual things with spiritual." The phrase "the Holy Spirit teaches" implies the inspiration and illumination of the Holy Spirit. The phrase "comparing spiritual things with spiritual" implies the use of Scripture in interpreting Scripture, as other translations indicate ("interpreting spiritual truths with spiritual language" - Amplified New Testament).

One of the oldest and most highly regarded adages of hermeneutics is: "Scripture interprets Scripture." This communicates to us that the Bible, to a large degree, is self-explanatory and that the Holy Spirit will use Scripture to interpret Scripture. This underscores the value of the context principle as the **"First Principle of Hermeneutics."**

A further amplification of the context principle would be to say that a part can never be understood without the whole. This balances the burden of exegesis which contends that the whole cannot be understood without knowing the meaning of its parts. This paradox has been referred to by interpreters as the **"hermeneutical circle"**, which rotates from part to whole, and from whole to part.

The interpreter must interpret the whole with a knowledge of its parts and interpret each part in the light of the whole.

In other words, the interpreter and expositor must constantly keep in mind the fact that The Context Principle is the "principle of all principles" for interpreting properly the Word of God. The interpretation of a word, a verse, a passage, a chapter, a book, a testament — all must be done within the context circles. Any interpretation of a word, a passage, a chapter or a book that contradicts any other word, verse, passage, chapter or book of either Old or New Testament is not sound hermeneutics.

Though true of the total Bible, we speak especially here of the Book of Revelation. No word, verse, passage, or chapter of Revelation can be used to contradict or violate any other word, verse, passage or chapter in the total Bible. The Bible is one harmonious whole and no Scripture will be used to contradict another Scripture. The numerous interpretations of Revelation are so contradictory and violate so many other passages of Scripture in other books of the Bible. All of this shows a failure to use or properly use "the context principle".

Categories of Scripture Context:

The context of Scripture falls into four major categories, or concentric circles:

1. The Whole of Scripture Context

The context of any specific verse is the whole of Scripture. No one verse should be used on its own apart from its relationship to the whole body of Scripture. The phrase "Scripture interprets Scripture" means that the best interpreter of a Scripture is the Scripture itself.

2. The Testament Context

Within the whole of Scripture the context of any verse is the Testament in which it is found. Each of the two Testaments has its own distinctive character and emphasis. The general emphasis of the Old Testament is law; the emphasis of the New is grace. That which is the dividing point between the Testaments is the cross. As a general rule, the New is the interpreter of the Old.

"The New is in the Old concealed, the Old is in the New revealed."

"The New is in the Old enfolded, the Old is in the New unfolded."

3. The Book Context

Within the Scripture and the Testaments, the context of any verse is the specific book in which it is contained. Each of the sixty-six books of the Bible has its own particular purpose, message and style (e.g., The general theme of Romans is justification by faith, while the general theme of James is justification by works. Any verse in either book must be interpreted within the context of its respective message).

4. The Passage Context

Within the whole of Scripture, the Testaments and the books of the Bible, the context of any verse is the passage in which it occurs. Each book of the Bible is divided subject-wise into passages, each consisting of a group of consecutive verses pertaining to a particular subject. Any single sentence or verse within a passage must be interpreted in the light of the subject-context of that passage (e.g., Romans 11:26 must be interpreted in the light of the subject-context of Romans chapters 9,10,11, which actually constitutes the passage).

These four categories may be illustrated by four concentric rings showing contexts within contexts:

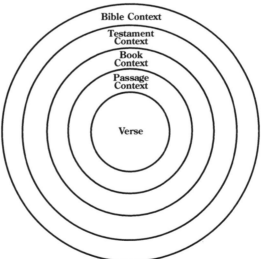

* The context of a verse is the passage
* The context of the passage is the book
* The context of the book is the Testament
* The context of the Testament is the whole Bible

So it may be said, "a text out of context of the whole Bible is a pretext." The context of any verse is not only the passage, but also the book, and the Testament and the whole Bible.

C. Demonstration

From the Book of Revelation, we consider the following example of "the golden lampstand". This illustrates and demonstrates the use of the context principle within each of its concentric circles.

1. Verse Context - Revelation 1:12,13

The verse context speaks about seven golden candlesticks (lampstands) and Christ being in the midst of them. This is what the context of the verse is telling us.

2. Passage Context - Revelation 1:10-20

The passage context is clearly seen to be verses 9-20. Here John writes of the glory of the risen Christ in the midst of the golden lampstands. The symbol of the seven golden lampstands is interpreted for us as being symbolic of the seven churches in Asia.

3. Chapter Context - Revelation 1:1-20

Within the chapter, as defined in most translations of the Bible, we see John's greetings and salutations to the churches, and then the vision of the risen Christ in the midst of the seven churches. Within this chapter context, we have several passages. One would have to check out the Greek passage beginnings and endings where they begin and end. Or else refer to a good translation of the Bible having the passage beginnings and endings.

4. Book Context - Revelation 1:11 with 22:9-21

The book context is the Book of Revelation. John is expressly told to write it in a book and send it to the seven churches which are in Asia.

5. Testament Context - The New Testament

The Testament context is the New Testament. It is the dispensation (arrangement) of the Holy Spirit and the New Covenant era. The Old Covenant has been fulfilled and abolished. The New Testament, the New Arrangement, the New Covenant is now in order. The New Covenant Church is now God's light (lampstand) in the world. (Matthew 26:26-28; Hebrews 8; Matthew 5:14-16; John 8:12).

6. Bible Context - Old and New Testaments

A consideration of the whole Bible shows the following about the golden lampstand.

(a) It was given to Moses by revelation and made according to Divine pattern and placed in the Tabernacle of Moses (Exodus 25:31-40; 37:17-24; 40:24-25).

(b) Ten golden lampstands were placed in the Temple of Solomon (1 Kings 7:49; 2 Chronicles 4:7).

(c) God worked in judgment on Babylon in connection with the golden lampstand (Daniel 5).

(d) The Lord gave visions to Zechariah about the golden lampstand, the golden bowl and the two olive trees (Zechariah 4).

(e) John sees seven golden lampstands in Revelation and these are clearly interpreted to be symbols of the New Testament churches, God's light-bearers (Revelation 1:9-10,20).

(f) John also saw the two witnesses who are also spoken of as being lampstands and olive trees (Revelation 11:1-4).

The **interpretation** of the golden lampstands is saying that God has set light-bearers in the midst of a darkened world. **Application** is to the New Testament churches specifically and also to the two witnesses.

Using the concentric circles, nothing is in any way contradictory. Verse context, passage context, chapter context, book context, Testament context and Bible context are all brought together in the full use of the context principle. Together these "contexts within contexts" provide a most insightful study of God's light-bearers in the midst of a darkened world.

This principle is indeed the **"First Principle of Hermeneutics"** and should constantly be used in expounding and interpreting the Book of Revelation.

Using the context principle, within Revelation alone, provides very rewarding studies.

The example given here shows the use of the context principle in the full concentric circles as in the following diagram:

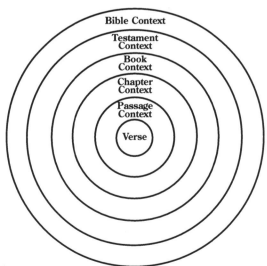

1. The Word - lampstands -1:12
2. Verse Context - 1:12,13
3. Passage Context - 1:10-20
4. Chapter Context 1:1-20
5. Book Context - Revelation
6. Testament Context - New Testament
7. Bible Context - Exodus, Kings, Daniel, Zechariah, Revelation or,
   Moses, Solomon, Daniel, Zechariah and John working in harmony together.

CHAPTER TWELVE
THE FIRST MENTION PRINCIPLE

A. Definition

The First Mention Principle is defined as that principle by which the interpretation of any verse is aided by considering the first time its subject appears in Scripture.

B. Amplification

In general, the first time a thing is mentioned in Scripture, it carries with it a meaning that is consistent throughout the whole Bible.

The First Mention Principle is likened to:

1. **A Key** which unlocks the door into the full room of truth

2. **A Gateway** into the long pathway of Divine truth

3. **A Guide** to discovering truth in its progressive unfolding

4. **A First Link** in a long chain of Divine revelation

5. **A Seed** which has within it all the subsequent mentions of a truth

6. **A River** which begins in the mountains of Genesis, and flows through every book of the Bible into the **Sea of Fulfilment** in the Book of Revelation (Ecclesiastes 1:6).

Understanding this will help us to understand and more properly interpret the Revelation.

It is to be recognized that, though each book of the Bible is complete in itself, no one book is the total Bible. The sixty-six books are to be viewed as one complete book, rather than merely a compilation of many books. Though there are about forty different writers of these sixty-six books, there is really only one Author - God! The writers of Scripture were God's mouth-pieces, but God was the one Divine speaker throughout Scripture (Jeremiah 15:19; Hebrews 1:1-2). The Bible is the Word of God. Because God knew the end from the beginning, as an Author He was able to formulate in the first mention of a thing that which would characterize it in its progressive unfolding.

In writing Scripture, God used the literary method of first mention in that He indicated by the first mention of Scriptural subjects the truths, in His mind, that were to be connected with those subjects in susequent mentions.

This is seen in six major areas which involve the use of first mention, and all find their ultimate in the Book of Revelation. These six areas are (1) Principles, (2) Events, (3) Symbols, (4) Persons, (5) Places and (6) Prophecy.

C. Demonstration

In demonstrating the use of first mention, we will use it in connection with both Revelation and Genesis; the Book of Endings and the Book of Beginnings!

1. **First Mention of a Principle**

    Generally, the first mention of a principle is rather to be seen in its demonstration rather than in its being represented in a word .

    An example is seen in Genesis 15:6 where the first use of the **word** "believe" is mentioned. However, the **principle** of faith is seen in Genesis 3:20-21, where Adam and Eve accepted God's sacrificial covering for their sinful nakedness. So one is to look for the first mention of a truth in **principle** more than just the first mention of a **word**.

    Following is an example of the first mention principle in both Revelation and Genesis. It is the first mention principle of the "agreement of the Word and the Spirit".

    In Revelation 1:2,4 we have the first mention of "the word of God", and the first mention of "the seven Spirits of God". This is the first mention in the Book of Revelation.

    However, the very first mention of the principle of **"the Word"** and **"the Spirit"** is found in Genesis 1:1-3. There we see "the Spirit of God" moving on the face of the waters of the deep. There we see "God said", or God speaking the Word. Ten times in Genesis chapter 1 we have "God said". The Spirit moved. God said. The Spirit preceded the Word. The Spirit made way for the Word.

    Therefore the principle here is the Word and the Spirit agree. The Spirit of God will never contradict the Word of God. Nothing in Revelation (the end) will contradict anything in Genesis (the beginning).

2. **First Mention of Events**

    The first mention in Revelation of the tree of life, which man lost in the event of the Fall, is found in Revelation 2:7.

    In order to properly interpret the significance of this promise to the overcomer, one would need to go back to the first mention of man's fall and the forfeiture of the tree of eternal life. This is found in the Book of Beginnings, Genesis 3:1-7. In Genesis and in Revelation, the beginning and the ending are brought together.

3. **First Mention of Symbols**

    This will be considered more fully under the chapter on The Symbolic Principle. Revelation has numerous symbols in its chapters. One example is appropriate here in conjunction with the first mention principle.

    The first mention of the number **"seven"**, which becomes a symbolic number, is found in Revelation 1:4, which speaks of "the **seven** churches." The first specific mention of the word and number **"seven"** is found in Genesis 2:23. Here God ended His work of creation on the seventh day, and blessed and sanctified this day from the six working days.

The first mention of **"seas"** in Revelation is found in Revelation 4:6. However, the first mention of **"seas"**, which becomes symbolic in due time, is found in Genesis 1:9,10.

The use of the first mention principle is necessary to properly interpret Revelation as to its symbols.

4. First Mention of Persons

The first mention in Revelation of **"Satan"** is Revelation 2:9. However, the first mention of Satan is understood under the symbol of **"the serpent"**, as in Genesis 3:1.

However, if, as many Bible expositors believe, Job was written before Genesis, the first mention of **"Satan"** would be Job 1:6.

By a consideration of the first mention in Genesis of the nature and character of Satan, it certainly is the seed of the doctrine of Satan as unfolded throughout the Bible unto Revelation.

Another example of the first mention of a person is the first mention of **"Balaam"**. Balaam is mentioned in Revelation 2:14. However, the very first mention of Balaam in the Bible would be found in Numbers 22:5. Consideration of this first mention, plus subsequent mentions of Balaam, would be necessary in order to understand the truth about Balaam and the evil doctrine that Christ rebukes in the church of Pergamos.

5. First Mention of Places

The first mention of the place called **"Sodom"** in Revelation is found in Revelation 11:8. In order to understand and properly interpret the truth and significance of this verse, it would be necessary to go to the first mention of Sodom in Scripture.

The first mention of **"Sodom"** is in the first book of the Bible, Genesis 10:19. Its further mention is in Genesis 13:10-13 and so on.

The same is true of **"Babylon"**. The first mention in Revelation of this place is in Revelation 14:8. The first mention of **"Babylon"** (or Babel) is found in Genesis 10:10 and the seed of its significance begins there.

In order to understand and interpret places mentioned in Revelation, one would need to use the first mention principle.

6. First Mention of Prophecy

The first mention of Christ's coming in Revelation is found in Revelation 1:7. There it says, **"He comes with clouds."** This is the burden of the prophecy of Revelation.

However, the first Messianic prophecy of Christ's coming is implied in Genesis 3:15. There the seed of the woman was prophesied to bruise the seed of the serpent. Though implicitly speaking of the first coming, it also involves in enigmatic form the second coming. The first coming of Christ is incomplete without the second coming of Christ. The second completes that which began in the first. Each are incomplete without the other.

The first coming is also implicit also in the "seed promises"; that seed that was to bless all the nations of the earth (Genesis 22:18).

The second coming is implicit also in the coming of Shiloh, unto whom the gathering of the people would be (Genesis 49:10).

Revelation is the consummation of numerous prophecies, having their first mention in Genesis, and flowing through other books of the Bible into Revelation, the book of Divine ultimates! Revelation is the book of Christ's second coming.

The expositor of Revelation should realize the importance of the use of the first mention principle. Numerous things are mentioned in Revelation, and such would not be able to be properly interpreted without referring back to their first mention. Most of the first mention subjects are found in the first five books of the Bible, the Pentateuch. However, such are not limited to these books.

However, the first mention principle has its limitations, and must be used in conjunction with other principles, which brings us to the next chapter, "The Comparative Mention Principle".

CHAPTER THIRTEEN
THE COMPARATIVE MENTION PRINCIPLE

A. Definition

The Comparative Mention Principle is defined as that principle by which a certain verse or group of verses may be interpreted by comparing and/or contrasting it with another verse or group of verses.

B. Amplification

To **"compare"** means to bring things together in order to examine the relationships they bear to each other, especially with the view of ascertaining their agreement or disagreement; points of resemblance or difference.

To **"contrast"** means to place together in view things widely differing from each other, though of the same catergory or class, in order the make the difference more vividly marked.

In the comparative mention principle, these words denote a bringing together of Scriptures which deal with a certain subject area in order to clarify the interpretation of each by comparison or contrast. This principle can then be seen to be an integral part of the context principle in that Scripture is used to interpret Scripture. As Paul says, "Comparing spiritual things with spiritual" (1Corinthians 2:13). The Bible writers themselves used the literary method of comparison and contrast in their writing of Scripture.

As with the First Mention Principle, so with the Comparative Mention Principle. This principle also can be illustrated in six major areas that involve comparison and contrast.

These areas are (1) Principles, (2) Events, (3) Symbols, (4) Persons, (5) Places and (6) Prophecy. These "Mention Principles" should be used in interpreting Scripture as a whole, but here we use such in our demonstration with regards to the Book of Revelation.

C. Demonstration

1. Comparative Mention of a Principle

Bible writers used comparison and contrast in dealing with a wide range of principles. The Book of Revelation has many principles underlying its chapters.

The principle of **"eating the Word before you speak"** the Word of God, or before prophesying, is seen in this brief comparison between the apostle John and the prophet Ezekiel. Both men experience the same in principle; one man from the New Testament, the other from the Old Testament. This comparison shows the truth of this.

Revelation 10:8-11	Ezekiel 3:1-4
(a) The little book	(a) A scroll of a book
(b) Take and eat the book	(b) Eat this scroll
(c) Sweet as honey in the mouth	(c) Sweet as honey to eat
(d) Belly was bitter	(d) Belly was bitter
(e) You must prophesy	(e) Speak to Israel

Undoubtedly using the comparative mention principle helps one to understand this passage in Revelation. The same principle underlies both passages. One must spiritually eat God's Word before one can speak for God. Divine things are sweet in the mouth, to the taste, but bitter in the inward working and experience. The Word of God has both the sweetest and the bitterest things to say to mankind in relation to Divine things.

2. Comparative Mention of Events

Bible writers used comparison and contrast in dealing with historical events. John in the Book of Revelation does the same, as the following example passage shows.

Revelation 11:6-8	Old Testament History
(a) Heaven shut up for three and a half years - no rain	(a) Elijah shut heaven for three and a half years - no rain
(b) Waters turned to blood	(b) Moses turned waters to blood
(c) Earth struck with plagues	(c) Egypt struck with plagues
(d) Sodom	(d) Sodom destroyed, fire, brimstone
(e) Egypt	(e) Eygpt destroyed by plagues

Read these Scriptures pertaining to Old Testament history and compare such with John's passage in Revelation (1 Kings 17:1; James 5:16-17; Genesis chapters 18,19 and Exodus chapters 6 through to 12).

It is evident that the comparative mention principle should be used to help the expositor in interpreting the passage in Revelation. Historical events find their ultimate in the book of ultimates - Revelation!

3. Comparative Mention of Symbols

As in the First Mention Principle, so with the Comparative Mention Principle, the subject of Symbols is fully dealt with in the chapter on The Symbolic Principle. However, a brief comparison and contrastive example is seen here from the Book of Revelation.

Revelation 2:17	Historical Symbolical
(a) Hidden manna	(a) Manna for Israel
(b) A white stone	(b) Stones in Aaron's breastplate
(c) A name in the stone	(c) Names of 12 tribes in stones

Comparing and contrasting Revelation and Exodus (Exodus chapters 16, 28), we discover rich truth that helps one properly interpret the Book of Revelation as to the numerous symbols used therein.

4. Comparative Mention of Persons

Bible writers used comparison and contrast in dealing with various persons. John does this in Revelation also, the following being an example in the mysterious prophet Balaam.

Revelation 2:14-16	Old Testament Person
(a) Doctrine of Balaam	(a) Balaam, the prophet
(b) Balak - a stumbling block to Israel	(b) Numbers 22:1-24:25
(c) Eat things sacrificed to idols	(c) Numbers 25:1-3
(d) Commit fornication	(d) Numbers 25:1-9
(e) Fight them with sword of My mouth	(e) Numbers 31:16 - Balaam slain with sword of Israel.

The interpreter must use the comparative mention principle here in this passage of Revelation in order to understand what the doctrine of Balaam was, and the evil effect it had in Israel, God's chosen people. The same evil effects were seen here in the church at Pergamos by those who held the same doctrine. The same judgment, by the sword that fell on Balaam, would also come on this church if the guilty ones did not come to repentance.

5. Comparative Mention of Places

Bible writers also used comparison and contrast in dealing with various places. John does the same in Revelation. Only by using the comparative mention principle will one be able to discern and discover the fuller significances of places mentioned in the Book of Revelation. The following provides an example.

Revelation 18	Old Testament Place
(a) Babylon, city of riches, and earthly glory	(a) Babylon, city of riches and earthly glory
(b) Babylon destroyed	(b) Babylon destroyed

Again, the following chapters from Revelation, though involving prophecy, provide another example of comparative mention of this same place - Babylon. These chapters, including Jeremiah chapter 51, are concerned with the fall of Babylon. In viewing these chapters together, we find they are indeed comparable, as set out here with regards to the major points of comparison.

Revelation 17,18	Jeremiah	Comparative Points
17:1,15	51:13	The great whore
17:4	51:7	The cup

17:2	51:7	Drunken Babylon
17:4	51:13	Her raiment
17:6	51:49	Killing the saints
18:2,21	51:8	Fall of Babylon
18:21	51:63	The millstone of judgment
18:2,3	51:37	Evil and corrupt birds
18:20	51:48	Rejoicing over her downfall

Thus New Testament prophecy and Old Testament history are woven together, as seen in the use of the comparative mention principle. By using this principle, the details of the glory of Babylon, its fall and judgments in the Old Testament, foreshadow the glory, fall and judgment of the New Testament Babylon.

6. Comparative Mention of Prophecy

Bible writers used comparison and contrast in dealing with prophecy and fulfilment. The apostle John does the same, for Revelation is the ultimate fulfilment of all prophecies concerning Christ and His people. Following is a brief example of the use of comparative mention principle in relation to prophecy.

Revelation 13	**O.T. Prophecy-Daniel 7**
(a) A beast	(a) Four beasts
(b) Seven heads	(b) Seven heads in total
(c) Mouth of a lion	(c) Lion with eagle's wings
(d) Feet of a bear	(d) A bear
(e) Body of a leopard	(e) A leopard
(f) Non-descript beast	(f) The fourth beast
(g) Ten horns	(g) Ten horns
(h) Persecutes the saints	(h) Persecutes saints
(i) For time, times, and half a time	(i) For time, times, and half a time

Again it should be evident that, by using the comparative mention principle, the expositor will have a clearer understanding of the passage and chapter in Revelation. By comparing and contrasting Daniel 7 with Revelation 13 one can discover the truth more fully.

As with the First Mention Principle, so with the Comparative Mention Principle. Neither on their own can provide the complete truth. It is only when internal evidences in the passages under consideration are dealing with the same subject can they be truly compared and/or contrasted.

Each of these principles belong to each other. Discover the first mention, then see if here are other passages that have similar content and then use the comparative mention principle.

CHAPTER FOURTEEN
THE PROGRESSIVE MENTION PRINCIPLE

A. Definition

The Progressive Mention Principle is defined as that principle by which the interpretation of any verse is aided by a consideration of the progressive mentions of its subject in Scripture.

B. Amplification

It is important to realize that the Word of God is a progressive revelation given, over the centuries, by God to man. The method of progressive revelation may be implied from the Scripture in Isaiah 28:13 within the context of God's dealings with Israel. The prophet says, "But the word of the Lord was unto them precept upon precept, precept upon precept; line upon line, line upon line, here a little, and there a little . . ."

By "**progressive revelation**" we mean the successive unfolding of a continuous theme to its consummation. God, as the virtual Author of Scripture, was able to progressively reveal His person and purpose. These themes in Scripture can be symbolized as "**rivers of truth**" that begin in Genesis and run through the books of the Bible into the "**sea of fulfilment**", the Book of Revelation.

God did not give the full truth all at once, rather He unfolded it progressively to man step by step, detail by detail, each portion giving further amplification and clarification. Thus, God spoke "in many separate revelations, each of which set forth a portion of the truth..." (Hebrews 1:1 Amplified New Testament).

There are some expositors and interpreters of the Word that do not see that the Bible is one progressive whole, but rather see that each book is complete in itself. Undoubtedly this is partly true, for, each book of the Bible is a complete book in itself, but no one book on its own is the complete Bible. The 66 books complete the one Bible, and together they are a progressive unfolding of the revelation of the plan and purposes of God in creation and redemption.

As with the First Mention Principle and the Comparative Mention Principle, so it is the same with the Progressive Mention Principle. This principle can be illustrated in six major areas, these being (1) Principles, (2) Events, (3) Symbols, (4) Persons, (5) Places and (6) Prophecy.

This principle, along with the previous principles should all work together in discovering the truth of God's Word, and especially in the interpretation of the Book of Revelation.

Because our purpose is to help provide principles of interpretation for Revelation, our examples will more especially be concentrated on this book though involving Scriptures from previous Bible books.

C. Demonstration

1. Progressive Mention of Principles

God used the method of progressive revelation in developing a wide array of principles in Scripture. This is an example of the principle of the ministry of the Spirit of God at work in creation and redemption.

" The Spirit of God moved ..." (Genesis 1:1-3)

" The Spirit spake by me ..." (2 Samuel 23:2).

" The Spirit of the Lord is upon Me because He has anointed Me to preach the gospel..." (Isaiah 61:1).

" The sword of the Spirit, which is the Word of God ..." (Ephesians 6:17).

These Scripture references are sample Scriptures showing the underlying, yet progressive ministry of the Holy Spirit in creation and redemption.

This same progressive mention of the Holy Spirit's ministry is seen also in the Book of Revelation. This has been seen more fully in the chapter dealing with **The Theology of The Revelation** under the section on **The Doctrine of the Holy Spirit.** However, for the present example, we note some of this progressive mention of the Holy Spirit in Revelation.

There are "seven Spirits of God before the throne" (Revelation 1:4).

The Lord Jesus Christ, as head of the church, is the One who has "the seven Spirits of God" (Revelation 3:1).

The "seven Spirits of God are like seven lamps of fire burning before the throne" (Revelation 4:5).

"The seven Spirits of God are sent forth into all the earth" (Revelation 5:6).

Believers in all the churches are called to "hear what the Spirit is saying to the churches" (Revelation 2:7,11,17,29).

Finally, the Book of Revelation closes with the last mention of the Holy Spirit in the Bible. There "the Spirit and the bride say, Come" (Revelation 22:17).

The principle of the Holy Spirit's ministry certainly has variety as seen in the progressive mention in the Bible, and as seen in these sample verses from Revelation itself.

2. Progressive Mention of Events

God used the progressive mention in dealing with events in Scripture and their significance.

In the event of man's Fall, Adam forfeited the tree of eternal life. There are links in the chain of Scripture in their progressive mentions from Genesis to Revelation concerning the tree of life lost in the Fall. These sample Scriptures show the truth of these links.

Man sinned by partaking of the Tree of Knowledge of Good and Evil (Genesis 3:1-7).

Job speaks of Adam who covered his transgressions (Job 31:33).

Paul tells us, "By one man sin entered the world, and death by sin..." (Romans 5:12-21).

And again, "In Adam all die ..." (I Corinthians 15:22).

Then in 1 Timothy 2:13,14, Paul says, "Adam was not deceived ..."

When we come to the Book of Revelation, we see this theme taken up as a continuation of this progressive mention.

In Revelation 2:7, the overcomer is given the promise to eat of "the tree of life which is in the midst of the Paradise of God".

The city of God, New Jerusalem, has a river (as earthly Eden's Paradise did!), and the tree of life is seen on the banks thereof (Revelation 22:2). The leaves of the tree of life are for the healing and health of the nations.

Finally, the one who obeys God's commandments is given the right to the tree of life, which Adam forfeited through disobedience to the commandment of God (Revelation 22:14). Surely there is a progressive unfolding in the mentions of the tree of life in Scripture!

3. Progressive Mention of Symbols

God utilized the method of progressive mention in developing the truths connected with that which He would use and did use as symbols in Scripture.

Think of the symbols of the sun, moon and stars. God took these created things and used them in symbolic sense as well as literal and actual sense in Scripture.

Genesis 1:14-18. The sun, moon and stars were set in the heavens as signs.

Genesis 37:9-10. Joseph's dream of the sun, moon and stars symbolized his family.

Psalm 148:3. The sun, moon and stars are told to praise the Lord.

Ezekiel 32:7. The sun, moon and stars would be darkened in judgment.

Luke 21:25. Jesus said there would be signs in the sun, moon and stars.

1 Corinthians 15:41,42. The glory of the sun, moon and stars is used to symbolize the glory of the resurrected saints.

The same truth in these symbols is seen in the Book of Revelation, as these Scriptures confirm.

Christ's face shines with the glory of the sun (Revelation 1:16).

Under the sixth seal, the sun, moon and stars are darkened (Revelation 6:12,13).

A third part of the sun, moon and stars are smitten by God (Revelation 8:12).

There is an angel seen standing in the sun (Revelation 19:17).

The holy city of God has no need of the sun (Revelation 21:23; 22:5).

These Scriptures, as well as many others, show a progression of thought concerning the literal and symbolic significance of these heavenly bodies. This progression is true whether they refer to the sun, moon and stars actually or symbolically.

4. Progressive Mention of Persons

God utilized the method of progressive mention in presenting the name, character, office and function of persons in Scripture. This is seen in the progressive revelation of the redemptive names of God Himself, all of which consummate in the greatest redemptive name ever to be revealed - the name of the Lord Jesus Christ. Note the progressive revelation in these names of God.

Genesis 2:4	The Lord, the Creator
Genesis 14:22	The Lord, the Most High God
Genesis 22:14	The Lord, the Provider
Exodus 15:26	The Lord, the Healer
Exodus 17:15	The Lord, the Banner
Judges 6:24	The Lord, our Peace
Psalm 23:1	The Lord, our Shepherd
Jeremiah 23:6	The Lord, our Righteousness

The consummation of all redemptive names is found in the greatest name ever to be revealed, in this world, or the world to come. That is, in the name of the LORD Jesus Christ.

On the day of Pentecost, this was the first revelation that the Holy Spirit gave to the apostle Peter. That was, "Let all the house of Israel know assuredly that God has made this same Jesus whom you crucified both LORD and Christ" (Acts 2:34-36).

In the Book of Revelation, we see various names of the Son of God. In Revelation 1:5, He is the Faithful Witness, the First Begotten of the Dead, and the Prince of the Kings of the earth.

In Revelation 1:8,11, He is the Alpha and Omega, the Beginning and the End.

In Revelation 1:13, He is the Son of Man.

In Revelation 5:6, He is the Lamb slain from the foundation of the world.

In Revelation 19:16, He is the King of Kings and Lord of Lords.

The final and ultimate name above all names is found in Revelation 22:21. "The grace of our LORD JESUS CHRIST be with you. Amen."

These verses, together with numerous others, unfold the progressive revelation of the glorious compound redemptive names of God in Christ.

5. Progressive Mention of Places

God also utilized the method of progressive mention in dealing with places in Scripture and their significance.

The place of Babylon has been mentioned previously, but the progressive revelation in the mention of Babylon finds its consummation in Revelation.

Genesis 10. The origin of Babylon and its tower.

Joshua 7:21. A garment of Babylon was part of Achan's transgression.

Isaiah 13-14. The burden of Babylon is given to Isaiah in these chapters.

Isaiah 47-48. Further utterances are given to Isaiah concerning Babylon's fall.

Jeremiah 50-51. Jeremiah also predicts the fall and judgment of Babylon.

Zechariah 5. Zechariah has a vision of two women flying to Babylon.

The Book of Revelation shows the final and ultimate of the progressive revelation of the place of Babylon.

Revelation 17 gives the whole chapter to the description of the great harlot church, under the figure of a woman named, "BABYLON, Mystery the Great, the Mother of Harlots and Abominations in the earth."

Revelation chapter 18 gives a vivid description of the great commercial city of Babylon, using mostly Old Testament references throughout, to describe its glory, fall and final judgments.

In these chapters, there is a definite progressive development of God's estimate of Babylon, all of which consummate in Revelation.

6. Progressive Mention of Prophecy
God used the method of progressive mention in developing prophetic themes in Scripture.

An example of this is found in Messianic prophecy, beginning in the Old Testament and consummating in the Book of Revelation. The example Scriptures given here show the progressive mention of Christ's kingship and the church, His body, being a kingdom of priests.

Genesis 14:18. Melchisedek was a king and priest and ministered to Abraham the communion, as well as receiving tithes from him.

From Abraham and Sarah were to come kings of nations (Genesis 17:6,16).

From Jacob's loins, kings were to come (Genesis 35:11).

From Judah, the fourth son of Jacob, the sceptre would never depart (Genesis 49:8-12).

David was promised a continual line of kings by Divine covenant (Psalm 89).

Jesus was born to be king and receive the throne of David (Luke 1:26-35).

Consummating in the the Book of Revelation, there we see the people of God as "kings and priests unto God and His Christ" (Revelation 1:6).

The twenty-four elders rejoice that they are "kings and priests unto God", and represent the thousands of the redeemed, out of every kindred, tongue, tribe and nation (Revelation 5:9-10).

The order of Melchisedek was an order of "kings and priests", and the saints reign with Christ for 1000 years (Revelation 20:6).

When Jesus comes the second time, it is as King of Kings and Lord of Lords (Revelation 19:16).

Anyone interpreting the Book of Revelation must recognize the need to use the progressive mention principle, to help in a proper exposition of this wonderful book. The examples in these six areas confirm that truth. All begin in Genesis (First Mention), and progress through the Scriptures unto Revelation (Complete Mention).

CHAPTER FIFTEEN
THE COMPLETE MENTION PRINCIPLE

A. Definition

The Complete Mention Principle is defined as that principle by which the interpretation of any verse is determined upon a consideration of the complete mention of its subject in Scripture.

B. Amplification

The Word of God contains countless subjects to which there are more than a single reference. In order to understand these subjects, every reference to them must be gathered and considered as a whole. The term **"complete mention"** is used here to refer to the total aggregate of references to any individual subject in Scripture.

God, who had in mind, as a whole, the full truth of that which He desired to reveal to man, nevertheless communicated to man in a very fragmentary fashion. He gave to each writer certain fragments to record, thus making it necessary for an interpreter to assemble these fragments. Only as these parts are pieced together can the full truth be seen as a whole.

One may use the illustration of a zig-saw puzzle. The puzzle has many parts to it. The parts of the puzzle have to be laid out fully before being assembled together to see the picture. No one part of the puzzle is the whole. In putting the puzzle together, one must not force the parts or else the puzzle will be distorted. In putting the puzzle together, one must work from part to whole and whole to the part. So it is with numerous themes in Scripture. In studying a theme of truth through the Scripture, one must lay out all the parts (the verses) pertaining to that truth, then assemble them together to see the picture. One must not force the parts (the Scriptures), or else the truth becomes distorted. This is how heresy arises. The expositor must work from whole to part and part to whole. When this is done, we have used the complete mention principle.

As in the previous mention principles, this can be illustrated in the same six major areas, which involve the complete mention principle. These areas are listed again here, these being (1) Principles, (2) Events, (3) Symbols, (4) Persons, (5) Places and (6) Prophecy.

However, because of the similarity between this principle and the previous mention principles, rather than illustrate each in these six areas, we will only illustrate in one area. This will be the complete mention with regard to a symbol .

Any reader of the Scripture immediately sees that God uses actual colours, numbers, objects and so forth in symbolic sense. The symbol is used to convey Divine truth.

C. Demonstration

God used the method of complete mention in presenting a vast assortment of symbols in Scripture. Following are two examples and these also find their consummation in the Book of Revelation.

1. The Symbol of a Key

The word **"key"** is used in both actual and symbolic sense in Scripture. Following is every reference in the total Bible of the use of the word "key". In setting such out, we have used the complete mention principle.

Judges 3:25.	A key is used to open the door to the king's parlour.
Isaiah 22:22.	The key of the house of David is laid upon the shoulders of Eliakim giving him authority to open and shut doors.
Matthew 16:19.	The keys of the kingdom of heaven are used in binding and loosing ministry.
Luke 11:52.	The scribes had taken away the key of knowledge from the people of God.

The Book of Revelation is the consummation of Biblical mentions of the key, as these references show us.

Revelation 3:7.	These things saith He that is holy, He that is true, He that has the key of David, He that openeth and no man shutteth; and shutteth, and no man openeth..."
Revelation 1:18.	The keys of death and hell.
Revelation 9: 1.	The key of the bottomless pit.
Revelation 20:1.	The key of the bottomless pit.

The complete mention listed above of the symbol of the key is interpreted by Scripture as being the authority to open and shut doors. It reveals that the one who holds the key has the power and authority to bind or exercise control.

2. The Colour White

Another example in the use of the complete mention principle is following the subject of **"white"** in Scripture. The colour white is used in both actual and symbolic sense. The following references are the complete references only from the New Testament. To do this fully would involve every use of the word "white" in the total Bible. However, for the purpose of this text, we list the complete mention of the word "white" in the New Testament only, and then note the use of this colour in the Book of Revelation.

Matthew 5:36.	One cannot make a hair white or black.
Matthew 17:2.	His raiment was white as the light.
Matthew 28:3.	His raiment was white as snow.
Mark 9:3.	Shining, exceeding white as snow.
Mark 9:3.	No fuller on earth can white them.
Mark 16:5	Clothed in a long white garment.
Luke 9:29.	His raiment was white.
John 4:35.	The fields are already white to harvest.

John 20:12.	Two angels in white sitting.
Acts 1:10.	Two men stood by them in white apparel.

It is significant to note the use of the word "white" in the Book of Revelation. Here we provide the complete mention of every reference. The word white is used at least 19 times in Revelation.

Revelation 1 :14.	White like, white as snow.
Revelation 2:17.	I will give him a white stone.
Revelation 3:4.	They shall walk with Me in white.
Revelation 3:5.	They shall be clothed in white raiment.
Revelation 3:18.	White raiment, that you may be clothed.
Revelation 4:4.	Sitting, clothed in white raiment.
Revelation 6:2.	And I saw, and behold a white horse.
Revelation 6:11.	White robes were given unto every one of them.
Revelation 7:9.	Clothed with white robes.
Revelation 7:13.	Arrayed in white robes.
Revelation 7:14.	Made them white in the blood of the Lamb.
Revelation 14:14.	And I looked, and behold a white cloud.
Revelation 15:6.	White linen.
Revelation 19:8.	Arrayed in fine line, clean and white.
Revelation 19:11.	Heaven opend, and behold a white horse.
Revelation 19:14.	Followed Him upon white horses.
Revelation 19:14.	Clothed in fine linen, white.
Revelation 20:11.	And I saw a great white throne.

A study of the use of this word "white" in Revelation shows that it is always used with regards to God, Christ, the angels and the saints. The consistent use of the word "white" in Revelation with regards to that which is good should help clarify the different interpretations of "the white horse" in the opening of the first seal (Revelation 6:1-2).

The references to the word "white" do give an illustration of how the complete mention principle should be used in seeking to arrive at the full truth on any given subject.

Because the Book of Revelation is indeeed **"the book of ultimates"**, and **"the sea of fulfilment"** of all prophetic streams flowing from Genesis through every book of the Bible into it, the "Mention-Group Principles" should be used in helping one to interpret this wonderful book.

The "Mention-Group Principles" can be safely used within the limits of the book itself, as has been demonstrated in these last several chapters. However, in the use of such and the final results, nothing will contradict the use of these same principles in the rest of the total Bible.

In concluding these several chapters on the "Mention-Group Principles", some final observations, along with an example, will be helpful.

The Complete Mention Principle is really the ultimate end of the (1) First Mention Principle, (2) the Progressive Mention Principle, and (3) the Comparative Mention Principle. All these will be used together. These three principles may be likenend to "first the blade, then the ear, and then the full corn in the ear" (Mark 4:28).

In using the complete mention principle, every relevant verse is important in formulating the teaching of any subject. Each relevant verse is an integral part of the whole; supplementing, adding to, clarifying and illuminating the others. The full truth on any given subject can only be realized by a consideration of its complete mention in Scripture.

An example of the use of the "Mention-Group Principles" being used together is seen in the following and is used within the Book of Revelation itself as well as the total Bible. The theme is the truth of the golden candlesticks, or golden lampstands.

"The Golden Candlesticks"

The Bible	The Revelation
1. **First Mention** - Exodus 25:31-40 Golden lampstand revealed to Moses Oil for lamps - Exodus 27:20-21	**First Mention** - Revelation 1:10-20 Seven golden lampstands revealed Seven churches in Asia
2. **Progressive Mention** - Exodus 37:17-24 Lampstand fashioned for tabernacle of God Covered in Israel's journeys-Numbers 4:9	**Progressive Mention** - Revelation 2:1 Christ walks in midst of the seven golden lampstands
3. **Comparative Mention** - 1 Kings 7:49 Ten lampstands in Solomon's temple 2 Chronicles 4:7	**Comparative Mention** - Revelation 11:3-4. Two witnesses likened to two lampstands
4. **Complete Mention** - Daniel 5:5 Writing on Babylon's wall in the unknown tongue over against the lampstand Vision of gold lampstand, golden bowl, golden oil, and the two olive trees. Zechariah 4:1-14.	**Complete Mention** - As above in the Book of Revelation

As this example shows, in using the "Mention - Group" of principles, both within Revelation itself, and the whole Bible, nothing is used to contradict anything else.

The golden candlestick in the Old Testament in the nation of Israel was God's light-bearer. The whole purpose of the existence of this article of furniture in both the tabernacle of Moses, and the temple of Solomon, and also in Babylon, was to give light. All of this was symbolic truth.

In the New Testament, the golden candlesticks are used to symbolize people, the people of God who are called to be light-bearers (Philippians 2:15-16). Jesus said to His disciples, "You are the light of the world" (Matthew 5:14-16). He Himself is the light of the world (John 8:12).

In Revelation, the golden lampstands are used to symbolize or represent the seven local churches in the cities of Asia. Later on they are used to represent the two witnesses. They shine as lights in the midst of a crooked generation, and a darkened world.

By a serious study of each and all of these references to the golden candlesticks, and the fragments of truth each passage provides, the expositor will have used the Context Principle. He will more fully understand the truth conveyed in the symbolic use of the golden lampstand.

Each and all of the "Mention-Group Principles" used together constitute the CONTEXT Principle!

CHAPTER SIXTEEN
THE ELECTION PRINCIPLE

This and the following number of chapters have to do with the Theological Group of Principles mentioned in previous chapters; those chapters dealing with "The Theology of The Revelation", and "Hermeneutical Principles of The Revelation". Here we consider the Election Principle and use it in order to help us understand the Book of Revelation.

A. Definition

The Election Principle may be defined as that principle by which the interpretation of any verse or group of verses is determined by considering its relation to the election involved in the purposes of God.

B. Amplification

According to Webster's Dictionary, the word "election" means "to choose out, a choosing out or choice." In theology it refers to the selection of, or giving preference to, certain persons or nations relative to the purposes of God pertaining to time or eternity.

The Hebrew word **"Bachiyr"**. as used in these sample Scripture references means "to select, choose, or the person chosen." It is translated in English, "choose, chosen one, elect" (2 Samuel 21:6; Psalm 89:3; Isaiah 42:1).

The Greek word **"Ekloge"**, as used in these Scripture references, mean "selection, choice, the act of picking out, the person chosen" (Acts 9:15; Romans 9:11; 2 Peter 1:10).

Another Greek word **"Eklectos"** also means "picked out, chosen by God", and it is translated "chosen, elect" in these sample Scripture references (Matthew 20:16; Matthew 24: 22,24,31).

The word "election" in its simplest meaning refers to the intention, process and result of making a choice. It refers to an act of the will, but more especially in the Scriptures refers to an act of the Divine will.

C. Demonstration

In any study of the Book of Revelation, especially as one seeks to understand the various groupings and designated companies of people, the truth of election needs to be understood. And, while not a doctrine that may be seen on a surface reading of Revelation, the doctrine of election is underlying and woven throughout the book, as will be considered here.

The doctrine of election is particularly seen in verses such as Revelation 13:8 and 17:8. There the Scriptures tell us: "And all who dwell on the earth will worship him (the beast), whose names have not been written in the book of life of the Lamb slain **from the foundation of the world**"(13:8). And again, "And those on the earth will marvel, whose names are not written in the book of life **from the foundation of the world**" (17:8).

The doctrine of election is seen underlying these Scriptures. The Lamb was slain FROM the foundation of the world. The names of the redeemed were written in the Lamb's book of life FROM the foundation of the world.

It is worthy of consideration to note that the phrase, **"the foundation of the world"** is used ten times in the New Testament. Three times it is used in the words, "BEFORE the foundation of the world", and seven times it is used in the words, "FROM the foundation of the world." All of this implies the principle of Divine election.

We consider the references to these words **"before"** and **"from"** the foundation of the world, and see their finality in the Book of Revelation.

1. Before the Foundation of the World

The Father loved His Son **before** the foundation of the world. The Son asked the Father to glorify Him with the glory that He had with the Father **before** the world began (John 17:5,24). Such is the love between the Father and the Son and from which the whole plan of redemption came.

Believers are redeemed with the precious blood of Christ, who was as a lamb without blemish or spot, foreordained **before** the foundation of the world. God foreknew that man would fall and was prepared with the redemptive plan in mind for those who would respond to His call (1 Peter 1:18-20). The theme of Revelation is that slain Lamb, slain before the foundation of the world.

In Ephesians 1:4, Paul tells the believers that God had chosen them **before** the foundation of the world, chosen to be holy and without blame before Him in love.

This is election! God loved the Son before the foundation of the world. The Son was chosen to be the Lamb before the foundation of the world. People were chosen of God in Christ before the foundation of the world.

2. From the Foundation of the World

Here we consider those references to the phrase, **"from** the foundation of the world".

Jesus uttered things which had been kept secret **from** the foundation of the world (Matthew 13:35).

The blood of the prophets and the righteous, which had been shed **from** the foundation of the world, would be required of Christ's evil generation (Luke 11:5).

God prepared a rest for His people **from** the foundation of the world (Hebrews 4:3).

Christ's offering for sin was once-for-all, so He did not have to suffer since **(from)** the foundation of the world (Hebrews 9:26).

The Father has prepared a kingdom for His own and this kingdom was prepared **from** the foundation of the world (Matthew 25:34).

The final references are found in Revelation. Here we see that the Lamb was slain **from** the foundation of the world (13:8), and the names of the redeemed were written in the Lamb's book of life **from** the foundation of the world (17:8).

In Revelation, we see various companies of the people of God who are chosen or elected of God in His redemptive purposes.

The church is the "ekklesia", the "called out ones", called out from the world and they are gathering to the risen Christ. Christ's word is to the seven churches, the elect of God (Revelation 2-3 chapters).

The innumerable multitudes, out of every kindred, tongue, tribe and nation, who are redeemed by the blood of the Lamb, called to be a kingdom of priests, are also the chosen of God, elected to salvation (Revelation 5:9-10).

When it comes to the controversial passages in Revelation 7:1-8 and 14:1-5, concerning the 12,000 chosen out of the twelve tribes of Israel, the election principle is evident. One has to discover whether it speaks of "natural Israel", or "spiritual Israel" from which the 12,000 out of each tribe is chosen. Election is evident here.

The same is true concerning the controversial chapter, Revelation 12. There are several companies of the people of God, designated as "the woman", "the manchild" and "the remnant of her seed" (verse 1,5,17). These have been chosen of God.

The ones who are riding with the Lamb on white horses are "called, chosen and faithful" (Revelation 17:14).

In the finality of things in Revelation, there are the redeemed inside the city of God, and there are those who are outside the city of God (Revelation 21:1-8,27).

Regardless of who these groupings or companies of the people of God are, there are basically two divisions of mankind. There are the redeemed and the unredeemed; the saved and the lost; those who enter the city of God, and those who are cast into the lake of fire. Every person's destiny is pre-destined according to the elective purposes of God based on His foreknowledge.

The election principle has to do with God's eternal choices based on His eternal, essential and moral attributes; the attributes of foreknowledge, omniscience, omnipresence, omnipotence, as well as the immutability and spirituality of His being.

As has been mentioned in previous chapters, undergirding and woven throughout Revelation are these essential and moral attributes of God. Sound theology and sound hermeneutics are joined together in sound Biblical exposition. Without both, it would be impossible to properly exegete the Book of Revelation.

Because God is omniscient, omnipresent and omnipotent, He knows all things beforehand. He knows all things at all times, and is everywhere present at all times. He is able to see the end decision of all and every creature, angelic or human. Time past, present and future is but one eternal present to Him who is eternal. It is on this basis, that eternal destinies of mankind are settled in time for eternity. On this basis God's elective purposes stand.

From **"The Foundations of Christian Doctrine"** (pages 249-250 - Conner), we adapt in brief several major facts concerning God's elective purposes in redemption. These things involve both election, predestination and foreknowledge.

In relation to the plan of redemption, election may be defined as that sovereign act of God, in grace, whereby He chose in Christ Jesus all those whom He foreknew would accept Him.

1. Election is a **sovereign act of God,** whereby certain are chosen from among mankind for Himself (John 15:19). God was under no obligation to elect or save anyone, since all had lost their standing before Him.

2. Election is wholly of **grace,** apart from human merit (Romans 9:11; 11:5,6). He chose those who were utterly unworthy of salvation. Man deserved damnation, but in His grace God chose to save some.

3. Election is applicable only to those **"in Christ".** God could not choose man in himself because of his sinfulness, and ill-deserving state. God could only choose man in the merits of another; that is, His sinless Son.

4. Election is according to and soundly based on **God's foreknowledge** (1 Peter 1:1-2). God chose only those whom He foreknew would accept Christ. We are chosen of God in Christ (Ephesians 1:4).

5. **Election and predestination** are founded in God's **foreknowledge.** Whom He did foreknow, them He also did predestinate to be conformed to the image of His Son (Romans 8:28-30). Foreknowledge always precedes predestination (Ephesians 1:3-12).

Though election and predestination go hand in hand, the following distinctions should be noted.

Election means that God has chosen to save those He foreknew would accept His Son. Predestination means that God has fixed the destiny beforehand of those who are not of His election. Therefore, predestination can be viewed as the bringing to pass of God's election. While election looks back to foreknowledge, predestination looks forward to eternal destinies, yet both are based on God's foreknowledge, and neither violate man's free-will choice! Man can either choose to accept or reject Christ to his eternal joy or sorrow. God's foreknowledge does not stem from election or predestination. Election and predestination are solidly founded in God's foreknowledge! An improper understanding of the doctrine of election teaches that God has predestined some to heaven and some to hell, and people have no choice in the matter. Scriptures in Revelation have been misused to teach this.

Revelation deals with the eternal states. Though God did choose or elect some people in TIME for temporal purposes, election of people for ETERNITY has to do with

Divine foreknowledge. A balanced understanding of the principle of election is absolutely necessary in order to gain a proper interpretation of the Book of Revelation.

The New Testament teaches that, since the cross, the people of God, the elect of God, are only those who have been redeemed. The church, composed of believing Jew or Gentile, becomes THE people of God this side of Calvary. These Scriptures all show that the church is the elect of God. The truth is so in Revelation (Romans 8:33; Colossians 3:12; Titus 1:1; Romans 11:5; 1 Thessalonians 1:4; 2 Timothy 2:10).

Their names have been written in the Lamb's book of life "from" and "before" the foundation of the world (Revelation 13:8; 17:8). And the Scripture shows that it is possible to have one's name blotted out of the book of life (Revelation 3:5 with Exodus 32:32; Psalm 68:28). Because of this, Peter exhorts believers to "make their calling and election sure" (2 Peter 1:10).

A clearer understanding of the election principle will help in a clearer exposition of the Book of Revelation!

CHAPTER SEVENTEEN
THE COVENANTAL PRINCIPLE

Another heremeutical principle which will be necessary to use for a proper interpretation of Revelation is the "Covenantal Principle".

A. Definition

The Covenantal Principle is defined as that principle by which the interpretation of a verse or group of verses is determined by a consideration of its covenantal language or setting.

B. Amplification

The English word **"covenant"** signifies a mutual understanding between two or more parties, each binding himself to fulfill certain obligations. In Scripture, the Hebrew and Greek words denote a somewhat different meaning.

The Hebrew word **"Beriyth"** means "to cut, to contract", because of being made by passing between pieces of sacrificial flesh (Genesis 15:17; Jeremiah 34:18). The nation of Israel knew about covenant. They were a covenant people with a covenant book in a covenant land (Exodus 2:24; 6:1-8; Psalm 89:3,4; Daniel 9:27).

The Greek word **"Diatheke"** means "a dispensation, arrangement, testament, will". It is translated by the English words "testament" (Matthew 26:28; Hebrews 9:15-20), and "covenant" (Romans 9:24; Ephesians 2:12; Hebrews 13:20).

Another Greek word **"Suntithemai"** means "to put together, place together, to make arrangement." It is translated by the English words "covenanted"(Luke 22:5), "agreed" (Acts 23:20), and "assented" (Acts 24:9).

It was God who was the initiator of covenants between Himself and man. Man did not come to God with a proposal, seeking God's approval. God came to man declaring His will and seeking man's adherance. It is a contract between God and man, drawn up by God and presented to man. Man can either accept it or reject it, but he cannot change it.

The Scriptures show there are two kinds of Divine covenants; revocable and irrevocable covenants. These differences should be observed in any study of the covenants.

A revocable covenant is a covenant in which God obligates Himself to fulfill the promises of the covenant only upon man's obedience to the conditions set forth by God. This kind of covenant is dependant on, "If you will", then "I will" (Exodus 15:22-27; Deuteronomy 28:58,59).

An irrevocable covenant is a covenant in which God obligates Himself to fulfill the promises of the covenant regardless of man's response. An irrevocable covenant is simply based on the "I will" of the Lord (Genesis 9:11; Exodus 6:3-8).

It should be understood that there is no such thing as an unconditional covenant! Revocable and irrevocable covenants, but there are NO unconditional covenants!

For man to receive the benefits of any of the covenants God makes, he must meet God's conditions. The covenant, if irrevocable, will be fulfilled, but for man to receive the benefits of any of God's covenants, then the conditions of faith AND obedience are necessary.

There is a difference of opinion as to the number of Divine Covenants in Scripture among expositors, but the number mentioned here would be nine covenants. These are defined as the Edenic, Adamic, Noahic, Abrahamic, Mosaic, Palestinian, Davidic and the New Covenants and the Everlasting Covenant.

Undergirding all the covenants pertaining to time, dealing with both creation and redemption, is the covenant made in the eternal counsels of the Godhead. The eight covenants of God pertaining to this earth constitute an unfolding expression of God's eternal covenant in time.

A study of the covenants in Scripture show that, in order for such to be truly a Divine covenant, there are basically three parts to a valid covenant. Without these three parts, the covenant is invalid. These three parts are:

1. The **promises** or words of the covenant

2. The body and blood **sacrifice** of the covenant

3. The **seal** or token or sign of the covenant.

These three things complete the testimony of a Biblical covenant, and a study of the above covenants, with these things in mind, provides a rich and rewarding gold mine of spiritual truth. For fuller exposition of these things, the student is referred to the Bibliography for text-books dealing with **"Covenants"**.

It is not the purpose of this text to deal with the covenants, but, as one studies the Book of Revelation, covenantal language is to be found woven throughout the book. Only by using the covenant principle will one be able to unlock the truths in the use of covenantal language. Revelation is the consummation of all covenants that God ever made with man.

C. Demonstration

Though the word "covenant" or "testament" is used only once in Revelation 11:19, speaking of the "ark of the testament" (Grk. "Diatheke"), covenantal language is used through the book. In fact, an important truth to keep in mind through the whole of the New Testament epistles, is to constantly remember that the New Testament writers use Old Covenant language to describe New Covenant realities, passing all through the cross.

Because this text seeks mainly to present principles of interpreting The Revelation, examples of covenantal language are set out here in the following references and allusions to covenants.

1. The Edenic Covenant

Under the Edenic Covenant, God placed the tree of eternal life in the midst of the garden of God (Genesis 2:8-9), the garden being watered by a river that flowed into four heads.

The Book of Revelation closes the earthly scene with the vision of the heavenly Paradise, having a river flowing from the throne of God and the Lamb, and the trees of life on either side of the banks of the river. The tree of eternal life was the seal of Edenic Covenant (Revelation 22:1-4). This is covenantal language.

2. The Adamic Covenant

The tree of life was forfeited because of Adam's sin and disobedience to the Divine commandment. Adam violated the words of the covenant God had given him (Genesis 3: 1-6).

In the Book of Revelation, the first promise to the first church, given to the overcomers, to those who had washed their robes in the blood of the Lamb, and to those who had kept His commandments, was the promise to eat of the tree of life. That which was lost in Adam is restored in Christ (Revelation 2:7; 22:1-2). This is covenantal language.

3. The Noahic Covenant

In Genesis, we see the first mention of the bow, or the rainbow. This was given to Noah and all the earth, as the seal of the covenant God had made, promising never to flood the whole earth with water. Every time one sees the rainbow in the heavens, after rain, one is reminded of the covenantal promises of God in the Noahic Covenant (Genesis 9:8-17). This covenant was an everlasting covenant.

In the Book of Revelation, John sees in vision, the sign and token of the Noahic Covenant - the rainbow. First, John sees the rainbow of promise around the throne of God (Revelation 4:3). Later on he sees the rainbow on the head of the angel-messenger, who is clothed with a cloud, who seems to be none other than the Lord Jesus Himself (Revelation 10:1-3). This is covenantal language.

4. The Abrahamic Covenant

Allusions to the Abrahamic Covenant are also seen in some references in Revelation. Two examples are given here of covenantal language. Melchisedek appeared to Abraham at the time of covenant and gave to him the communion, and was blessed of Melchisedek. Melchisedek was a king and priest unto the Most High God (Genesis 14:18-20). The order of Melchisedek is spoken of in the prophetic Psalm of David many years later (Psalm 110).

Abraham, Isaac and Jacob were also promised a city whose builder and maker was God (Hebrews 11:10-16). This is the promise of covenant.

The Book of Revelation shows the finality of these things. The church, the people of God, are called to be "kings and priests" (a kingdom of priests) unto God and His Christ (Revelation 1:5-6; 5:9-10).

It is in Revelation chapters 21-22 that we see the city of God, New Jerusalem, the city that Abraham, Isaac and Jacob were looking for; the city whose builder and maker is God. This is the fulfilment of the promises of the Abrahamic Covenant.

5. The Mosaic Covenant

Under the Mosaic Covenant, God gave to Israel the way of approach to Himself, by means of the Tabernacle and its particular furnishings and priestly ministrations (Exodus chapters 25-40). These chapters provide full details.

Revelation uses much of the language of the Mosaic Covenant. It is impossible to understand Revelation without some understanding of the Tabernacle of Moses. The golden lampstand, the golden altar, the brass altar, the ark of the covenant, and numerous other things from the Tabernacle order are mentioned in Revelation. These will be dealt with more fully in subsequent chapters on the Typical and Symbolic Principles.

Moses himself is alluded to in Revelation 11:3-6, where one of the two witnesses has power to "turn the waters to blood, and smite the earth with plagues" as often as he wills. Moses is the only Old Testament prophet who was given such power.

The saints who overcome the beast and his mark are seen standing on the sea of glass, and they sing the song of Moses and the Lamb. Here Moses is specifically named (Revelation 15:1-3). Such language is covenantal language, language pertaining to the Mosaic Covenant.

6. The Palestinian Covenant

There seems to be no specific references to the Palestinian Covenant, which involved the land of Israel in the Old Testament. However, a study of New Testament writings show that the land of promise, the earthly land of Canaan, pointed to something greater. This was "a heavenly country".

In Hebrews 11:8-16 we are clearly told that Abraham, Isaac and Jacob, lived in tents in Canaan land, because they were pilgrims and strangers, looking for a city and a country, a better country, a heavenly country! Surely this promise is fulfilled in the Book of Revelation, in the vision of the heavenly city and heaven itself, as the heavenly country!

Paul goes further in Romans 4:13 and tells that Abraham was "heir of the world", not just Canaan land. In Revelation 5:9-10, the 24 elders sing redemption's song, saying we shall reign on the earth. These things are indeed allusions to a greater land that Palestine. The saints shall inherit the earth (Matthew 5:5).

7. The Davidic Covenant

God gave covenant to David concerning his seed, his throne, his kingdom and dominion (2 Samuel 7). David set up the "Tabernacle of David" in Mt Zion, and established there a whole new order of worship, with singers and musicians worshipping the Lord (1 Chronicles chapters 15,16,17).

In Revelation there are a number of allusions to that which pertains to the Davidic Covenant, as the following things reveal. These things are covenantal language.

Christ, the Lamb, is spoken of as "the lion of the tribe of Judah, the root of David" (Revelation 5:5). In Revelation 22:16 He is called "the root and offspring of David".

In Revelation 5:8-12 and 14:1-5 we see the order of worship as established in the Tabernacle of David. There are the singers, the worshippers with harps, singing a new song unto the Lord. There John sees the Lamb on Mt Zion with the 144,000 worshippers. All such are references and allusions to the Psalms of Zion and the worship order established there by David. How often did David tell us to sing to the Lord with a harp and a new song, and such was sounded forth from Mt Zion. Such is indeed covenantal language.

David was promised that he would always have one to sit on his throne. When Jesus was born of Mary, He was promised the throne and kingdom of David (Luke 1:30-33). Surely Jesus fulfills, as the Son of David, the glorious throne and kingdom of David. He is David's Son and David's Lord, and comes as King of Kings and Lord of Lords (Matthew 1:1; Revelation 19:16).

8. The New Covenant

Underlying and undergirding the whole of Revelation is the reality of the New Covenant. Even though covenantal language of other covenants is used throughout the book, it must constantly be kept in mind that John and all believers in Christ are under the NEW Covenant! The church is not under previous covenants or the Old and Mosaic Covenant.

A sound hermeneutical principle is to pass everything from previous covenants through the cross. Certain things were fulfilled and abolished at the cross. Some promises from some covenants pass to the cross and through the cross, and are repeated in the New Covenant. The cross really becomes what may be called "the hermeneutical filter".

Because the New Testament writers lived at the overlapping of dispensations, under the old covenant, and then, through the cross, coming into the new covenant, they continually use old covenant language to describe new covenant realities!

So John is a new covenant apostle, who lived at the cross-roads of covenants, crossing from the old into the new covenant.

Therefore the expositor of Revelation must not place new covenant believers back to the other side of the cross, or back under the old covenant, just because John is using old covenant language!

Each of the covenants pointed to Christ, to the New Covenant. The Revelation is written by a new covenant apostle, and must be interpreted through new covenant principles. By failing to do this, a number of expositors have interpreted passages of Revelation from the Mosaic point of view, from the Mosaic period of time.

The Mosaic Covenant will never be restored as to its ritualisms and ceremonies, as all were abolished at the cross. So was much of the other covenants. Animal sacrifices, festival occasions, circumcision, the Aaronic and Levitical priesthood, earthly tabernacles and temples - all were done away with at Calvary. Such will be never be restored in this age or the age to come, or any other age, as some expositors teach.

If the expositor of Revelation does not use this major hermeneutical principle of covenant, there will certainly be an improper interpretation of this book. Things will be placed in the end of this age, or even in a Millennial Age that really belong to the Law Age and were abolished at the cross. The Book of Revelation is a New Covenant book!

In bringing this chapter to its conclusion, we see in Revelation the three parts of a valid covenant, and here especially the New Covenant.

1. The Promises or Words of the Covenant

Revelation 1-2-3 given seven special overcomers promises. There are other promises throughout the book.

2. The Body and Blood Sacrifice of the Covenant

The constant reminder of the slain Lamb is evidence of the body and blood of the Lord Jesus Christ, who becomes the sacrificial Saviour of the covenant (Revelation 5:9-10).

3. The Seal or Token of the Covenant

The Revelation shows those who have the seal of God in their forehead. They are sealed with the seal of the living God, by His Spirit and by His name (Revelation 7:1-4; 9:4; 14:1-14).

The New Covenant in Revelation brings man back to the Edenic Covenant, and all that was lost in Adam there in creation is now restored in Christ in redemption! The language of the covenantal principle is evident indeed.

(**Note:**- The student is referred to the Bibliography to the text-books, **"The Covenants"** (Conner/Malmin), and **"New Covenant Realities"** (Conner).

CHAPTER EIGHTEEN
THE ETHNIC DIVISION PRINCIPLE

The Ethnic Division Principle is a very important principle to use in interpreting Revelation. This is especially so when we consider the various companies or people groupings in the Book of Revelation. Are they all referring to one and the same people, or do they represent different companies of God's people? If they are different groupings or companies of the people of God, then how does this affect the church, and the unity of the one body of Christ These are things that need to be considered in using this principle.

A. Definition

The Ethnic Division Principle is defined as that principle by which the interpretation of any verse or group of verses of Scripture is determined upon a consideration of God's appointed ethnic divisions.

B. Amplification

The word **"ethnic"** has to do with the basic divisions of mankind distinguished by culture, as both Hebrew and Greek words show.

1. Old Testament Hebrew

In the Old Testament, there are several Hebrew words used to speak of ethnic groupings of people.

(a) **"Ummah"** - meaning "a collection, or community of persons". It is translated as "nations" (Ezra 4:10; Daniel 3:4,7,29), and "people" (Numbers 25:15; Psalm 117:1).

(b) **"Gay"** - meaning "a massing; a foreign nation, hence a Gentile". It is translated by several English words as "Gentiles" (Genesis 10:5; Isaiah 11:1-10); "heathen" (Psalm 2:1,8; Malachi 1:11); "nation" (Psalm 22:27-28; Malachi 3:12), and "people" (Daniel 11:23).

(c) **"Leom"** - meaning "to gather; a community". It is translated by several words in English as "nation" (Psalm 47:3; 57:9); "people" (Genesis 25:23; Isaiah 55:4); "folk" (Jeremiah 51:58).

(d) **"Am"** - meaning "a people, as a congregated unit; specially a tribe". This word is translated by "folk" (Genesis 33:15; Proverbs 30:26); "nation" (Deuteronomy 30:3; 1 Chronicles 16:24), and "people" (Psalm 29:11; Zechariah 8:22).

2. New Testament Greek

In the New Testament there are two Greek words speaking of ethnic divisions.

(a) **"Ethnos"** - meaning "a race, a tribe; specially a foreign or non-Jewish one". This word is translated "Gentile" (Matthew 10:5; Romans 9:24,30); "heathen" 2 Corinthians 11:26; Galatians 3:8); "nation" (John 11:50-52; Romans 4:17-18), and "people" (Romans 10:19).

(b) **"Genos"** - meaning " offspring, family, nation, the aggregate of many individuals of the same nature, kind, sort or species." It is translated by a number of words, such as "born" (Acts 1:8; 2:24); "country-man" (Acts 4:36); "diversity" (1 Corinthians 12:28); "generation" (1 Peter 2:9); "kindred" (Matthew 13:47); "nation" (Mark 7:26); "offspring" (Acts 17:28-29) and "stock" (Philippians 3:5).

The Hebrew and Greek words together indicate that an ethnic group is to be viewed as a community of persons sharing the same ancestry and participating in the same culture.

C. Classification

The apostle Paul recognized that, while God is no respecter of persons, He has instituted certain ethnic divisions. Paul noted the three basic ethnic divisions in the human race. This is seen in 1 Corinthians 10:32, where he says that we are not to give offence to:

1. The Jews

2. The Gentiles

3. The Church Of God.

In God's mind, these are the only ethnic divisions of the human race. All the world of mankind falls into either of these three classes of people.

D. Ethnic Divisions

1. Old Testament Ethnic Divisions

In Old Testament times, mankind was basically divided into two ethnic groupings; the chosen nation, Israel and all other nations were Gentiles.

The history of the chosen nation of Israel fills the Old Testament. All Gentile nations are dealt with accordingly. God's choice of Israel was ultimately to bless all other nations (Deuteronomy 4:6-8; Genesis 12:1-3; 17:1-7; Deuteronomy 7:6-9; 9:1-6; Romans 9:4-5; 3:2; Galatians 3:8).

Some Gentiles did come into blessing in Israel even under Old Testament times. However, full blessing would come under Messianic times.

2. New Testament Ethnic Divisions

Once Christ came and established the New Covenant, there is added another ethnic division in mankind. As seen in 1 Corinthians 10:32, since the cross there are three groupings; the Jews, the Gentiles and the Church.

The Jews and the Gentiles continue their respective history from pre-cross times right through to Christ's coming.

The old natural, national Israel (or Jew) continues as such. The promises that Abraham's seed would be as "the sand" or "the dust" continue in this age. The Gentiles also continue as such. Both Jew and Gentile remain such as long as they are outside of Christ.

However, once a Jew or Gentile accepts Christ as Lord and Saviour, they come into the NEW ETHNIC, which is THE CHURCH. The church is a new ethnic division of mankind (Matthew 16:18-20). The New Testament is composed of believing Jews and Gentiles; those who have accepted Christ. Paul clearly states that Christians, whether Jews or Gentiles, are one body in Christ (Ephesians 1:22-23; 2:15-16; 3:6; 1 Corinthians 12:13; Galatians 6:15).

The church is God's olive tree, the branches being believing Jews and Gentiles. It is a faith olive tree, as the book of Romans clearly shows (Romans chapters 9,10,11). The only hope for Jew or Gentile to be in the olive tree is by faith in Christ. The natural, the unbelieving natural Jew was cut off because of unbelief. Those of the natural birth can only come into the olive tree by spiritual birth. To offer to the Jew or Gentile any other way than the way of faith in Christ, and salvation through His blood, is to exalt the natural, fleshly birth above the spiritual and heavenly birth. All must be born again, born from above (John 3:1-5). There is not one way for the Jew and another for the Gentile. All must come the same way. Jesus said, "I am THE Way, THE Truth, and THE Life; no man comes unto the Father but BY ME" (John 14:6).

The church is Abraham's seed in Christ (Galatians 3:16,29).

The church is now God's holy nation, His royal priesthood, His temple and habitation by the Spirit (1 Peter 2:5-9; Revelation 1:6; 5:9-10; Ephesians 2:19-22).

The church is God's true and spiritual Israel; for, "they are not all Israel which are of Israel" (Romans 9:6-8). He is not a Jew which is one outwardly but one inwardly (Romans 2:28-29). The new Israel of God are those who are new creatures in Christ (Galatians 6:15-16). This is God's new ethnic.

The church is the great mystery, the bride of Christ (Ephesians 5:23-32).

All of this sets the unbelieving Jew and unbelieving Gentile in their respective ethnic groupings and by themselves before God. They are not part of the new covenant church. They are the unredeemed, and outside of Christ. In Christ there is neither Jew nor Gentile (Galatians 3:28). The church is "one NEW MAN" (Ephesians 2:15-16).

These things have to kept in mind as one interprets Revelation. In this book we have many designations of people; there are various companies of people. All must find their respective place in one of the three basic divisions of mankind. All will either be Jews, or Gentiles, or the church. Only by a skilful use of the Ethnic Division Principle will these ethnic groupings be discerned.

E. Demonstration

Following is a list of most of the designations of people or the various companies of people mentioned in Revelation. It is for the student to discern which ethnic division is being spoken of in order to do a proper exposition of the passages under consideration. The list also includes angelic beings. However, these do not belong to the ethnic divisions of mankind. Following are designations of the companies and personages in Revelation:

1. The seven local churches in Asia, symbolized as lampstands (1:12,20)
2. The seven stars, the "angels" or messengers of the seven churches (1:16,20)
3. The Nicolaitanes (2:6,15)
4. The Balaamites (2:14)
5. The woman Jezebel (2:20)
6. Jews who say they are Jews but are of the Synagogue of Satan (2:9; 3:9)
7. The 24 elders around and on their thrones (4:4)
8. The four living creatures (4:6-10)
9. The souls under the altar (6:9-11)
10. The 144,000 sealed ones of the tribes of Israel (7:1-8)
11. The twelve tribes of Israel (7:1-8)
12. The great multitude who come out of great tribulation (7:9-17)
13. The locust army out of the bottomless pit (9:1-12)
14. The four angels bound at the river Euphrates (9:13-15)
15. The two million army of horsemen (9:16-21)
16. The two witnesses, likened to two lampstands and olive trees (11:3)
17. The servants who are the prophets (11:18)
18. The saints (11:8)
19. Those that fear His name (11:18)
20. Angel messengers (Refer to "Doctrine of Angels", Chapter 9)
21. Those that destroy and corrupt the earth (11: 18)
22. The sun-clothed woman (12:1)
23. The manchild (12:5)
24. Michael and his angels (12:7)
25. The dragon and his angels (12:7)
26. The remnant of the woman's seed (12:17)
27. The first beast, with seven heads and ten horns (13:1-10)
28. The second beast, the false prophet (13:11-18)
29. The 144,000 with the Lamb on Mt Zion (14:1-5)
30. The saints who are slain (13:7-10)
31. Those that dwell in heaven (13:6; 14:12-13)
32. Those that receive the mark of the beast, the earth-dwellers (14:9-11)
33. The company that stand on the sea of glass (15:1-4; 20:4)
34. The ten horns who are the ten kings (12:3; 13:1-2; 17:3,9-17)
35. The seven heads on the dragon (12:3; 17:9-17)
36. The kings of the east, the sun-rising (16:12)

37. The kings of the earth (16:14;19:19)

38. The great whore, the harlot, Mystery Babylon (17:1-7,18)

39. The nations (11:18; 19:15)

40. The image worshippers who take the mark of the beast (19:20)

41. The remnant (19:21)

42. The bride and the marriage of the Lamb's wife (19:7-8)

43. Those who are called to the marriage supper of the Lamb (19:9)

44. The white horse rider and the armies with Him (19:11-14)

45. Those who reign on thrones for 1000 years (20:4)

46. The first resurrection company of saints (20:1-6)

47. Gog and Magog in the four quarters of the earth (20:8)

48. The wicked dead raised in the second resurrection (20 :11-15; 21:8; 22:15)

49. The camp of the saints (20:9)

50. The bride-city (21:9)

51. The twelve apostles of the Lamb (21:14)

52. The twelve angel-messengers standing in the gates of the city (21:12)

53. The twelve tribes of the children of Israel (21:12)

54. The kings of the earth (21:24)

55. The nations of them who are saved who enter the city (21:24,26)

56. Those who are cast into the lake of fire (21:8; 22:15)

57. Those who have the right to the tree of life (22:1-5, 14)

In the resurrection, all will stand in their lot (Daniel 12:13). All will arise to judgment. The saints will arise to their various resurrection glories (1 Corinthians 15:41-42). The saints from the patriarchal age, the redeemed of natural and national Israel of Old Testament times, the redeemed of the church age, Jews or Gentiles, saints and believers, the church as the bride of Christ — all will stand in their place in the resurrection of the dead.

Paul said that he would bow his knees to the Father of our Lord Jesus Christ, of whom **every family in heaven and earth is named** (Ephesians 3:15). There is one Father God, and one blessed Lord Jesus Christ, yet God has many families of His people over the ages of time. Each family has its glory, and each stand in their appointed places in the end of time. All will be under the Lordship of the King of Kings and Lord of Lords. It is God Himself who makes distinctions in families. He promised Abraham that in him all the **families of the earth** would be blessed (Genesis 12:1-3). In eternity, Abraham will see the fulness of that promise in the redeemed out of every kindred, tongue, tribe and nation (Revelation 5:9-10).

Therefore, even though there is a full list of designated people of God, all such, apart from the angelic beings (good or evil), basically fall into one or the other of the three ethnic groupings of mankind on earth. That is, (1) Unsaved Jews or

Israelites, (2) Unsaved Gentiles, or (3) Saved Jews and Gentiles, the people of God, the families of God, or the church of the living God.

An excellent exercise for the earnest student would be to study the above list of peoples and classify them into a three-column approach, placing them in the particular groupings to which each belong. This would be the use of the ethnic division principle in helping to understand the Book of Revelation.

CHAPTER NINETEEN
THE CHRONOMETRICAL PRINCIPLE

Undoubtedly, one of the most problematical and difficult areas of interpretation of Revelation is that which pertains to the use of the Chronometrical Principle. The Book of Revelation, as Daniel and Ezekiel (Babylonian Exilic books), and Zechariah (Post-Exilic book) is the major apocalyptic book in the New Testament. Various "time elements" in Revelation have to be properly interpreted as to their literal or symbolic use.

Perhaps it would be profitable, at the beginning of this chapter, to consider in brief, the various Schools of Interpretation pertaining to the three most controversial issues in the field of eschatology, as most of it pertains to the "time element". (The reader is also encouraged to read afresh Chapter Two as it pertains to these several Schools of Interpretation).

The three major issues could be classified as (1) The Great Tribulation period of time, (2) The Rapture of the Church and Revelation of the Christ, and (3) The Millennial Kingdom of God and His Christ. Each of these involve some "time element". The question is 'WHEN?' Such has to do with the Chronometrical Principle!

A. Schools of Interpretation

The Schools of Interpretation pertaining to these things fall into three main views as follows:

1. The Great Tribulation, Rapture and Revelation

(a) Pre-Tribulationists

Hold the view that there will be a secret rapture of the saints at the beginning of a seven year period of tribulation. The revelation, or actual coming of Christ is at the end of the seven year period of time.

(b) Mid-Tribulationists

Hold the view that the rapture of the church takes place in the middle of the great tribulation period of seven years. Christ comes at the end of the seven year period.

(c) Post-Tribulationists

Hold the view that the rapture of the church and the second coming of Christ are at one and the same time.

It will be seen that each of the varying views all have to do with some "time element" pertaining to the Great Tribulation, the Rapture and the Revelation of Christ.

2. The Second Coming and the Millennium

This period of time, spoken of as the Millennium, is undoubtedly the most controversial passage as far as the "time element" is concerned. Revelation 20:1-10 speaks of a period of time of 1000 years. Is it an actual period of time or is it a symbolic period of time? When did this period begin and when does it end? Where does it find its place in the plan of God in redemption? These are the questions that arise in dealing with this "time element". We consider in brief the various Schools of Interpretation of Millennialism and the general order of eschatological events each set out. The passage in Revelation 20:1-10 becomes the major foundational passage for the differing views.

(a) A-Millennialism

This view holds that there is no such period of time as a literal or actual 1000 years reign of Christ on the earth with His saints. The general idea is that Christ is reigning now with His own, in a spiritual reign. He reigns with and over His saints in this present period of time. Hence it is referred to as A- (no) Millennialism. It is counted as a figurative period of time. This is because it is the only passage in the total Bible that speaks of 1000 years. Although there are some slight variations in this school, their general order of eschatological events are:

1. The first resurrection is a spiritual resurrection, the new birth.
2. Satan is bound at the cross, and no longer deceiving the nations now as the Gospel is available for nations.
3. The millennium is an indefinite period of time between first and second comings of Christ.
4. The saints are reigning with Christ in heavenly places now.
5. At the close of the age, Satan will be loosed a short season to deceive nations.
6. The second resurrection is physical and is a general resurrection of the wicked and the righteous.
7. Judgment takes place and all are ushered into the eternal states.

(b) Post-Millennialism

This view holds that the second coming of Christ is after or at the end of the millennium period; hence it is called "post-millennialism". This view teaches that the millennium is not an actual or literal time period of 1000 years, but is figurative. The period is counted as a period of time between the first and second comings of Christ. We are now living in this period of time. The church conquers the nations with the Gospel of Christ and Christ comes to receive for Himself the kingdom. Though there may be slight variations in this school, their general order of eschatological events is as follows:

1. The first resurrection is spiritual.
2. The millennium follows the cross as the heathen are converted by the Gospel.
3. Satan is bound now, inactive as to his previous power.
4. The church triumphs and fills the whole earth.
5. The age closes with Satan being loosed for a short period of time, leading a rebellion against God and His Christ, but comes into judgment.
6. After a general resurrection, and judgment, eternal states are ushered in.

As can be seen, A-Millennialism and Post-Millennialism have much in common. The one believes we are in the millennium now, while the other believes the millennium will be ushered in by the victory of the Gospel proclaimed by the church.

(c) Pre-Millennialism

This view holds that Christ will come to the earth after a period of great tribulation, either seven years or three and one-half years duration. His coming will be before the millennium is established. Christ will rule and reign with His saints for an actual period of 1000 years, during which time, Satan is bound. Again, though there may be slight variations in this school, their general order of eschatological events is as follows:

1. The church age lasts for about 2000 years, symbolized in Revelation 1,2,3.

2. About the close of this age, the rapture of the church takes place, symbolized in Revelation 4:1 as John hears the trumpet call up to heaven.

3. There is a period of seven or three and one-half years tribulation, symbolized in Revelation chapters 6-18 with its details.

4. Christ returns the second time in Revelation 19.

5. Antichrist and his armies are judged.

6. The first resurrection take place, a physical resurrection of the righteous.

7. Satan is bound in the bottomless pit for 1000 years, no longer deceiving nations, as seen in Revelation 20.

8. The saints reign with Christ on the earth for 1000 years, while a Mosaic and Jewish kind of millennium is established for unsaved nations, Jerusalem and the new temple being the governing power.

9. At the end of the 1000 years, Satan is loosed, He deceives the nations once more. But judgment takes place and he is cast into the lake of fire.

10. The great white judgment takes place, and eternal destinies are settled; the righteous taken to a new heaven and new earth and the wicked cast into the eternal lake of fire (Revelation 20,21,22).

Sufficient overview has been given to show the truth of the need for understanding the various "time elements" in the Book of Revelation. The difference of opinion and the controversy is over time periods. This necessitates the proper use of the Chronometrical Principle, which we now consider.

B. Definition

The Chronometrical Principle is defined as that principle by which the interpretation of a verse or passage is determined upon a consideration of its chronometrical setting.

C. Amplification

The word **"chronometrical"** is taken from two Greek words: **"chronos"** meaning **"time"**, and **"metron"** meaning **"measure"**. From the Dictionary the following relevant words give further definitions and clarifications.

Chronometry - "The art of measuring time; the measuring of time by periods or divisions."

Chronometer - "An instrument that measures time; specifically, a compact time-keeper of the highest possible accuracy."

Chronographer - "One who writes concerning time or the events of time."

The Scriptures clearly reveal that God is the great chronographer of the ages. God Himself is eternal. God is not limited to time or by time (Psalm 90:1-4). Man is subject to time, but God is the guardian of time, and the designer of its ages. Hebrews 11:3 tells us that "the worlds (Grk. "ages") were framed by the word of God". What is time then? Time is but a fragment of eternity in which God is working out His eternal purposes in relation to both creation and redemption.

The Scriptural basis upon which this principle is built is the usage of these words: age(s), time(s), and season(s), as in the Old Testament Hebrew and New Testament Greek.

Old Testament Hebrew

The Old Testament has several Hebrew words pertaining to subject of time.

1. **Mowadah** - meaning "an appointment, a fixed time or seasons; specifically a festival". The word is translated by "feasts" (Leviticus 23:2,4,37, 44), "seasons" (Genesis 1:14; Leviticus 23:4), and "times" (Exodus 23:15; Habakkuk 2:3).

2. **Eth** - meaning "time". It is translated "season(s)" (Exodus 18:22,26; Psalm 1:3), and "time" (Ecclesiastes 3:1-17; Zechariah 10:1).

3. **Yowm** - meaning "a day, lit. or fig. (a space of time)". This word is translated "day(s)" (Genesis 5:1-8; Isaiah 2:2), and "time(s)" (Deuteronomy 10:10; Psalm 27:5).

New Testament Greek

The New Testament has several words also pointing to time or periods of time.

1. **Aion** - meaning "an age; by extension, perpetuity of time; by implication, the world; an unbroken age, or segment of time, an era, a period of time viewed in relation to what takes place in it." The word is translated . "age(s)" (Ephesians 2:7; Colossians 1:26), "course" (Ephesians 2:2); "eternal" (Ephesians 3:11; 1 Timothy 1:17), "forever" (1 Timothy 1:17; Philippians 4:20), and "world" (Matthew 13:39,40,49, Hebrews 1:2; 11:3).

2. **Genea** - meaning "a generation; by implication, an age, a period of time (of limited duration)". It is translated "age(s)" (Ephesians 3:5,21), "generation(s)" (Luke 1:48,50; Colossians 1:26), "nation" (Philippians 2:15), and "time(s)" (Acts 14:16; 15:21).

3. **Kairos** - meaning "an occasion; a set or proper time; a measure of time; a fixed and definite time; a seasonable time; the right time; a period of time; a limited portion of time." It is translated " season(s)" (Acts 1:7; 1 Thessalonians 5:1), and "time(s)" (Mark 1:15; Luke 19:44).

4. **Kronos** - meaning "a space of time (in general); a period of time; by implying delay." It is translated "season(s)" (Acts 19:22; 20:18), "space" (Acts 15:33; Revelation 2:21), and "time(s)" (Acts 3:21; 17:30; Galatians 4:4).

Together these Hebrew and Greek words confirm the fact that God has divided and arranged time into a series of successive ages, times and seasons.

D. Clarification

An important point that needs clarification here is the misunderstanding concerning the use of the word "dispensation". The confusion surrounding the word has centred around its application to the ages of time. Certain Dispensational Schools have confined the various dispensations to limited periods of time. This misses the meaning of the word.

The Greek word **"oikonomia"** means "administration (of a household or estate); specifically a religious economy." This Greek word is translated "dispensation" (1 Corinthians 9:17; Ephesians 1:10; 3:2; Colossians 1:25), and "stewardship" (Luke 16:2,3,4).

The word "dispensation" involves God's administrative dealings with man, but it contains no direct allusion to the ages of time! The Dispensationalists use the word to limited ages of time. However, the word does not refer to an age of time, but rather to an arrangement or administration of religious affairs.

It is really a misunderstanding and misinterpretation of the word, and therefore a misapplication of the chronological principle.

The Dispensationalist teaches there are seven Dispensations, these being:

1. The Dispensation of Innocence, beginning with Adam.
2. The Dispensation of Conscience, beginning with the Fall of man.
3. The Dispensation of Human Government, beginning with Noah after the Flood.
4. The Dispensation of Promise, beginning with Abraham.
5. The Dispensation of Law, beginning with Moses and Israel.
6. The Dispensation of Grace, beginning with Christ's redemptive work.
7. The Dispensation of the Kingdom, beginning at the second coming and the establishment of the millennial kingdom.

However, the dispensations find their proper foundation in the covenants in that they refer to the different methods of God's dealings under these arrangements.

The dispensations, though having no definite reference to time, do have a point of commencement. However, each arrangement was not abolished when another arrangement was ushered in.

Conscience was not abolished when Human Government was brought in. Human Government was not abolished when Promise was brought in. Nor was Promise abolished when Law came in. Grace did not abolish Divine Law, although the Ceremonial Law was abolished at Calvary. Kingdom did not abolish Grace! Conscience, Human Govemment, Promise, Law, Grace and Kingdom — all are with us today and continue in parallel form through to the completion of God's eternal purpose and plan.

Each of these Dispensations belong to Covenants:

1. Innocence belongs to the Edenic Covenant.

2. Conscience belongs to the Adamic Covenant.

3. Human Government belongs to the Noahic Covenant.

4. Promise belongs to the Abrahamic Covenant.

5. Law belongs to the Mosaic and Palestinian Covenants.

6. Grace belongs to the New Covenant.

7. Kingdom belongs to the Everlasting Covenant.

This matter of "dispensation" needed clarification because of its effect on various interpretations and expositions of Revelation..

(Note:- Adapted from **"Interpreting the Scriptures", Chapter 15 – Dispensations Redefined.** Conner/Malmin).

E. **Demonstration**

In Revelation we do find various periods of time and in order to properly interpret them, a proper use of the chonometrical principle is necessary.

It is not the purpose of this text to interpret these things fully, but to draw attention to the principles that do need to be used for a proper exposition of the Book of Revelation.

Following are some of the references having to do with time or periods of time. Any student who has read various interpretations of Revelation will immediately discern the right or faulty use of the chronometrical principle.

1. **The Lord's Day (Revelation 1:10)**

Is this "day" Sunday, the first day of the week, or does it refer to "the day of Christ 's second coming", or " the day of the Lord" ? The proper interpretation lends itself more to the events pertaining to that which many of the Old Testament prophets have spoken of as "The Day of the Lord" (i.e., Christ's second coming).

2. **Tribulation Ten Days (Revelation 2:10)**

The church at Smyrna was to have tribulation "ten days". Various expositors have made this a period of "ten years" (a day for a year theory). Some have made it to correspond with the periods of church persecution under the ten major emporers of the Roman Empire, therefore ten periods of time.

What did it mean to the church at Smyrna? Interpretation must precede application!

3. The Day of Wrath (Revelation 6:17)

The wrath of the Lamb is spoken of as "the day of wrath". Is it a period of time, or an actual day of twenty-four hours, or is the day of wrath the day of Christ's actual second coming? The aggregate of Scripture about this "day" shows that it involves a period of time, consummating in the day of Christ's coming!

4. Five Months Torment (Revelation 9:5)

In this verse we have a period of five months torment of the locust-like plagues out of the bottomless pit. Some expositors have made this an extended period of time beyond five months. In the days of Noah, it took five months for the waters of the flood to recede (Genesis 7:24). That was an actual period of time. There is no need to make it symbolic of an extended period of time. The same rule should apply in Revelation.

5. The Forty-Two Months (Revelation 11:2,3; 12:6,14; 13:5)

Another period of time that has generated much difference of opinion and interpretation is the period of three and one-half years. This period of time is designated as:

"forty and two months" (11:2),
"1260 days" (11:3),
"1260 days" (12:6),
"time, times and half a time" (12:14), and
"forty and two months" (13:5).

By a faulty use of the chronometrical principle, expositors have made this time period to mean 1260 years ("a day for a year" theory), or three and one-half actual years. Some have made it to be the whole of the period of time from Christ's first coming to His second coming. Some have also added the time periods together in Revelation 11,12, and 13, making the total ten and one-half years!

The expositor should use the Comparative Mention Principle in conjunction with the Chronometrical Principle and study the notable Seventy Week Prophecy (Daniel 9:24-27). There the controversial final week of that prophecy is divided into two periods of "three and one half years", and spoken of as "the midst (middle) of the week". Sufficient for this study is for the student to see the need to properly use the chronometrical principle in interpreting this "time period". What does it really refer to? What period of time does it really speak of ?

6. The Thousand Years (Revelation 20:1-10)

The expression, "one thousand years", is mentioned six times in these verses. As already seen, this time period has generated some of the most controversial interpretations of church history. The time period has been called "The

Millennium" and out of this has arisen the various Millennial Schools; the A-Millennial, the Post-Millennial, the Pre-Millennial.

This "time period" has been taken as a symbolic or indefinite period of time. Others have taken it as an actual period of time, based on the 1000 year-day theory, based on Psalm 90:4; 2 Peter 3:8. A few writers have taken it to speak of a "Utopian period of time on earth", a period of peace, prosperity and blessing, ushered in by the church having subjugated the world to Christ.

Again, it is not the purpose of this text to do an exposition of this subject, but simply to draw attention to the fact that the problems, in the author's mind, arise out of not using properly the chronometrical principle.

Other "days" mentioned in Revelation are found in 7:15; 9:15; 11:11. Also other "time periods" are mentioned, such as "for ever and for ever" (Revelation 14:11; 20:10).

Revelation does not contain the totality of eschatological teaching. What eschatology is in Revelation must harmonize and fulfill – not contradict – all the previous eschatological revelation. Things that are found in 1 Corinthians 15, 1 Thessalonians 4 and 2 Thessalonians 2 are all part of the eschatological teaching. Millennial teachings arise out of the events of these chapters and the order the expositor places them in.

This author believes that Revelation is basically written in chronological order as to its events. The basic order unfolds throughout, like a video, just as it is, with the exception of a verse here and there anticipating the end. If the book is not in chronological order, then the whole book is up to anyone's fanciful arrangement. Hopeless confusion abounds through not accepting the basic outline and progressive order of the book, as it is. This writer believes it is the key to the "time element" since the first advent of Christ and from His ascension to His second advent.

Therefore the Book unfolds as follows:

1. From the church at Pentecost through the church age to the second coming of Christ, there is about 2000 years of time (History has brought us to the 1990's!). The seven churches in Revelation 1,2,3 were local churches in Asia. They have truth that is applicable to all churches of all time. The seven churches do not have to be placed in "seven church ages", but truths from each church are always applicable in all time. Revelation chapters 4-10 provide much truth and spiritual lessons for the church.

2. Revelation chapters 10-18 especially deal with the beast and the terror of his reign of three and one-half years, immediately preceding the coming of the Lord Jesus. The writer believes this fills out the final half of the "seventieth week" of Daniel 9:24-27. (The student is referred to the Bibliography and textbook of this notable prophecy).

3. Revelation 19 deals with the actual second coming of Christ. The writer believes the rapture of the saints and the revelation of Christ take place at one and the same time.

4. The millennial age is bounded by the first and second resurrection, during which time Satan is bound and no longer deceives the nations. Deception abounds today! At the end of this period Satan will be loosed, the wicked dead will be raised for judgment, and eternal states are settled (Revelation 20). The writer believes in a Christian Millennium, NOT a Jewish Millennium — a textbook in itself!

5. After the great white throne judgment, eternity is ushered in and destinies are settled, either heaven or hell (Revelation 21,22).

This is a simple and basic unfolding of Revelation without rearranging it to fit some inconsistent interpretation and exposition. All unfulfilled Scripture has to find its fulfilment in the book of ultimates and the time of Christ's coming.

In conclusion, whatever one's understanding of the "time periods" in Revelation, it is evident that a proper use of the chronometrical principle is needed. Such must be used in conjunction with the whole Bible and God's master plan of the ages!

(The Student is encouraged to refresh his reading of "The Structure of The Revelation", Chapter Four).

CHAPTER TWENTY
THE BREACH PRINCIPLE

Another hermeneutical principle that should be used, with care, in the interpretation of the Book of Revelation is the Breach Principle. This principle is not a common one amongst expositors. However, some expositors do use it, though not under this designation.

Because this principle will be "new" to many interpreters, a larger amount of this chapter will be given to its development before its application, where appropriate, to the Book of Revelation. The Breach Principle is virtually linked with the Chronometrical Principle. Therefore, Chapters 19 and 20 need to be studied together.

A. Definition

The Breach Principle is that principle by which the interpretation of a certain verse or passage in Scripture is aided by a consideration of certain breaches, either breaches of promise or breaches of time.

B. Amplification

Following we consider the definition of the word **"breach"** as in Webster's Dictionary and in its use in the Bible, especially the Old Testament words.

1. Webster's Dictionary

According to Webster's Dictionary, a "breach" is:

A state of being broken ; a rupture; a break; a gap, A hole or an opening, as in a wall or fence, made by breaking or parting, An interruption of continuity; a blank space, A break or interruption in friendly relations.

In common language, other phrases are used which speak of a breach in human relationships. These phrases are defined as:

(a) Breach of faith - a failure to keep faith.

(b) Breach of privilege - an act in violation of rules, order, privileges or dignity of a legislative body.

(c) Breach of promise - failure to fulfill a promise.

(d) Breach of the peace - a violation of the public peace.

(e) Breach of trust - a violation by fraud or omission of any duty imposed on a person in a position of trust.

2. Old Testament Hebrew

There are at least seven Hebrew words which speak of a breach and such are translated by a wide variety of English words. Such can only be dealt with in brief here.

(a) **Begeq** - meaning "a gap or leak (in a building or a ship); fissure or rent". It is translated "breaches" (2 Kings 12:4-8), and "calkers" (Ezekiel 27:9,27).

(b) **Baqa** - meaning "to cleave; generally to rend, break, rupture or open; to break through or into". It is translated "make a breach" (Isaiah 7:6; 22:9); "break" (Genesis 7:11; Isaiah 58:8); "cleave" (Numbers 16:31; Amos 6:11); "divide" (Exodus 14:16,21; Psalm 78:13); "rend" (Joshua 9:4; Job 26:8), and "tear" (Hosea 13:8).

(c) **Miphrats** - meaning "a break (in the shore); a haven". It is translated "breaches" (Judges 5:17).

(d) **Parats** - meaning "to break out, break through, break down, make a breach in, break into, break open, break up". It is translated "make a breach" (1 Chronicles 13:11; 15:13), and "break" (Exodus 19:22,24), and "breach" (Psalm 106:29).

(e) **Perets** - meaning "a break (lit. or fig); bursting forth, a breach". It is translated "breach" (Genesis 38:29; Amos 9:11); "breaking forth" (Job 30:14; Psalm 14:4 "gap" (Ezekiel 13:5; 22:30).

(f) **Sheber** - meaning "a fracture, figuratively a ruin; a breaking; breach; crushing". It is translated "breach" (Psalm 60:2; Isaiah 30:26); "breaking" (Isaiah 30:13,14); "broken" (Leviticus 21:19) and "destruction" (Proverbs 16:18; Isaiah 1:28).

(g) **Tenuwah** - meaning "alienation; by implication, enmity; opposition". The root word means "to hinder, restrain, frustrate, forbid, dissuade, refuse". It is translated "breach of promise" (Numbers 14:34), and "occasion" (Job 33:10).

A perusal of these words provides the basic meaning of a division or gap. As already mentioned, some expositors use this principle under the designation of "the gap theory" when interpreting various passages in the Bible.

C. Illustration

Examples in Scripture of the Breach Principle fall into two basic classifications. These have to be properly distinguished. These two classifications are (1) Breaches of Promise, and (2) Breaches of Time.

1. Breaches of Promise

It must be kept in mind that God keeps His promises. These are two immutable things concerning God; that is His own person and His own word. It is impossible for God to lie (Hebrews 6:13-20). However, there are "breaches of promises" which are caused by unbelief and disobedience on the part of man. It is never the fault of God, but the fault is on the part of man. These examples show the truth of these things.

(a) Breach of Promise Concerning Entering Canaan

God had promised the land of Canaan to Abraham, Isaac and Jacob and their seed (Genesis 15:13-21; 22:16-18; 28:13-15; Psalm 105:8-12; Exodus 3:15-17). However, the first generation of Israel experienced God's breach of promise for forty years in the wilderness when they rejected the land of promise through unbelief.

It was not that God broke His promise, but He did postpone the fulfilment of it for forty years until the new generation entered Canaan land (Numbers 14:26-38). This "breach of promise", speaks of the "altering of God's purpose", or "the revoking of His promise" (Amp.O.T.) UNBELIEF was the cause of this forty year breach-period in the wilderness. The wilderness was never God's perfect will, but He permitted it because of their unbelief and disobedience to His word (Hebrews Chapters 3-4)

(b) Breach of Promise Concerning Dominion in Canaan

God promised Abraham, Isaac and Jacob that their seed would also have dominion in the land over the Canaanites (Genesis 15:18-21; 22:16-18; 24:60). They were to possess the gate of their enemies. This promise was confirmed to the nation through Moses (Deuteronomy 28:14; 30:1-20), and Joshua (Joshua 1:1-9; 21:43-45). All was dependant upon faith and obedience to the law of the Lord.

However, the historical books of the Old Testament, from Judges onward, show Israel's unbelief and disobedience to the word of the Lord. Servitudes and various captivities mark their history until both Israel and Judah were cast out of the land and subjugated by their enemies.

Where was God's promise of dominion? Israel knew God's breach of promise time and again. The root cause was the sin of disobedience and unbelief. Time, for them, was lost as they served their enemies. The conquerors became the conquered!

(c) Breach of Promise Concerning Occupancy of Canaan

God promised Abraham, Isaac and Jacob that their seed would inherit the land of Canaan, have dominion over their enemies, and also that their seed would possess the land for "an everlasting possession" (Genesis 17:8; 48:4).

Biblical history as well as secular history has shown that Israel has only ever, ever possessed the land for several hundred years. As a nation, Israel has been absent for more time outside the land than in it. What of God's promise of "everlasting possession?"

Again, the breach of promise is experienced because of Israel's unbelief and disobedience to God's laws for living in the land. All has to do with covenant promises of the Abrahamic Covenant. There God promised the land for an everlasting possession. However, under the Mosaic and Palestinian Covenants, God laid out the conditions for keeping the land as an everlasting possession. Israel was to keep the sabbaths of the land every seventh year, plus the jubilee year, which was every fiftieth year (Leviticus 25:1-22). If they failed to do this, then the people, the cities, the sanctuaries and the land would be brought to desolation (Leviticus 26:14-46; 18:24-30; 20:22-26; Deuteronomy 28:56-68). All such came to pass.

The House of Israel was carried captive to Assyria about BC 721. The House of Judah was carried into Babylonian Captivity about BC 606, and this for a period of seventy years (Jeremiah 25:12; 29:10; Daniel 9:2). The House of Judah was, at the conclusion of the seventy years, restored to the land unto the first coming of Messiah. However, after the rejection and crucifixion of their long promised Messiah, in AD70 the Romans desolated the people, the cities, the temple and the land.

Jewry has been desolate ever since. From AD 1917 onwards, a remnant has been returning to the land amidst constant turmoil, and all this according to the prophecy of the Lord Jesus (Luke 19:41-44; 21:20-24).

Israel's history in and out of the land has been the result of their unbelief and their disobedience; not the fault of the promise of God. Jewry has experienced God's breach of promise! Time for them, out of the land, has been lost time!

(d) Breach of Promise Concerning the Sceptre

Israel has also experienced God's breach of promise concerning kingship. The word to Jacob's son, Judah, was that the sceptre would not depart until Shiloh came (Genesis 49:8-12).

David was the first king of the tribe of Judah over all Israel. God confirmed the covenant of kingship to David, that he would never lack a man to sit on his throne (2 Samuel 7; Psalm 89). This is spoken of as the Davidic Covenant.

From David to Zedekiah, there was an unbroken dynasty of Davidic kings reigning over Judah. But, when Zedekiah was dethroned, about 600 years before Christ, there came about a breach, a gap, in the throne of David. Jewry has never had a Davidic king reigning over it from about BC 600 until this day, almost 2600 years!

What of the promises of God? What of the promise of the sceptre of Judah? When Christ was born, He was promised the throne of David (Numbers 24:17; Luke 1:30-33). The 600 years from Zedekiah to Christ provides another example of the breach of promise.

Again, the promise of God was not at fault. It was, again, the unbelief and the disobedience of Israel and Judah that caused, to them, the breach of promise of the kingship!

2. Breaches of Time

It is important to understand the distinction between **"breaches of promise"** and the **"breaches of time"**.

The "breaches of promise" are caused by man's unbelief and disobedience; two sides of the same coin, so to speak. The "breaches of time" are caused by God's outworking of His plan and purpose as revealed to and through the prophets.

God Himself is the great I AM (Exodus 3:14-15). Time past, time present and time future are one eternal present to God. God is not bound by time, but He does work in time. As noted under the Chronometrical Principle, time is simply a fragment of eternity in which God is working out His purposes in creation and redemption. Man is, however, a creature of time.

When God revealed His purposes to and through the prophets, they were caught up in what has been spoken of as "the prophetic perspective". They would see things from the Eternal's point of view. As a result of this, they would sometimes group together certain passages of Scripture, prophetic events, and include the past, the present and the future. They saw things from God's eternal present.

The Old Testament prophets did not always understand their own utterances concerning the coming of Christ. They searched what was meant by their prophecies. They tried to discover the time of fulfilment of the Spirit's utterances through them when He spoke of the "sufferings of Christ and the glory that should follow". It was revealed to them that their prophetic words were not just for their generation but also for future generations (1 Peter 1:10-12).

The historical fulfilment of some prophecies has proved that there is "a time gap", or **"a breach of time"** involved in their fulfilment. This is especially so concerning the events pertaining to the first and second comings of Christ. It is this "time element" that makes the interpretation of prophecy so difficult.

Following we note several brief examples of prophetic "breaches of time".

(a) **The Pre-existence, Incarnation and Crucifixion of Christ**

In Micah 5:1-2 we have a remarkable prophecy pertaining to Christ's first coming. In these verses three important facts are woven together. No "time element" is mentioned. The facts run together as if they were to be fulfilled all at one and the same time. However, the historical fulfilment of such shows that there was really a "breach of time" in fulfilment.

(1) **Messiah's Pre-existence**

The Ruler in Israel had His goings forth from of old, from everlasting, from the days of eternity. This is pre-existence, and eternity of being (John 1:1-3).

(2) **Messiah's Incarnation**

The Ruler would come out of Bethlehem of Judah. The virgin birth was Messiah's incarnation (Matthew 2:1-6).

(3) **Messiah's Crucifixion**

The Ruler of Israel was to be smitten with a rod on the cheek. This was fulfilled at Christ's crucifixion, about 34 years after His virgin birth (Matthew 27:30).

These truths, these prophetic facts, cover TIME! From eternity, to Micah's prophetic word (about BC 620), then Christ's virgin birth at

Bethlehem (BC 4), and then Messiah's crucifixion (AD 34), about 34 years later - all is covered in TIME! In other words, "breach of time" is seen in the fulfilment of this Messianic prophecy, though this could not be seen when Micah uttered the prophecy. History and time proved the prophecy!

(b) The Day of the Lord

Many times, in the Old Testament, the expression "the day of the Lord" is used by the prophets. It is used to speak of, sometimes, a local "day of the Lord" judgment falling on Israel or Judah. Most of the time, it is used to refer to either the first or more especially the second coming of the Lord. A study of the details in the verses surrounding this expression will help to determine whether it speaks of the first coming or the second coming of Christ.

An example of "the day" of Christ's first and second coming is found in the prophet Malachi.

(1) Messiah's First Coming

Malachi 3:1-2 speaks of Christ's first coming as "the messenger of the covenant" which was preceded by John the Baptist's ministry (Mark 1:2). This is spoken of as "the day of His coming". History proved this to be Christ's first coming.

(2) Messiah's Second Coming

Malachi 4:1 speaks of Christ's second coming. It is spoken of as "the day that cometh", and it is a day of judgment on the wicked. Time will prove this to be the Christ's second coming.

As we consider these references, between Malachi 3:1-2 and Malachi 4:1 there is indeed a "breach of time", and this is seen in the first and second comings of Christ. This "breach of time" is called the "dispensation of the Holy Spirit". It is called the "church age", during which the Lord is gathering a people for His name out of every kindred, tongue, tribe and nation (Revelation 5:9-10). This was in the eternal purpose of God (Ephesians 3:10-11).

Once again, we see a breach of time involved in the expression, "the day of the Lord", in prophetic fulfilment, as God allows His plan and purposes to be worked out in the earth.

(c) The First and Second Comings of Christ

One other example will be sufficient before applying the breach principle to some passages in the Book of Revelation.

A comparison of Isaiah 61:1-2 with Luke 4:16-21 implies the first and second comings of Christ. This being so, we have another example of the breach principle.

(1) Messiah's First Coming

Jesus in the synagogue of Nazareth was given the scroll of Isaiah. He opened it and began to read Isaiah 61:1-2. However, He stopped reading at the clause, "the acceptable year of the Lord", and closed the book and sat down.

The Gospels show the historical fulfilment of the clauses He read from verse 1-2. The Spirit of the Lord anointed Jesus at His baptism in Jordon. His ongoing ministry showed how He preached the Gospel to the poor, healed the broken-hearted, proclaimed liberty to the captives, opened the prison door to those who were bound, and proclaimed the acceptable year of the Lord (Read 2 Corinthians 6:2 and Isaiah 49:8 also).

(2) Messiah's Second Coming

The next clause of the same passage speaks of "the day of vengeance of our God" (Isaiah 61:2b). Undoubtedly the reason Jesus did not read that clause then was because, in His first coming, there was no vengeance in His heart. On the cross, He asked His Father to forgive His crucifiers. However, it is the second coming that "the day of vengeance of our God" finds fulfilment. The student should read Isaiah 63:4 with 2 Thessalonians 1:7-9 along with Revelation 6:9-17. Each of these verses and passages speak of the Lord's coming "with vengeance in His heart".

Here once again, we have an implied "breach of time". Though the details of the prophecy are woven together in a couple of verses in Isaiah, the details of history show there is a gap - a breach of time - in fulfilment of certain clauses. Though the prophet spoke of these two events in the same passage, history confirms that these clauses actually reach from the first coming to the second coming - a breach of time in their realization.

D. Demonstration

The expositor must use this principle with great caution due to its limited relevance in interpreting Scripture. It is obvious also, that this principle must be used along with other principles.

The writer believes that there are several examples in the Book of Revelation where the breach principle should be applied. Each of these examples involve a "time period" which have to be interpreted.

1. Christ's Second Coming

As John received the Revelation on Patmos, Jesus told him on several occasions, **"Behold, I come quickly"**, and **"the time is at hand"** (Revelation 1:3; 22:10,12,20).

Revelation is actually the book of Christ's second coming. "Behold, He cometh" is the theme of the book (Revelation 1:7; 2:25; 3:11; 22:5,20).

There was certainly some misunderstanding among the apostles and even the believers at Thessalonica about Christ's coming. In John 21:20-25, when Jesus talked to Peter about John, He said, "If I will that he tarry till I come", the saying went abroad that John would not die but live to the second coming of Jesus. They did not understand that there would be some "time period" before Jesus returned. He had taught this in the parables of the kingdom, but they still had not comprehended this (Note the Parable of the Kingdom in Luke 19:11-27).

The early church thought He would come **"quickly"** - that is, in their time. The believers in Thessalonica were concerned for their fellow Christians who had died and they feared they would miss out on the second coming of Jesus. Paul had to write to them to clarify and correct those views. Paul told them that certain events were to take place, in time, before Jesus came again. Before Christ came, there would be a great apostasy, and the man of sin (the antichrist) would be revealed. However, all this would take place "in his time". The believers who had died in faith would not miss out on the Lord's coming. They would be raised first, and the the living believers would be caught up together with them to meet the Lord in the air (2 Thessalonians 3:6-15; 2:1-12; 1 Thessalonians 4:13-18; 5:11). Then all would be with the Lord for ever.

Almost nineteen centuries of time have passed since Jesus said, "I come quickly", and "the time is at hand", and Jesus has not yet returned.

This church age has certainly become a **breach of time** between the first coming and the second coming. But it is not "lost time" or wasted time, as far as God is concerned. For in this period of time, He is building His church, composed of believing Jews and Gentiles, building them together as one body in Christ (1 Corinthians 12:13; Ephesians 2:19-22).

2. **The Three and One Half Year Period**

As noted under the Chronometrical Principle, we find there are certain "time periods" in the Book of Revelation that need to be properly interpreted. It is recommended that the student refresh his memory on the contents of Chapters 2 **(Revelation - History or Prophecy)**, and 18 **(The Chronometrical Principle)**.

One of the most controversial of the "time periods" that are found in Revelation is the period of three and one-half years, found in Revelation chapters 11,12,13. This three and one-half years period is spoken of as fortytwo months, 1260 days, and time, times and half a time (Revelation 11:2,3;12:6,14; 13:5).

In seeking to understand and interpret this time period, the Chronometrical Principle and the Breach Principle, along with other hermeneutical principles need to be used.

What is this three and one-half year time period in which the beast reigns in the world-system, persecuting the saints, and seeing his name, mark and number enforced on the peoples of the world? Is there any other time period like this in Scripture? Is there any other period like this that seems to await fulfilment? The answer is in the affirmative.

Using the Comparative Mention principle, along with the Chronometrical and Breach principles, in Daniel and Revelation (twin eschatological books), we find what, the writer believes, is the answer. Let us consider these twin books and this time period that is used in both of them. Let us seek to discover if there is a "breach of time" in the fulfilment of such.

(a) **The Book of Daniel**

In Daniel 9:24-27, we have the notable and controversial "Seventy Weeks Prophecy".

A comparison of Daniel 7, Daniel 9, Daniel 12 provides us with the following facts.

(1) Daniel 7:25 speaks of the little horn who makes war with the saints for a time, times and half a time; that is, three and one-half years. This period of time is revealed to Daniel before he received the seventy week prophecy!

(2) Daniel 9:24-27 shows us the overall view of the seventy weeks, or 490 years of time relative to Judah and the Messiah's manifestation and crucifixion. The angel interpreter, Gabriel, gives Daniel seven weeks of 49 years, and 62 weeks of 434 years, then takes Daniel to the middle of the seventieth week of seven years, and, as it were, leaves him there. That is, Gabriel takes Daniel to "midst of the week", that is, three and one-half years. This is to Messiah's crucifixion, for, it is Christ NOT Antichrist - who causes the sacrifice and oblation to cease, by His once-for-all, perfect sacrifice. Gabriel provides no details here about the final three and one-half year period of this seventieth week.

(3) Daniel 12:5-11 speaks of "the time of the end", and in verses 7-9 it speaks of a time, times and half a time. Daniel heard this, but he understood it not. The word came to him that the explanation of this time period, of time, times and half a time was sealed up and closed to "the time of the end".

We may ask, Is there any other book in the Bible that speaks of a similar period of time? Is there a time period like this which seems to be unfulfilled? The answer is seen in the Book of Revelation.

(b) **The Book of Revelation**

When we come to the Book of Revelation, we discover that there are five given references to a period of time of three and one-half years.

(1) Revelation 11:2 speaks of a time period of 42 months when the holy city is trodden under foot of the Gentiles.

(2) Revelation 11:3 tells of the two witnesses who prophesy for a period of 1260 days. This is a period of three and one half years.

(3) Revelation 12:6 speaks of a woman who is preserved in the wilderness for a period of 1260 days. Again, it is a period of three and one half years.

(4) Revelation 12:14 tells us that this woman is preserved from the face of the serpent for a time, times and half a time; or, three and one half years.

(5) Revelation 13:5 mentions the same period of time, as time, times and half a time, in which the beast makes war with the saints and overcomes them.

It is worthy of much consideration that, in Revelation Chapter 10, John is told to "eat the little open book", and then prophesy to many people. This a little open book, not a sealed book, as in Daniel 12. The moment John eats the little book, and begins to prophesy, he immediately takes up the language of Daniel from Daniel Chapter 7. He speaks of the beast who makes with the saints, and also John speaks of the same time period of "time, times and half a time".

Using the Comparative Mention principle (as previously done), we compare Daniel 7 and Revelation 13 to see if we can discover clues that will help us in interpreting the Revelation.

The Book of Daniel	**The Book of Revelation**
Four beasts	One beast
A lion with eagles wings	The mouth of a lion
A bear	The feet of a bear
A leopard with four heads	The body of a leopard
Seven heads in all	Seven heads
Ten horns	Ten horns
Little horn makes war on the saints	The beast makes war with the saints
Time, times and half a time	Forty and two months

Who cannot see that this is a proper use of the Comparative Mention principle? To add to this, we will apply the Chronometrical and the Breach principles in the following diagram.

The Four Gospels	**Daniel and Revelation**	
Christ ministered for three and one half years Daniel 9:24-27	The Breach of Time Church Age About 2000 years	Antichrist reigns for three and one half years Daniel 7:25 Daniel 12:5-11 Revelation 11:2 Revelation 11:3 Revelation 12:6 Revelation 12:14 Revelation 13:5

The writer believes that this church age, the dispensation of the Holy Spirit, is actually a breach of time (the breach period) between the first coming and the second coming of Christ. It is the "breach period" between the first half of the seventieth week prophecy and the last half of that same week.

If this time period in Revelation is not the final half of the seventy week prophecy, then what is it? Where is its fulfilment to be found in history? As seen in previous chapters, this time period has suffered much at the hands of some expositors. The writer has set forth what he believes is consistent interpretation and application of hermeneutical principles of interpretation.

The student must be reminded that, God's prophetic clock did not stop with Jewish unbelief. He foreknew the Jewish nation would reject the Messiah in the midst of the seventieth week. He foreknew the coming in of the Gentiles in this time period of the church - "the breach period" - and, in His plan, set the final half of the seventieth week prior to Christ's second coming. Thus, the first and second comings of the Messiah are bounded by three and one-half years; at the beginning and at the end.

(3) The Thousand Year Period

There is one other "time-period" in Revelation that needs our consideration, and that is, the period of time called "the millennium" (Revelation 20:1-10). Again, as previously mentioned, this period is a difficult and controversial period of time, and this period has also suffered much at the hands of expositors. This has been considered in the previous chapter, the Chronometrical Principle. However, further comment relative to the Breach Principle needs to be made here.

The passage in Revelation 20:1-10 speaks of "the first resurrection" and "the second resurrection" as being 1000 years apart. Some expositors interpret the first resurrection as being a spiritual resurrection, when those who are "dead in trespasses and sins" come to resurrection life in Christ (John 5:24-30 with Ephesians 2:1,5; Colossians 2:13). These expositors also teach that the second resurrection is physical, taking place at the second coming of Christ. The period of 1000 years is reckoned to be symbolic of the "time-period" between the first and second advents of Christ. This is basically the view called A-Millennialism. It may be asked, On what grounds can one say the first resurrection is spiritual and the second physical? Such seems to be inconsistent exegesis!

Other expositors see both the first and second resurrections to be physical. In the first resurrection, which takes place at Christ's coming, only the righteous and holy are raised. One thousand years later, the second resurrection takes place, and this is of the wicked. The period between these two resurrections is called the millennium, and this view is held by those called Pre-Millennialists.

It is worthy to note that, whichever view one holds, both see some "time-period" involved in the two resurrections, though both differ in their view on how to interpret this period of time. Such implies a "breach of time".

In a study of the Biblical doctrine of Resurrection, these are several verses of Scripture that simply speak of the two resurrections in the one verse. A general reading of these verses would convey to the reader that the resurrection of the righteous and, the resurrection of the wicked, take place at one and the same time, and is simply a general resurrection. Here we see several verses that would confirm this.

(a) Daniel 12:2 speaks of "some who shall awake to everlasting life, and some to everlasting shame".

(b) John 5:29 also speaks of the fact that there is a resurrection of life and also a resurrection of damnation.

(c) Acts 24:15 speaks of the resurrection of the just and the resurrection of the unjust. These sample verses link both resurrections together with no time period between them.

However, when we get to Revelation, it is John the beloved apostle who speaks of 1000 years being between these resurrections. This being so makes a "breach of time" between the resurrections. Therefore, in Revelation 20:5,6 we discern that there are two resurrections and they are 1000 years apart. The first resurrection is for the blessed and holy. The second resurrection is for the rest of the dead, the wicked dead. The first resurrection takes place at the beginning of the 1000 year period. The second resurrection takes place at the end of the 1000 year period.

Regardless of how the different Schools of Interpretation interpret these resurrections, there is a "breach of time" between them; that of the righteous and that of the wicked. Therefore, even though the several sample verses link both resurrections together, there is implied in them a breach of time - a gap. Only John in Revelation clearly states it. In other words, John, writing under the inspiration of the Holy Spirit applies "the breach principle" to the matter of the resurrection of the righteous and the unrighteous.

When Paul writes about the resurrections, the breach principle is implicit in his statement about the resurrections. In 1 Corinthians 15:23-25,28 Paul tells us that every man will be resurrected in order; Christ the firstfruits, then afterwards, they that are Christ's at His coming. Then comes the end when the Son returns everything to the Father and God is all in all.

The following diagram links Paul's thoughts and John's thoughts on the resurrections in diagramatic form to focus more sharply what the writer believes.

"The Breach Principle"

Christ's Death and Resurrection The Firstfruits	Christ Reigning Church Age	Christ's Coming The End of Age The First Resurrection Believers	The 1000 years	The End
				The Second Resurrection Wicked
			The Kingdom	The Kingdom to the Father

In concluding this chapter, the student will see that this chapter is dealt with more fully and this is because of the difficulty and the limited relevance of this principle to Scripture.

The **"breaches of promise"** are not because God has broken His promises but the promises are unrealized or postponed because of unbelief and disobedience and go to a believing and obedient generation.

The **"breaches of time"** are because of God's plan and purposes. Time may be lost to man, but time is never lost to God. Contrary to some teachers, God's "prophetic time-clock" has never stopped. God is eternal. God is not limited to or by time, though He works in time. Because time is one eternal present to God, He was able to inspire the writers of Scripture to record these various breaches throughout Scripture.

Whatever view the student may hold, it should be seen that any expositor of Revelation should correctly discern the nature of a breach, and cautiously and skillfully apply this principle, where necessary. The Chronometrical and Breach Principle especially have to do with TIME, and it is these "time-periods" that have caused the most controversy.

The writer has found that the Breach Principle gives much understanding of these "time-periods" in the Book of Revelation, as dealt with here. For the writer, the view that "the three and one-half years" and "the thousand years" refer to one and the same period of time (that is, time between the first and second comings), is a rather inconsistent view. This is the view of Progressive Parallelism. For this view, time between first and second comings fulfills these controversial periods of time. For this writer, the breach principle provides an answer to the gap between the first and second half of Daniel's seventieth week prophecy, and also an answer to John's first and second resurrections!

CHAPTER TWENTY-ONE
THE CHRISTO-CENTRIC PRINCIPLE

Without doubt, one of the more simple principles of hermeneutics to be used in any exposition of the Book of Revelation is the Christo-Centric Principle. After all, the Book of Revelation is the revelation or unveiling of Jesus Christ. It is given to Him. It is about Him in his ultimate triumph over evil. It is "The revelation of Jesus Christ ..." (Revelation 1:1).

Regardless of eschatological controversy, and leaving aside eschatological order of events, all expositors see that Christ is central in Revelation. To speak of Him is to be sure of standing on redemption ground. He is the central theme of the book.

A. Definition

The Christo-Centric Principle is that principle by which Scripture is interpreted in relation to its center - Christ.

B. Amplification

As already mentioned, regardless of which School of Interpretation one may be in, when it comes to the events in Revelation, the person of Christ in Revelation shines brightly and provides messages that indeed glorify Him.

The basis for this principle is in the fact that Christ is the central person of the Bible. He is the central One in the eternal Godhead.

The written Word revolves around Him who is the living Word (John 1:1-3,14-18). In the wheel of Divine revelation, Christ is the HUB and all other truths are as spokes of the wheel relating to Him Who is the Truth. Who He is (as to His person), what He has done (as to His redemptive work), and what He has spoken (as to His words), becomes the very heart of the Bible. These example Scriptures attest to this.

"In the volume of the book it is written of Me..." (Hebrews 10:7).

"Search the Scriptures...they are they which testify of Me ..." (John 5:39).
"He expounded unto them in all the Scriptures the things concerning Himself..." (Luke 27,44).
Read also Acts 10:43; John 1:1,14,45; 5:46-47; Matthew 5:17-18; 11:13; Acts 3:18; John 14:6.

The Bible is Christ-centred. In all things the Father has caused His Son to have the pre-eminence (Colossians 1:18).

Many writers have provided types and titles of Christ through every book of the Bible. The student is referred to these. The purpose of this chapter is to illustrate and demonstrate the centrality of Christ in Revelation by using the Christo-Centric Principle.

C. Demonstration

The first verse of Revelation clearly says, "the revelation of Jesus Christ which God gave unto Him ..." (Revelation 1:1). It is a revelation given TO Him, but it is also a revelation OF Him. The Greek word for **"revelation"** is **"apokalupsis"**. It means "an unveiling, or a revealing" of Jesus Christ. It is not the word **"apocrypha"**, which is exactly the opposite, and means **"concealing"**, or that which is hidden and veiled. The Book of Revelation is a book given to Him and it is about Him, and about His final triumphs over the enemies of God the Father, the elect angels, the people of God and the church of all ages.

In this book Christ is seen acting in His various titles and offices of administration. The fulness of the Godhead bodily dwells in Him (Colossians 1:19; 2:9). The titles and designations of Christ in Revelation touch every area of things in the universe of worlds.

Christ is seen in relation to:

1. The Church,
2. The Earth-dwellers,
3. Jewry,
4. The Angelic and Spirit realm,
5. The Kingdom of Satan and darkness, and
6. The Throne of God His Father.

All power is given to Him in heaven and in earth, and all angels, principalities and powers are subject to Him (Matthew 28:18-20; 1 Peter 3:22). In Revelation we have both **Theophany**; that is, visions of the eternal Godhead relative to the throne (Revelation 4-5), and we also have **Christophany**; that is, visions of Christ in His administration power and glory. Consider the many titles and designations pertaining to the Christology of Revelation.

1.   He is Jesus Christ - 1:1,2,5,9,9
2.   The Faithful Witness - 1:5 with John 5:31,36
3.   The First Begotten of the dead - 1:5 with Colossians 1:18
4.   The Prince of the Kings of the earth - 1:5
5.   The Alpha and Omega - 1:8,11; 21:6; 22:13 with Isaiah 44:6; 48:12
6.   The Beginning and the End - 1:8; 21:6; 22:13
7.   The Lord - 1:8,10
8.   The One which is, which was and which is to come - 1:8
9.   The Almighty - 1:8
10. The First and the Last - 1:11,17; 22:13
11. The Son of Man - 1:13; 14:14
12. He that liveth and was dead, and is alive forevermore - 1:18; 2:8
13. The Amen - 1:18; 3:14
14. He that has the keys of Death and Hades - 1:18
15. He that has the Seven Stars in His Right Hand - 1:20
16. He that walks in the midst of the Seven Lampstands - 2:1
17. The Son of God - 2:18
18. He that is Holy - 3:7
19. He that is True - 3:7

20. He that has the Key of David - 3:7
21. The Faithful and True Witness - 3:7
22. The Beginning of the Creation of God - 3:7
23. The Lion of the Tribe of Judah - 5:5
24. The Root of David - 5:5
25. The Lamb slain - 5:6,8,11,12,13,13; 6:1 (The Lamb, used 28 times in Revelation)
26. The Mighty Angel clothed with the Rainbow and Cloud - 10:1-11; 11:3
27. Jesus - 14:12;19:10; 22:16
28. Lord God Almighty - 15:3;16:7
29. King of Saints (The Ages) - 15:3
30. Lord of Lords - 17:14; 19:16
31. King of Kings - 17:14; 19:16
32. Faithful and True - 19:11
33. The Word of God - 19:13 with John 1:1-3,14-18
34. Christ - 20:4,6;11:15; 12:10
35. The Lamb and the Temple - 21:22
36. The Light - 21:23
37. The Root and Offspring of David - 22:16 with Isaiah 11:10
38. The Bright and Morning Star - 22:16
39. Lord Jesus - 22:20
40. Our Lord Jesus Christ - 22:21

In bringing this chapter to its conclusion, the reader is encouraged to refer again to Chapter 9, **"The Theology of The Revelation" (Section E).** In this section we dealt with the doctrine of angels as in Revelation. There we saw that the word **"angel"** is used in a threefold manner. It is used of (1) Ministers of the Gospel over local churches, or the saints of God (1:20; 2:1,8,12,18; 3:1,7,14; 21:12; 22:6,8,16); or (2) Angelic spirit beings who serve the throne of God and the Lamb (5:11; 7:11-12), or, (3) it seems to refer to the Lord Jesus Christ as the Jehovah-Angel.

If this is so - and a number of expositors follow this line of interpretation - then these "Jehovah-Angel" manifestations are really Christophanies; appearances and manifestations of our Lord Jesus Christ.

Without repeating in full what has already been covered in Chapter 9, we just list briefly those passages in Revelation that we believe are Christophanies.

1. The Sealing-Angel points to the Lord Jesus Christ, who alone has the seal of the living God for His own redeemed - 7:1-3; 14:1-2 with Ephesians 1:13-14; 4:30.

2. The Priestly-Angel who offers the prayers of the saints mingled with His own prayers also points to the Lord Jesus Christ - 8:1-5.

3. The Rainbow-Clothed Angel with the little open book, who speaks of "My two witnesses", points to none other than the Lord Jesus Christ - 10:1-5; 11:3.

4. The Angel whose glory lightens the whole earth points to the Lord Jesus Christ - 18:1.

5. The Binding-Angel who binds Satan, the author of sin, and casts him into the bottomless pit points to the Lord Jesus Christ - 20:1-3 with Matthew 12:28-29.

In the Old Testament, there are a number of Christophanies, seen in the appearances of "the angel of the Lord", or "the Jehovah-Angel". Only by a careful study of the details in the passages of Scripture involved will these Christophanies be clearly substantiated (Study carefully passages like Genesis 16:7-11; 22:11-15; 48:16; Exodus 3:2; 14:19-24; Judges 6:11-22; 13:3-21; Daniel 3:10).

The same is true of "the angel" manifestations in the Book of Revelation. The language used will provide the clues as to who is particularly being spoken of in either of the above three major groupings.

However, apart from these "Jehovah-Angel" appearances (concerning which there are scholarly differences), there are enough titles and designations of Christ in Revelation for devotional meditation. The Christo-Centric Principle can always be appropriately used in Revelation as the Lord Jesus Christ is exalted and worshipped as the head of the church, the redeeming Lamb of God, and the King of Kings and Lord of Lords.

CHAPTER TWENTY-TWO
THE MORAL PRINCIPLE

The Moral Principle is also one of those principles that a teacher or preacher or expositor of the Word has more confidence to use within its proper boundaries. This is true of much teaching from the Book of Revelation.

Each of the various Schools of Interpretation would use this principle in interpreting Revelation. The Preterist School and the Idealist School would major on this principle in their interpretation of Revelation. All Schools would use it to discover the principle truths and lessons from the Book of Revelation. Some would rather major on this principle than seeking an explanation and interpretation of its complex visions and symbols.

A. Definition

The Moral Principle is that principle by which the interpretation of a verse or passage of Scripture is determined by discerning the moral it contains.

B. Amplification

Webster's Dictionary defines the word "moral" in its noun form as "the practical lesson taught by any story or incident; the significance or meaning; (plural) principles and practice in regard to right, wrong and duty; ethics, general conduct or behaviour."

One of the chief purposes for the existence of the Bible is to instruct men in the way of righteousness. Most of its contents are written to teach man both what he should BE and what he should DO (2 Timothy 3:16,17). Many portions of Scripture are written as clear, concise instructions, such as in the Epistles and the clear teachings of Jesus. On the other hand, much of Scripture contains indirect instruction and the moral of it must be drawn out (Proverbs 25:2).

This may be illustrated in the following areas of literary styles in Scripture:

1. History

The Historical sections of Scripture were written, not only to record historical facts, but also to teach spiritual lessons.

(a) **The Death of Saul** - 1 Chronicles 10:13,14
The books of Samuel record Saul's life-story. The Chronicles passage provides the moral lessons for us to avoid involvement in witchcraft.

(b) **The Miracles of Jesus** - John 20:30,31
Behind all of Christ's miracles was a moral. Many experienced the miracle, but missed the moral (John 6:26-29), which was to believe that Jesus Christ is the Son of God.

(c) **The Exodus of Israel** - 1 Corinthians 10:1-11
Paul refers to a number of Israel's historical experiences but shows that such were written for our admonition, and for the moral lessons we can receive from such.

2. Poetry

The Poetical books have numerous lessons for the believer (Job 19:23). A number of the Psalms are Psalms of Instruction (Psalm 78,88,89. Inscription). The Book of Ecclesiastes concludes with the moral of its content (Ecclesiastes 12:13-14).

3. Proverbs

Proverbs 1:1-6 clearly sets forth the purpose of the Book of Proverbs. The "wise sayings" of the book contain numerous lessons for all who are of a humble and a teachable spirit.

4. Parables

The many Parables that Jesus Himself taught had a moral behind them. Many of the multitude heard the parables but missed the moral of the parables because of their own spiritual state (Matthew 13:10-13; Mark 4:1-2). The moral of the parable becomes the key to its interpretation.

5. Prophecy

Prophecy also provides numerous spiritual lessons and numerous morals. This is seen throughout the writings of the prophets. These prophetic utterances were all founded on Divine principles, including the moralisms of the Law.

As noted, most expositors use the Moral Principle when teaching the Word of God. In using the Moral Principle, there may be more than one moral, or spiritual lesson in the passage of Scripture under consideration, and this needs to be recognized. This principle must be kept in balance and used with other hermeneutical principles. Scripture was not intended to be only moralized. There must be harmony between theological interpretation and moral application for a proper interpretation of the Bible. And, of course, this is true when it comes to the need for a proper interpretation of the Book of Revelation.

C. Demonstration

The Moral Principle may be used in Revelation as long as it is not used to contradict sound theology, or, violate other hermeneutical principles.

The spiritual or moral lessons in Revelation are too many to list out here, but some of the major lessons are seen in the following chapter overviews.

1. Christ is the risen, glorified Son of God and to see Him in all His glory is to fall at His feet as dead (Revelation 1).

2. Christ is the head of the church, and He sees the internal spiritual condition of each church, and can remedy such upon genuine repentance (Revelation 2-3).

3. The throne of God rules and reigns over the universe and all the affairs of men. As one is related to the throne of God and the Lamb, one can only be a worshipper (Revelation 4-5).

4. The judgments of God in the earth are all subject to the power of God and the Lamb, as He opens the sealed book (Revelation 6-7-8-9).

5. God will preserve His own in all periods of tribulation and bring them triumphantly before His throne (Revelation 11-12-13).

6. Though the kingdoms of this world, as "wild beasts" may overcome many of the saints of God, the saints are the final overcomers (Revelation 14-15-16).

7. Christ will come and subdue all antichristial and Satanic powers under His feet in the Father's appointed time (Revelation 18-19-20).

8. The redemptive purposes of God will bring man into the city of God, the eternal paradise, and there restore to redeemed mankind the tree of eternal life (Revelation 21-22).

The student will notice that in the overview of moral lessons, as above, eschatological order of events, or interpretation of symbols and visions have basically been left alone. This shows that one can still receive many blessings from the Book of Revelation by use of the moral principle.

Numerous are the morals to be found in Revelation, and this principle of interpretation is generally a safe, sound principle with which to discover much blessing and spiritual and practical help for believers of all ages.

The Moral Principle may therefore be used to discover timeless truths that are applicable to each and every generation. Truth is eternal, truth is unchanged and unchanging. Truth in its multiplied facets is applicable in all circumstances of life. The Book of Revelation provides insightful truths - moral principles - that have encouraged the people of God in every generation, regardless of the eschatological school of thought they belonged to. However, the major safe-guard in using the moral principle is to make sure it is governed by sound theology. Application of truth must always be built upon proper interpretation of facts! The moral principle must be governed by sound theology. Proper observation leads to proper interpretation, and proper interpretation will lead to proper application. That is, using the Moral Principle.

CHAPTER TWENTY-THREE
THE SYMBOLIC PRINCIPLE

In this chapter, and the several chapters following, we consider several of **"The Figures of Speech"** group of Principles, which were mentioned in Chapter 10 of this text.

Without question, one of the most important principles in any exposition of the Book of Revelation is the Symbolic Principle. One cannot read the book without immediately seeing that it is a book of symbols, symbols that need to be interpreted properly, in order to understand the book. In Revelation 1:1 we are told that the Lord Jesus Christ "sent and **signified** it unto His servant John". The very word "signify" means to communicate by signs and symbols. So Revelation is a book that uses numerous symbols and signs in order to communicate God's mind to His church.

However, while various expositors do recognize this fact, some have fallen into extreme interpretation of these symbols, and brought the Book of Revelation into much disrepute. Therefore, there must be safeguards used with this principle to preserve one from extremes. The Revelation has many symbols, but the book is not all symbols. There are actualities and realities in the book that are not symbols and these must be discerned.

A. Definition

The Symbolic Principle is that principle by which the interpretation of a verse or passage in Scripture containing symbolic elements can be determined by a proper interpretation of the symbol(s) involved.

B. Amplification

According to Webster's Dictionary, the word **"symbol"** is made up of two Greek words: "syn" meaning "together", and " ballein" meaning "to throw". It means literally "thrown together", and denotes an object used to represent something abstract; an emblem; using one thing to stand for or represent another.

Though the word "symbol" is not specifically used in the Bible, God caused the writers of Scripture to employ the literary method of symbolization throughout Scripture. They often used one thing to represent another because of the common characteristics between them. This is what is meant by symbolization, in which the link between that which is used as a symbol, and that which is being symbolized is the characteristics which are common to both.

Things used as a Symbol ⋯⋯⋯⋯⋯⋯⋯⋯⋯⋯⋯⋯⋯⋯⋯⋯⋯⋯⋯ Things Symbolized

Common Characteristics

God, in authoring the Bible, dealt with both creation and redemption. The first two chapters of Genesis contain the record of the creation of the natural realm; the rest of the Bible contains God's plan of redemption. In Scripture, God uses the natural things He created to become symbols (Romans 1:19,20). In other words, the language of creation becomes the language of redemption.

The more one reads the Word of God, the more one sees that the language of creation is God's language of the sign and symbol. It is God's secret code, which will either veil truth or reveal truth according to the attitude of the listener. As noted, in Genesis chapters 1-2 we have the brief account of creation. The creation of the earth, the sun, moon and stars, the seas, seed, herb, grass, trees, fish and fowl, beast and man. And within this range of created things and creatures, God has hidden truth. In the rest of the Bible, and woven throughout the books of the Bible, God now takes the language of creation and makes it become the language of redemption, God's secret code. Only as the creature knows the Creator will he ever understand the language of the symbol. It is the glory of God to hide a thing, but it is the honour of kings to search out the matter (Proverbs 25:2 along with Psalm 19; Romans 10:17-18; Job 12:7-10).

The Book of Revelation is a book of symbols. Creation's sign-language, God's secret code, is the language which conceals or reveals truth. It either enfolds or unfolds truth. The truth is more often contained than explained in the use of the symbol.

The Lord Jesus Christ Himself especially used the Symbolic Principle in much of His teaching of the parables of the kingdom (Matthew 13). One needs to interpret the sign or symbol aright to discover the truth. The natural man receives not the things of the Spirit of God for they are foolishness to him. It is the spiritual mind who receives, believes and perceives the hidden truths of God (1 Corinthians 2:9-14). Many of the symbols in Revelation are interpreted in Revelation itself, or else the interpretation is given elsewhere in Scripture.

Basically there are eight catergories of symbols in Scripture, as set out in brief in the following. Rather than write out the full Scripture, the student is encouraged to read the appropriate Scripture references given in order to help understand the truths hidden in the language of the symbol.

1. **Symbolic Objects**

   In Scripture, God used inanimate objects, whether God-created or man-made as symbols (Hosea 7:8; Psalm 18:2; Proverbs 18:10; Deuteronomy 32:2; Psalm 119:105).

2. **Symbolic Creatures**

   In Scripture, God used living creatures, whether plants or animals, as symbols (Daniel 7:17; Hosea 7:11; Luke 13:31-32; Isaiah 40:31; 1 Peter 1:24; John 1:29,36).

3. **Symbolic Actions**

   In Scripture, God used actions in a symbolic sense (Psalm 141:1-2; Genesis 25:23-26; Joshua 1:3; Genesis 14:4).

4. **Symbolic Numbers**

   In Scripture, God attributed symbolic significance to numbers (2 Corinthians 13:1; Matthew 19:28; Genesis 14:4).

5. Symbolic Names

In Scripture, God uses names, both personal and national names, to be symbolic of the nature, character, office, experience or function of that person or nation (1 Samuel 4:21;25:25; Hosea 1:9; Matthew 1:21; John 1:42).

6. Symbolic Colours

In Scripture, God attributed symbolic significance to various colours (Isaiah 1:18; Mark 15:17,18).

7. Symbolic Directions

In Scripture, God attributed symbolic significance to directions (Jeremiah 1:14; Ezekiel 43:1-2; 2 Chronicles 4:4; Daniel 8:4).

8. Symbolic Places

In Scripture, God used various places to show forth symbolic significance (Hebrews 3-4), Canaan-Rest ; Exodus 13:3,14, Egypt, Land of Darkness and Bondage; Genesis 11 , Babylon, Confusion ; Sodom, Revelation 11:8).

Each of these catergories of symbols are seen in the Book of Revelation. A worthy exercise would be for the student to catergorize such into each category from Revelation.

C.   Classification

Merrill C. Tenney, in his excellent book, **"Interpreting Revelation"** (pages 186-193), says that symbols in Revelation basically fall into three catergories, adapted here as follows:

1.   The symbols that are definitely explained by stated equivalents;
2.   The symbols that are unexplained, that are drawn from the Old Testament background, and
3.   The symbols that have some connection with the apocalyptic literature or with pagan usage. There are very few that cannot be placed in one of these classes.

From Tenney we adapt in brief ten examples and references that fall into one of the above classifications.

1. Symbols Explained

* The seven stars – angels of the churches	1:20
* The seven lampstands – the seven churches of Asia	1:20
* The seven lamps of fire – the seven spirits of God	4:5
* The bowls of incense – the prayers of the saints	5:8
* The great multitude – those out of great tribulation	7:13,14
* The great dragon – the Devil, Satan	12:9
* The seven heads of the beast – seven mountains	17:9
* The ten horns of the beast – ten kings	17:12
* The waters – peoples, multitudes, nations and tongues	17:15
* The woman – that great city	17:18

2. Symbols Paralleled by Old Testament Imagery

* The tree of life	2:7; 22:2
* Hidden manna	2:17
* The rod of iron	2:27
* The morning star	2:28
* The key of David	3:7
* The living creatures	4:7ff
* The four horsemen	6:1ff
* The great angel	10:1ff
* The first beast	13:1-10
* The second beast	13:11-18

3. Unexplained Symbols

* The white stone	2:17
* The pillar	3:12
* The elders	4:4ff
* The seals	5:1; 6:1-17
* The two witnesses	11:3ff
* The woman clothed with the sun	12:1,2,14ff
* The winepress	14:20;19:15
* The supper	19:6-9,17
* The lake of fire	19:20
* The great white throne	20:11
* The city of God	21:2ff

(Adapted from **"Interpreting Revelation"** - Used by kind permission of Wm.B.Eerdmans Publishing Co.)

D. Qualification

Following are some safeguards that need to be used when interpreting symbols in Scripture, and more especially the Book of Revelation. These safeguards are taken from the textbook, **"Interpreting the Scriptures"** (Conner/Malmin, pages 142-143).

1. The first step in using the Symbolic Principle is to rightly determine which elements of the verse under consideration are meant to be interpreted as symbols.

    (a) If the language of the verse makes no literal or actual sense, then it must be interpreted as having symbolic sense (e.g., Revelation 12:1-4; 13:1-2 with Daniel 7:1-4).

    (b) If it does make literal or actual sense, then it can only be interpreted as having symbolic sense, when the Scripture interprets or intimates this to be the case in other verses (e.g., The Tabernacle, John 1:14, and The Temple, 1 Corinthians 3:17)

2. The interpreter must recognize the three fundamental elements of symbolism:

   (a) The significance of a symbol is based upon the literal or actual nature and characteristics of that which is being used as a symbol.

   (b) A symbol is meant to represent something essentially different from itself.

   (c) The link between that which is used as a symbol and that which it symbolizes is the common characteristic common to both.

Things used as a Symbol 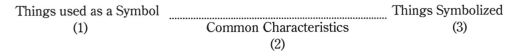 Things Symbolized
       (1)   Common Characteristics   (3)
                                 (2)

3. The use of this principle must be in constant conjunction with the Context-Group of principles. Because many symbols are used more than once in Scripture, every usage of them, beginning with the First Mention, must be compared in order to gain a complete understanding of the progressive unfolding of their symbolic significance in Scripture.

4. Generally speaking, the Bible interprets its own symbols. Thus, the interpreter must search through Scripture for the interpretation of the symbol under consideration.

5. A study of the usages of the symbol in Scripture must be based on a consideration of the original languages (e.g., there are several different Hebrew words for "lion" and each have their own significance).

6. The interpreter must keep in mind that something may be used to symbolize more than one thing in Scripture. The same symbol may represent different characteristic aspects. (e.g., Gold - used to represent the Divine nature, God, Wisdom, Faith, etc). Also, some symbols have both good and evil aspects to them (e.g., the Lion is used as a symbol of Jesus and His saints, as well as the Devil. Revelation 5:5; 1 Peter 5:8, etc). A safe adage is: One interpretation, but many applications!

7. When interpreting a symbol within a verse, its general Scriptural signficance should be used unless there are indications otherwise.

8. If the symbol is uninterpreted in the Word, investigate the context thoroughly for the thought or idea set forth. Check the Concordance for other references, and also consider the nature of the symbol used as it may give the clue (e.g., Lion, Swine, Lamb, Serpent, etc). The nature of such will give one the idea of the truth hidden therein.

The student must constantly keep in mind these guide-lines and safeguards to preserve from extreme or fanciful interpretations of Biblical symbols. Also, it is good to remember that the language of creation becomes the language of the symbol which becomes the language of redemption - God's secret code for either concealing or revealing truth, according to the attitude of the hearer!

E. Demonstration

From the author's textbook, **"Interpreting The Symbols and Types"** (Chapter 11), all the symbols used in the Book of Revelation are listed here, along with a brief interpretation of the symbol, and supportive Scriptures.

The Book of Revelation, the last book of the Bible, has many symbols therein. There are at least 130 symbols in Revelation, and without understanding them, it is virtually impossible to interpret this book. The student will note the Scripture references given where the symbol is interpreted, either specifically or by implication. (Bible books are abbreviated)

REVELATION	SYMBOL	INTERPRETATION	SCRIPTURES
1:10; 4:11	Trumpet	Voice of prophectic utterance	Isa 58:1; Num 10:1-10
1:11	Book	Written inspired records	2 Kgs 22:8-13; Neh 8:1-17
1:12, 13	Gold Candlesticks	Seven local churches	Rev 1:20
1:13	Garment to foot	Priestly clothing	Ex 28:2
1:13; 15:6	Golden girdles	Priestly service	Ex 28:40, 41
1:14	Hair white as wool	Wisdom, Ancient of Days	Dan 7:9
1:14	Eyes as flame of fire	Searching, penetrating insight	Dan 10:6
1:15	Feet as fine brass	Judgment against sin	Deut 28:23
1:15	Voice – many waters	Majestic, awe-inspiring	Ezek 43:2
1:16	The seven stars	Seven church ministers	Rev 1:20
1:16; 19:15	Two-edged sword	Word of God by the Spirit	Eph 6:17
1:16; 10:1	Glory of the sun	Glory of God the Father	Matt 13:43
1:18	Keys of Hell & Death	Authority over spirit realm	Matt 16:19
2:7	Tree of life	Eternal life	Gen 3:22
2:7	Paradise	Third heaven, Holiest of All	2 Cor 12:2-4
2:10	Crown of life	Eternal life	Jam 1:12
2:13	Satan's seat	Satan's throne of power	Rev 13:1,2
2:17	Hidden Manna	Word of God by the Spirit	Jhn 6:35
2:17	White stone	Priestly revelation	Ex 28:15-28
2:17	A new name	Priestly revelation, insight	Ex 28:21-29
2:22	Bed of adultery	Spiritual lusts, fornication	Jam 4:4
2:27; 19:15	Rod of iron	Power over nations	Psa 2:9
2:28	Morning star	Morning light, new day	2 Pet 1:19
3:4	Defiled garments	Garments defiled by the flesh	Jude 23
3:5,18	White raiment	Priestly, holy attire	Ex 28:39-41
3:5	Book of life	Register of heaven	Heb 12:23
3:7	Key of David	Kingdom power and worship	Matt 16:19; Isa 22:21-22
3:12	Pillar in temple	Stability, permanent position	Gal 2:19
3:18	Gold tried in fire	Faith of God; Divine nature	2 Pet 1:7
3:18	Eyesalve	Anointing of the Spirit	1 Jhn 2:20,27
3:21; 4:2-5	The throne	Sovereignty of God	Psa 45:6
4:1	Door in heaven	Access to heavenly places	Jhn 1:51
4:3	Jasper-sardine stones	Glory brightness of God	Rev 21:11

4:3	The rainbow	Covenant of God with earth	Gen 9:12-17
4:4	Crowns of gold	Royalty, reigning on thrones	Psa 21:3
4:4	Twenty-four elders	Priestly courses of ministry	1 Chron 24
4:5	Lightnings, voices, etc	Judgments of God in earth	Ex 19:16
4:5	Seven lamps of fire	Fulness of Holy Spirit	Zech 4:2
4:6	Full of eyes	Sight, perfection of insight	Ezek 1:18, 2Chron 16:19
4:6-8	Four living creatures	Four standards of Israel	Ezek 1:10
	The lion	King of beasts, royalty	
	The calf	King of sacrificial animals	
	The man	King of creation, intelligence	
	The eagle	King of birds, heavenliness	
5:1-7	Seven sealed book	Bible – Book of redemption	Jer 32:6-12
5:6	Slain Lamb	Sacrifice, atonement, Son of God	Jhn 1:29,36; Ex 12
5:6	Seven horns	Omnipotence, fulness of power	Psa 92:10
5:6	Seven eyes	Omniscience, perfect insight	Zech 3:9
5:8	Golden vials	Temple vessels, bowls, basins	1 Kgs 7:50
5:8	Odours, incense	Prayers of saints	Psa 141:1,2
5:9	New song	Songs of redemption	Ex 15:1
5:9	Blood atonement	Calvary, redemption	Lev 17:11-14
5:10; 1:6	Kings and priests	Order of Melchisedek	Heb 7:1-3
6:2	White horse & rider	Word & Spirit of revival	Rev 19:11-21
6:4	Red horse & rider	Spirit of war and bloodshed	Rev 12:3
6:5	Black horse & rider	Spirit of famine, hunger	Lam 5:10
6:8	Pale horse & rider	Spirit of pestilence & death	Matt 24:7
6:5	Balances	Scarcity, weighing out	Job 31:6
6:6	Wheat & barley	Passover, Pentecost harvests	Hos 2:22
6:6	Oil & wine	Tabernacles harvest	Hos 2:8,22
6:9	Altar of brass	Sacrifice, outpoured life	Ex 27:1-8
7:1	Four winds of earth	Powers of evil	Dan 7:2
7:2	The east	Sunrise, heaven, light	Gen 3:24
7:2	Seal of God	Holy Spirit, full redemption	Eph 4:30
7:9	Palm branches	Tabernacles, rejoicing, victory	Lev 23:39-44; Jhn 12:13
7:9,13,14	White robes	Priestly garments	Ex 28:40,41
7:14	Washed white	Cleansed by blood atonement	Ex 28:40,41
8:3,5	Golden censer	Intercessory prayers	Lev 16:12,13
8:3	Golden altar	Intercessory ministry	Ex 30:1-10
8:2,6	Seven trumpets	Feast of trumpets, judgments	Josh 6, Num 10:1-10
8:13 (Grk)	Eagle messenger	Translated saints	Isa 40:31
9:1	Fallen star	Antichrist, an apostate	Jude 13
9:1; 20:1	Key of bottomless pit	Authority over spirit realm	Matt 16:19
9:2	Smoke from pit	Religious, demonic confusion	Psa 37:20
9:3-12	Locusts armies	Demon spirits	Ex 10:1-20
9:13-21	Horsemen armies	Demon-inspired armies of hell	
		Counterfeit of God's armies	Rev 19:11-21
10:1-7	Little open book	Book of Daniel (Biblios)	Dan 12

10:2	Foot on earth & sea	Taking formal possession	Josh 1:2-5
10:3,4	Seven thunders	Secret sayings of God	Jhn 12:27-30, Psa 29:3-9
10:5	Lifted up hand	Oath to God	Gen 14:22
10:9-11	Eating the book	Feasting on the Word of God	Ezek 3:1-3
11:1	Reed or rod	Measuring, judge by standard	Ezek 42:15-20
11:1,2	Temple measured	Church measures up to Word	Eph 4:10-16
11:2	Unmeasured Court	Tribulation saints	Matt 5:13
11:2	Trodden under foot	Defeated, down-trodden	Lke 21:24
11:3	Sackcloth	Mourning, sorrow, judgment	Jonah 3:5-8
11:4	Two olive trees	Anointed witnesses	Zech 4:3,12,14
11:4	Two candlestickes	Light bearers	Zech 4:3,12,14
11:5	Fire out of mouth	Fiery judgment laws	2 Kgs 1:5-12; Deut 33:2
11:19	Heavenly temple	True sanctuary of God	Heb 8:1,2
11:19	Ark of Testament	Glory-throne of God	Psa 80:1; 99:1
12:1	A woman	True church, Christ's bride	Eph 5:23-32; Rev 21,22
12:1	Sun, moon, stars	Glory of God in resurrection	Gen 1:14-19; 1Cor 15:41
12:1	Twelve stars	Twelve last-day apostles	Rev 21:12-14
12:3	Red dragon	The devil serpent, Satan	Rev 12:3,9; 20:2
12:3	Seven heads	Seven world kingdoms	Matt 4:9; Rev 11:15
13:3	Ten horns	Antichrist's empire	Dan 7:7; Rev 17:3-16
12:4	Falling stars	Apostate, falling saints	Jude 13; Gen 15:5
12:6	Prepared wilderness	Preservation place of God	Ex 3:18; Deut 8:1-16
12:14	Eagles wings	Holy Spirit transport	Acts 8:39; Isa 40:31
12:15,16	Serpent's flood	Lies, propaganda of Satan	Isa 59:19
12:17	Remnant of seed	Remaining saints	Matt 25:1-13 (Left out)
13:1; 20:8	Sand of sea	Physical, flesh-seed of mankind	Gen 13:16; 22:17
13:1	The first beast	Antichrist & his kingdom	Dan 7
13:11	The second beast	The false prophet	Rev 19:20
13:15-18	Mark of beast	Triune man under Satan's sin	Rev 14:9-11 (Unpardonable)
14:1	Mt Zion	David's Tabernacle & reign	Heb 12:22-24; Acts 15:15-18
14:2; 15:2	Harps	Prophetic spirit, worship	1 Chron 25:1
14:14	Sharp sickle	Harvest reaping instruments	Mrk 4:26-29
14:14	White cloud	Shekinah glory of God	Ex 14:19,20
14:15	Harvest of earth	Reaping His saints	Matt 13:37-43
14:19,20	Winepress of wrath	Armageddon	Isa 63:1-4
15:2	Sea of glass	Tranquility of God's presence	Rev 4:6
15:2	Mingled with fire	Fiery tribulation trials	Job 23:10
15:7	Seven bowls of wrath	Temple vessels poured out	1 Kgs 7:50
15:8	Smoke of Glory	Blinding glory, permits no entry	Ex 19:18
16:13	Three frogs	Unclean, evil spirits	Rev 16:13, 14
17:1-7	Great harlot	The false church	Prov 7:6-23
17:1	Wine of fornication	Religion, deceptive doctrines	Isa 28:7,8
17:3	The wilderness	Godless, forsaken world	Jer 4:23-28
17:4	Cup of abominations	Evil communion table	1 Cor 10:19-21
17:9-10	Seven mountains	World kingdoms of Satan	Lke 4:5-8

17:15	Waters	Peoples, nations, tongues	Rev 17:15
18:2	Fallen Babylon	Religious, political confusion	Gen 11:1-10
18:2	Cage of birds	Unclean & foul spirits	Rev 18:2
19:7	Marriage of Lamb	Union of Christ & His Church	Eph 5:23-32
19:8	Fine bright linen	Righteousness of saints	Rev 19:8
19:9	Marriage supper	Kingdom communion time	Matt 26:26-29
19:11-16	White horse rider, armies	Christ, saints, angels in victory	Rev 19:11-14
20:1,2	A great chain	Satanic powers bound	2 Pet 2:4
20:8	Gog & Magog	Godless massess – wicked dead	Ezek 38-39; Rev 20:1-6
21:6; 22:17	Water of life	Eternal life by the Spirit	Jhn 4:13,14; 7:37-39
22:1	River of water of life	Flowing of the Holy Spirit	Jhn 7:37-39
21:16	Foursquare city	Heaven's Most Holy Place	Rev 21:10,11,16
22:15	Dogs	Unclean, vile, unredeemed	Phil 3:2
22:16	Root of David	Deity & pre-existence of Christ	Isa 11:1-4; Psa 110:1
22:16	Offspring of David	Humanity of Christ-David's Son	Matt 1:1; Jer 23:5,6

The student can see at a glance that the symbols of Revelation can be catergorized into the eight groupings as set out in this chapter. Revelation has symbolic objects, creatures, actions, numbers, names, colours, directions and places. The student will see that most of the symbols are clearly interpreted, others may be implied by the idea or thought. The symbolic principle is an important principle in interpreting the Book of Revelation.

CHAPTER TWENTY-FOUR
THE NUMERICAL PRINCIPLE

Closely linked to and actually a part of the Symbolic Principle is the Numerical Principle. This was briefly noted on "Symbolic Numbers".

Any reader of Revelation immediately sees that the book abounds with the use of numbers; numbers both specified and numbers implied. One cannot understand or properly interpret Revelation without some understanding of the significance of numbers therein. Again, much of the material in this chapter is adapted from **"Interpreting the Scriptures"** (Conner/Malmin), and **"Interpreting the Symbols & Types"** (Conner).

Numbers, or figures, as used in the Word of God, are never used promisciously, but take on spiritual meaning and significance. For the searcher of truth there is to be found "the treasures of wisdom and knowledge"(Colossians 2:3). And the writer of Proverbs says, "It is the glory of God to conceal a thing, but the honour of kings is to search out a matter" (Proverbs 25:2).

All creation is stamped with "the seal of God" in numerics. God has made man a creature of Time and therefore a creature of number. It is consistent with the very nature and being of God that His book, the Holy Bible, should be stamped with the "seal of Bible numbers". God is consistent throughout His book, and though the Bible was written by various men of God over different periods of time and generations, yet there is manifest throughout all the book the same marvellous meaning and harmony in the use of numbers. This begins in Genesis and flows through each book of the Bible and consummates in the Book of Revelation. All of this confirms the fact of Divine inspiration (2 Timothy 3:16; 2 Peter 1:21).

One of the principles of Biblical interpretation is the Numerical Principle. It is this principle, with its guidelines, that will help the student to keep within the safety limits of Bible Numerics.

It should be remembered that there is a fine line between the significance of Bible Numerics and the dangers of Numerology, the worship and idolatrous use of numbers. The Devil seeks to counterfeit all that God does. Bible astronomy is turned to astrology, the worship of the heavenly bodies. Bible numerics is turned into numerology, the worship and occultic use of numbers. But this should not stop the Bible student from the study of numbers as God used them. If the student does not go beyond the boundaries of Scripture in the interpretation and use of numbers, whether specified or implied, then there will be safety within Divine boundaries.

A. Definition

The Numerical Principle has been defined as that principle by which the interpretation of a verse or passage in Scripture containing numbers is aided by a recognition of the symbolic significance of the numbers involved.

B. Amplification

It is impossible to read the Scriptures without noticing the continuous use of numbers. From the first chapter in Genesis through to the closing chapter of Revelation, nearly every page contains some usage of numbers. God Himself is the Divine numberer, and He has stamped His numerical seal upon the whole of creation. This same seal has been placed upon His book - the Bible.

In Daniel 8:13,14, the saint who gives to Daniel the number of days concerning the cleansing of the sanctuary is referred to in a marginal rendering as Palmoni, "the numberer of secrets", or "the wonderful numberer". These several references show us that there is significance in numbers.

Job 14:16. "For now thou **numberest** my steps..."

Psalm 90:12. "So teach us to **number** our days..."

Psalm 147:4. "He telleth the **number** of the stars"

Daniel 5:26. "God has **numbered** thy kingdom.."

Matthew 10:30. "But the very hairs of your head are **numbered**..."

These verses point out God is in indeed **"the wonderful numberer."** This is more particularly seen to be in His dealings with the chosen nation, Israel. Israel's way of life was governed by numbers. This was especially evident in the Tabernacle of Moses, the Feasts of the Lord, and the Ceremonial and Moral Laws (Exodus 25-40 chapters).

Numbers, as used in the Bible, are not used promisciously, but do take on spiritual meaning and significance. They are a special form of symbol in Scripture.

There are basically two ways in which numbers are to be found in Scripture: by name (specified); and/or by implication (implied). An example of this is found in Genesis 15.

SPECIFIED NUMBERS	IMPLIED NUMBERS
Three years (vs 9)	Five sacrifices (vs 9)
Four hundred years (vs 13)	Eight pieces (vs 10)
Four generations (vs 16)	Ten nations (vs 19-21)

Though the Bible was written by various men of God over many generations, there is a marvellous consistency and harmony in its use of numbers. This is because God Himself is "the wonderful number", and was able, by His Spirit to inspire the writers to shape and maintain the significance of the numbers He desired to be used.

C. Qualifications

Following are safeguards in the use of this principle. By following such and staying within the boundaries, the student will be preserved from extreme or fanciful interpretations in the study of Bible numerics.

1. The first step in using this principle is to recognize the numbers involved in the verse or passage, whether specified or implied. The only possible difficulty in this is determining the implied numbers.

2. The first mention of a number in Scripture generally conveys its spiritual meaning.

3. God is consistent, and generally the significance of a number will be maintained throughout Scripture.

4. The spiritual significance of a number is not always stated; it may be veiled or hidden. Its significance can be seen by comparing it with other Scriptures using the same number.

5. Generally there are both good and evil, true and counterfeit, God and Satanic, aspects in the significance of numbers.

6. The numbers from one to thirteen are the basic numbers having spiritual significance. Multiples of these numbers generally carry the same meaning, only intensifying the truth symbolized by them.

7. This principle should be used in connection with many others, such as the First Mention, Full Mention and Symbolic Principles.

8. This principle must be used with discretion and kept in balance with the other Biblical principles in order to avoid extreme or eccentric interpretations.

D. Illustration (Specified and Implied)

Luke 10:1 tells us: "After these things the Lord appointed other **seventy** also, and sent them **two and two** before His face into every city and place, whither He Himself would come."

In this verse we have specified and implied numbers:

1. The Number Seventy

The first number mentioned in the verse is the number seventy. By context and comparison, we find that Scripture interprets the number seventy to be the number of imminent increase or representative of a multitude. Seventy souls went down into Egypt and there became a great nation (Genesis 46:17; Exodus 1:5). Seventy elders represent the nation of Israel before God (Exodus 24:1,9).

So Christ sends seventy disciples representing Him and the harvest that would come to Him through their ministry.

2. The Number Two

The second number mentioned is the number two. By contrast and comparison we find the Scripture shows that two is the number of testimony and witness. That is, when it is one with one. One against one is division. One with one is witness. There must always be the testimony of two witnesses before any matter is dealt with. This is confirmed by Old and New Testament. In the mouth of two or three witnesses shall every word be established; never in the mouth of one witness (Deuteronomy 19:15; 17:6,7; 2 Corinthians 13:1). One is dependant on the other. Two speaking the same thing is also unity of testimony.

3. The Number Three

The third number in this verse is by implication; that is the number three. By context and comparison we find that the Scripture interprets the number three to be the number of Divine completeness and perfect witness. God Himself is three; Father, Son and Holy Spirit. It is always in the mouth of two or three witnesses that every word is established (Deuteronomy 17:6,7; 2 Corinthians 13:1; Matthew 28:18-20). Therefore, every city was to have the testimony of two witnesses. Jesus sent them into every city and place where He Himself would later come, as the third witness, the completion, or final witness!

The student may see by the above the use of numbers, both specified (named) or implied (unnamed)!

E. Specification

Following is a brief list of some of the numbers most often used in Scripture. Such were interpreted by using the First Mention, Progressive Mention, Full Mention and Symbolic Principles of interpretation. The list is by no means complete and there are many shades of significance that could be added to it. The student should remember that some numbers are specified, others implied. For a fuller treatment of numbers in Scripture, the reader is directed to several publications mentioned in the Bibliography, and to authors who are far more qualified to handle this area. (Bible book names are abbreviated).

SYMBOLIC NUMBERS

NUMBERS	INTERPRETATION	SCRIPTURES
ONE	Number of God, Beginning, Source, First, Unity	Gen 1:1; Matt 6:33
	Compound Unity	Gen 2:21-24; Jhn 17:21-23
	Numerical One and Only	Gen 22:2; Jhn 3:16
TWO	Number of Witness, One with one	Deut 19:15; Jhn 8:17
	Number of Division, One against one	Gen 19; Matt 24:40-41
THREE	Number of Godhead, Divine Completness,	Matt 28:19; 1Jhn 5:6-7
	Perfect Testimony	Deut 17:6; Ezek 14:14,18
FOUR	Number of creation, earth, worldwide	Gen 2:10; Mrk 13:27
FIVE	Number of grace, atonement, life	Gen 1:20-23; Eph 4:11
	Number of Satan's self-will	Isa 14:12-14
SIX	Number of man, beast, Satan	Gen 1:26-31; 4:17-18
SEVEN	Number of perfection, completion, fulness	Gen 2:1-3; Jude 14
EIGHT	Number of resurrection, new beginning	Gen 17:12; 1Pet 3:20
NINE	Number of fulness, fruit, finality	Gen 17:1; Gal 5:22,23
	Nine fruit, gifts of the Spirit	1Cor 12:1-11
TEN	Number of Law, Order, Government	Ex 34:28
	Number of trial, testing, responsibility	Matt 25:1-13; Lke 19:13-25
	Number of Antichristal Kingdom	Dan 2; Dan 7
ELEVEN	Number of disorganization, disintegration,	Gen 27:9; 32:22
	Number of incompleteness, Antichrist	Ex 26:7; Dt 1:1-8
	One beyond 10, one short of 12	Dan 7 – The Little Horn
TWELVE	Number of Divine Government, Apostolic fulness	Gen 49:28; Matt 19:28
THIRTEEN	Number of rebellion, backsliding, apostasy	Gen 14:4; 10:10
	Number of double portion (12 plus 1=13)	Jesus & The Twelve
FOURTEEN	Number of Passover	Ex 12:6; Gen 31:41
SEVENTEEN	Number of Spiritual Order	Gen 37:2; Jer 32:9
TWENTYFOUR	Number of Priestly Courses in Temple	1Chron 24:3-5; 25:1-12
THIRTY	Number of Consecration, Maturity of Ministry	Num 4:3; Gen 41:46; Lke 3:23

FORTY	Number of Probation, Testing, ends in Victory or Defeat	Num 13:25; Matt 4:2
FIFTY	Number of Pentecost, Freedom, Liberty, Jubilee	Lev 23:16; 25:10-11; Acts 2:1-4
SEVENTY	Number of Increase, Represents a Multitude	Gen 46:27; Ex 1:5-7; Lke 10:1
ONE HUNDRED & TWENTY	Number of End of Flesh, Beginning in the Spirit	Gen 6:3; Deut 34:7; Acts 1:5
ONE HUNDRED & FORTYFOUR	Number of Elect, God's Ultimate in Redemption	1Chron 25:7
ONE HUNDRED & SIXTYSIX	Number of Antichrist, Satan, Mark of the Damned	Revelation 14:9-11

As will be seen, only the basic numbers have been dealt with for the purpose of this text. Other authors have dealt more thoroughly and exhaustively with the significance of numbers in Scripture. Enough has been covered here in order to consider some of the main numbers used in the Book of Revelation.

F. Demonstration

The whole purpose of this chapter is to help one see the significance of numbers as used in the Book of Revelation. It is not meant to be an exhaustive study, but enough clues are given for the student to see the importance of numbers and the part they play in the Book of Revelation. The listing has endeavoured to consider those numbers that are clear and specified rather than those that are implied. The reader is referred to the above brief definition of the number.

ONE/FIRST

There is one God, one throne, one Lamb, one Saviour, one city of God, one river of God, one way of redemption for Jew or Gentile. We are to seek first the kingdom of God (Matthew 6:33).

The first begotten of the dead	1:5
The Alpha and Omega, the first and the last	1:11
The first and the last	1:17
Left your first love	2:4
Repent and do the first works	2:5
The first and the last	2:8
Your works, the last to be more than the first	2:19
The first voice	4:1
The first beast	4:7
The first angel sounded	8:7
He gave power to the first beast	13:12
Caused them to worship the first beast	13:12
The firstfruits unto God	14:4
The first went and poured out	16:2
The first resurrection	20:5
Blessed and holy is he that has part in the first resurrection	20:6
The first heaven and earth	21:1
The first foundation	21:19
The beginning and the end, the first and the last	22:13

TWO/SECOND

The second death	2.11
A sharp two-edged sword	2:12
The second beast	4:7
The second seal	6:3
The second beast	6:3
The second angel sounded	8:8
Two woes more	9:12
The two witnesses	11:3
The second woe	11:4
The two olive trees	11:4
The two candlesticks	11:4
The two prophets	11:10
Two wings of a great eagle	12:14
Two horns like a lamb	13:11
The second angel poured out	16:3
The second death	20:6,14; 21:8
The second foundation	21:19

THREE/THIRD

The third beast	4:7; 6:5
The third seal	6:3
Three measures of barley	6:6
The third part of trees, sea, creatures, ships, rivers, waters	8:7,8,9,9,10,11
The third part of the sun, moon and stars shone not	8:12, 12, 12, 12, 12
The voice of the trumpet of the three angels yet to sound	8:13
The third part of men killed	9:15,18
By these three	9:18
Their bodies lay three and one half days	11:9
After three and one half days	11:11
The third woe comes	11:14
Tail drew third part of the stars	12:14
The third angel followed	14:9
The third angel poured out his vial	16:4
Three unclean spirits like frogs	16:13
City divided into three parts	16:19
On the east, north, south, west, three gates	21:13, 13, 13, 13
The third foundation	21:19

FOUR/FOURTH

Four and twenty elders	4:4,4,10; 5:8,14; 11:16; 19:4
Four beasts	4:6,8; 5:6,8,14; 6:1,6; 7:11; 14:3; 15:7;19:4
Four angels	7:1,2; 9:14,15
The four corners of the earth	7:1
The four winds of heaven	7:1
The 144,000 of all the tribes of Israel (Multiples of four)	7:4; 14:1,3
Four horns of the altar	9:13
Four quarters of the earth	20:8
Wall 144 cubits (Multiples of four)	21:17
The fourth beast like a flying eagle	4:7
Opened the fourth seal	6:7
The fourth beast	6:7
The fourth part of the earth	6:8
The fourth angel sounded	8:12
The fourth angel poured out	16:8
The fourth foundation	21:19

FIVE/FIFTH

When he opened the fifth seal	6:9
The fifth angel sounded	9:1
Tormented five months	9:5
Hurt men for five months	9:10
The fifth angel poured out his vial	16:10
Seven kings, five are fallen	17:10
The fifth foundation	21:10

SIX/SIXTH

Six wings about him	4:8
The sixth seal	6:12
The sixth angel sounded	9:13,14
His number is six hundred and sixty six (666)	13:18; 18
The sixth angel poured out his vial	16:12
The sixth foundation	21:20

SEVEN/SEVENTH

The seven churches which are in Asia	1:4
The seven Spirits which are before the throne	1:4
Send it to the seven churches	1:11
I saw seven golden candlesticks	1:12
In the midst of the seven golden candlesticks	1:13
In His right hand seven stars	1:16
The mystery of the seven stars	1:20
And the seven golden candlesticks	1:20
The seven stars are the angels (messengers) of the seven churches	1:20,20
The seven candlesticks are the seven churches	1:20,20
He that holds the seven stars in His right hand	2:1
Walks in the midst of the seven candlesticks	2:1

He that has the seven Spirits of God	3:1
And the seven stars	3:1
There were seven lamps of fire	4:5
Which are the seven Spirits of God	4:5
A book sealed with seven seals	5:1
No one worthy to loose the seven seals thereof	5:5
A Lamb with seven horns, seven eyes	5:6,6
The seven Spirits of God	5:6
When He had opened the seventh seal	8:1
Seven angels with seven trumpets	8:2,2
The seven angels, and the seven trumpets	8:6,6
The seven thunders	10:3,4,4
The seventh angel	10:7
Seven thousand slain	11:13
The seventh angel sounded	11:15
The great red dragon with seven heads	12:3
Seven crowns on his heads	12:3
Seven heads	13:1
The seven angels	15:1,6,7,8; 16:1
The seven last plagues	15:1,6,8
Seven golden vials full of the wrath of God	15:7
The seventh angel	16:7
One of the seven angels	17:1
The seven vials	17:1
Beast with seven heads and ten horns	17:3,7
The seven heads are seven mountains, and there are seven kings	17:9,9,10
He is the eight, yet of the seven	17:11
One of the seven angels	21:19
Which had the seven vials	21:19
Full of the seven last plagues	21:19
The seventh foundation	21:20
(Seven used at least 59 times in Revelation!)	

EIGHT/EIGHTH

Even he is the eighth, yet is of the seven	17:11
The eighth foundation	21:20

NINE/NINTH

The ninth foundation stone	21:20

TEN/TENTH

Tribulation ten days	2:10
Ten thousands times then thousands, thousands of thousands	5:11,11 (Multiples of ten)
Red dragon with ten horns	12:3
The tenth part of the city fell	11:13
A beast with seven heads and ten horns	13:1
Ten crowns	13:1
Beast having ten horns	17:3,7,12
Which are ten kings	17:12
The ten horns	17:16
The tenth foundation	21:20

TWELVE/TWELFTH

Twelve thousand out of each tribe, Juda, Reuben, Gad	7:5,5,5
Twelve thousand out of Asher, Nepthalim, Manasses	7:6,6,6
Twelve thousand out of Simeon, Levi, Issachar	7:7,7,7
Twelve thousand out of Zabulon, Joseph, Benjamin	7:8,8,8
Twelve stars	12:1
Twelve gates	21:12
Twelve angels	21:12
Twelve tribes	21:12
Twelve foundations	21:14
The twelve apostles of the Lamb	21:14
Twelve thousand furlongs (Multiples of twelve)	21:16
The twelfth foundation	21:20
Twelve gates	21:21
Twelve pearls	21:21
Twelve manner of fruit on trees of life	22:2

TWENTYFOUR

Four and twenty seals (thrones)	4:4
The four and twenty elders	4:4,4,10; 5:8,14; 11:16; 19:4

FORTYTWO

Outer court trodden under foot forty and two months	11:2
Make war with the saints and overcome them forty and two months	13:5
Time, times and half a time (Same period of time)	12:6,14
Twelve hundred and threescore days (1260 days – same time period)	11:3-6; 12:6

THOUSANDS

Thousands are multiples of tens or hundreds	
Angels worship ten thousand times ten thousands	5:10
And thousands of thousands	5:10
Sealed ones 144,000	7:4
Twelve thousand sealed out of the twelve tribes of Israel	7:4,5,6,7,7
Two hundred thousand thousand	9:16,16
One thousand, two hundred and sixty days	11:3; 12:6
Seven thousand were slain	11:13
The 144,000 on Mt Sion with the Lamb	14:1,3
One thousand, six hundred furlongs	14:20
One thousand years (Used six times)	20:2,3,4,5,6,7
Twelve thousand furlongs	21:16

In conclusion, a cursory glance at the listings of these basic numbers show that there is great significance in God's use of numbers. Multiples of them only intensify the truth that is symbolized in the number. There are certain "patterns" in the way numbers one through to seven are used, as well as other numbers. These "patterns" may be seen by way of comparison and contrast. It is because of these similarities that some expositors make such the same things. This may be seen by one example in a comparison of the seven trumpets and the seven vials. The writer believes that, though the judgments touch the same things, the latter is an intensification of the former.

THE SEVEN TRUMPETS	THE SEVEN VIALS OF WRATH
1. The earth – hail, fire and blood	1. The earth – boils on men
2. The sea – burning star	2. The sea – as blood
3. The rivers – bitter waters	3. Rivers – Waters to blood
4. Sun, moon, stars one third	4. Sun scorches men
5. Demon locusts plague	5. Plague of darkness
6. Demon horsemen plague/Euphrates	6. Euphrates river dried – Unclean spirits
7. Finished mystery of God	7. Great hail, cities fall – It is done

It will be seen that, though there are similarities, there are enough differences to let them be different from each other. The emphasis in the seven trumpet judgments is upon "the third part" (as seen in the significance of numbers), but the latter touches the greater earth.

God is indeed "the wonderful numberer" and we need to understand His use of numbers!

CHAPTER TWENTY-FIVE
THE TYPICAL PRINCIPLE

Understanding the Typical Principle is also another important key to the interpretation of the Book of Revelation as our comments here show.

Actually there are three principles which belong to the specialized Figures of Speech Group of principles, these being the Typical, Parabolic and Allegorical Principles. Most expositors and hermeneuticians of the Scriptures see that oftentimes there is an overlapping and interplay in types, parables and allegory. The Book of Revelation uses language that is found in types, parables and allegory from other books of the Bible.

However, this is not to say that Revelation is a book of types, parables or allegories, for it is not. But Revelation does use language from types, parables, allegories as well as using the language of the symbol, as seen in previous chapters.

If the expositor is going to interpret the symbols in Revelation, then he also must understand the types, the parables and the allegories of Scripture. The language of the symbol has been considered in the chapters on "The Symbolic Principle" and "The Numerical Principle".

In this chapter we consider the most outstanding Symbolic/Typical (Parabolic/Allegorical) language of Revelation as having its foundation in the Old Testament. For the purposes of this chapter, we will major on the Typical Principle, recognizing that this principle is inclusive of the elements in the other mentioned principles.

A. Definition

The Typical Principle is defined as that principle by which the interpretation of a verse or passage of Scripture containing typical elements can be determined only through a proper interpretation of the type or types involved.

B. Amplification

Webster's Dictionary provides the following definition of the word "type" as being:

1. An emblem; a symbol; that which has a symbolical significance; that which is emblematic.

2. An allegorical symbolic representation of some object, which is called the antitype; a symbol; a sign; theologically, the word is mainly applied to those prophetic prefigurings of the persons and things of the new dispensation, which occur in the Old Testament.

The word **"type"** comes from the Greek word **"tupos"**, which means "The mark of a stroke or blow; a figure formed by a blow or impression; the impress of a seal, the stamp made by a die; a figure, image, form, or mould; counterpart; example to be imitated; a model, pattern; an anticipative figure."

It is translated:

1. Print   John 20:25
2. Figure   Acts 7:43; Romans 5:14

3. Fashion	Acts 7:44
5. Manner	Acts 23:25
6. Form	Romans 6:17
7. Example	1 Corinthians 10:6; 1 Timothy 4:12
8. Ensample	1 Corinthians 10:11; Philippians 3:17; 1 Thessalonians 1:7; 1 Peter 5:3; 2 Thessalonians 3:9
9. Pattern	Titus 2:7; Hebrews 8:5

In summary, a type is defined as "a figure or representation of something to come; an anticipative figure, a prophetic symbol". By the definition from Webster's Dictionary, it is easy to see why the typical principle interplays and overlaps into symbols and allegories.

C. Distinction

Because Revelation is a book of many symbols, distinction needs to be made between types and symbols. Also, because of the inter-relatedness of types and symbols, this distinction does need to be understood. The following comments help us to understand the fine distinction and yet inter-relatedness of types and symbols.

Types are to be viewed as a select group of symbols having prophetic significance and having foreshadowing characteristics. Again, it must be recognized that types do involve symbols, but symbols, of themselves, are never types.

For example: Exodus Chapter 12 provides the account of the historical event of the Feast of Passover. The whole event is typical of Christ and His church. It was historical for the nation of Israel, but the historical becomes typical to the church. However, within this type, there are symbolic elements, such as, the lamb, the hyssop, the unleavened bread, the bitter herbs, and so forth. However, these symbols are not types by themselves. They are symbols within a type.

Another example is found in Exodus Chapter 17. Here we have the historical account of the smiting of the rock. It is historical but it also becomes typical. All this is typical and prophetic of the crucifixion of Christ. However, within this type, there are symbolic elements, such as, the rod, the rock and the waters. These things by themselves are not types, but they are symbols. They are symbols within the typical event. One has to interpret the symbols in order to properly interpret the type.

A Symbol may represent a thing, either past, present or future.
A Type is essentially a prefiguring of something future from itself.
A Symbol has no essential reference to time.
A Type has inherent within itself a reference to time - future time.

D. Classification

The Old Testament has many types which become prophetic of Christ's coming. These types may be divided into four main classifications: Persons, Offices, Institutions and Events.

1. Typical Persons

As God inspired the writers of the Old Testament to write, it is evident that certain persons were chosen to prefigure another person to come. These persons can be seen as foreshadowings in their character, office, function or relationship to the history of redemption.

"Adam ...who is the figure (Grk. "tupos") of Him that was to come..."(Romans 5:12-21, verse 14 especially).

Paul used Adam and his bride as a type of Christ and the church, as the language of Ephesians 5:23-32 clearly shows.

Abraham and Isaac are set forth as a type of God the Father, and His only begotten Son, Jesus (Genesis 22 with Hebrews 11:17-19). Abraham received his only son, Isaac, from the dead in a figure (Grk. "tupos"); the writer to the Hebrews tells us.

2. Typical Offices

God used various offices in Scripture to foreshadow offices to come.

"... as was Aaron...so also Christ ..." (Hebrews 5:1-10, verses 4-5 especially). Aaron was a type of Christ in his office as priest.

This is true also of the offices of Old Testament Judges, Prophets and Kings. All offices typified the offices of Christ as THE Judge, THE Prophet and THE King (Acts 3:18-26; Matthew 1:1; Revelation 19:16).

3. Typical Events

God used historical events in such a way as to be a foreshadowing of events to come. The things that happened to Israel happened to them for types and examples and are written for our admonition upon whom the ends of the age are come (1 Corinthians 10:1-11; verses 6 and 11 specially use the Greek word "tupos"). The wanderings in the wilderness were typical events, though historical to Israel as a nation (Read Numbers 13-14 with Hebrews 3-4 chapters).

The events in the order of creation (Genesis chapters 1-2), as pertaining to the sun, moon and stars, the grass, trees, beasts of the field, fish of the sea, the heavens and the earth - all find their ultimate in the Book of Revelation, either actually or symbolically.

4. Typical Institutions

God also set forth certain institutions in the Old Testament to be foreshadowings of things to come. The writer to the Hebrew believers says that the Tabernacle of Moses was a shadow and example in earth of things in the heavens (Hebrews 5:1-5 with John 1:14). The tabernacle pointed also to Christ, the Word made flesh.

The Book of Revelation actually refers directly or indirectly to many things in the Old Testament. Unless the Old Testament types are understood and interpreted properly, the interpreter will not be able to exposit clearly the Revelation.

The events were not types to those in Old Testament times; they were actualities. However, they become types to us because God used actualities as types, as prophetic prefigurings of Christ and His church. Of course, typical persons, offices, events and institutions may be inter-woven together. This is true especially of the Old Testament places of the Lord, such as the Tabernacle of Moses, Tabernacle of David and the Temple of Solomon, each of which find their consummation in the Book of Revelation.

It is important, however, to remember that there are no types in Revelation itself, but Old Testament types and typical/symbolical language is constantly used. This has to be understood in order to do a proper interpretation and exposition of the book.

E. Demonstration

A reading of Revelation reveals how much language is used of the typical institutions of the Old Testament. The Divine habitations of the Tabernacle of Moses, the Tabernacle of David and the Temple of Solomon were all shadows on earth of the heavenly tabernacle and the heavenly temple. The language of the tabernacle and temple become the language of Revelation. In Revelation we see the archetype of that which was the earthly type and shadow. In Revelation we see, as it were, Moses, David, Solomon and John all meet together. In this book all are seeing the same spiritual and eternal realities. Moses and David deal with the shadow and type; John deals with the substance, the reality. Moses and David deal with the earthly tabernacles; John deals with the heavenly tabernacle and temple.

A consideration of the following things in Revelation show that Revelation refers to and alludes to seven major Old Testament typical/symbolic realities in Israel's history.

1. The Tabernacle of Moses

The Tabernacle of Moses illustrates the way of approach to God. The details are covered in Exodus Chapters 25-40 inclusive.

The Tabernacle of Moses is another "key" to the understanding of Revelation. The language of the Tabernacle of Moses is also the language of the Book of Revelation. Under Moses we have the type, under John we have the archetype - the original of all things, that is, the heavenly original which cast its shadow on earth in Moses time. The Book of Hebrews tells us that the things on earth were but shadows of the real, the heavenly (Hebrews 8:1-5; 9:1-12). Both Moses and John saw the same heavenly pattern. It was Moses who built the shadow-tabernacle of earth. It is John who is taken up in the Spirit to see the real and heavenly tabernacle in the heavens.

It is not the intention of this author to classify everything in Revelation into what belongs to the Tabernacle of Moses, the Tabernacle of David or the Temple of Solomon. There is an overlapping of these things in Revelation. However, this would be a good exercise for the student to do. Following is an almost exhaustive list of things pertaining to these typical institutions in

Revelation. The list provides much food for thought and such could be superimposed on a diagram of the Tabernacle or Temple to bring all into sharper focus.

Revelation 1:1-20.	The Lord Jesus Christ, the great high priest, in sanctuary service, clothed in garments of glory and beauty.
Revelation 1:10.	The call of the trumpet as in the Feast of Trumpets.
Revelation 1:20.	The golden lampstands in the tabernacle.
Revelation 4:6.	The four standards of the camp of Israel; the lion, the ox, the man, the eagle.
Revelation 5.	The book as in the ark of the covenant.
Revelation 6:9-11.	The brazen altar, the poured out blood of the sacrificial victims.
Revelation 2:17.	The hidden manna for the overcomer.
Revelation 2:17.	The stone with the new name in it.
Revelation 2:26.	The rod of God.
Revelation 3:4-5,18.	The priestly garments of white linen righteousness.
Revelation 3:12.	The name of God, the name of the city of God, the new name for the overcomer.
Revelation 3:12.	The pillars in the temple of God.
Revelation 3:18.	The holy anointing or eyesalve
Revelation 4:2.	The throne of God's glory.
Revelation 11:19.	The ark of the covenant, the new testament.
Revelation 4:3.	The jasper and sardine stones.
Revelation 4:4.	The crowns of gold.
Revelation 4:6; 15:2.	The brazen laver, or molten sea of glass.
Revelation 5.	The sacrificial lamb for the altar.
Revelation 5:9; 12:11.	The blood atonement.
Revelation 5:9.	The book of redemption sealed with seven seals.
Revelation 1:6; 5:9-10	The order of Melchisedek, kings and priests.
Revelation 4:4.	The twenty-four elders, the priestly courses of the Tabernacle of David
Revelation 7:9.	The palms of rejoicing from the Feast of Tabernacles.
Revelation 8:1-5 ; 11:1.	The golden censer, the altar of incense, the Day of Atonement ministry.
Revelation 8:2,6.	The seven trumpets, like the Feast of Trumpets in Israel.
Revelation 9:13.	The horns of the golden altar.
Revelation 11:1; 19:15.	The rod of God.
Revelation 11:1.	The temple of God.
Revelation 11:1-2.	The outer court unmeasured and trodden under foot.
Revelation 11:4.	The golden candlesticks.
Revelation 11:12; 14:14.	The shekinah glory-cloud.
Revelation 11:19.	The temple of God in heaven (Also 7:15; 14:15-17; 15:5-8; 16:1,17).
Revelation 5:8.	The golden bowls of incense and priestly ministrations.
Revelation 13:6.	The name of God.
Revelation 13:6.	The heavenly Tabernacle.
Revelation 14 :1.	Mt Zion of the heavenly Tabernacle of David.
Revelation 14:2.	The harps of God, the Tabernacle of David and heavenly Temple orchestra.
Revelation 15:3.	The song of Moses and the Lamb (as at Passover in Exodus).
Revelation 15:5.	The heavenly Temple and Tabernacle of the Testimony.
Revelation 15:6.	White linen, golden girdles of priestly attire for service.
Revelation 15:8.	The smoke of the shekinah glory of God.

Revelation 16:1.	The temple vessels, vessels of wrath.
Revelation 20:1-6.	The Most Holy Place, as measured in the Tabernacle of Moses, 10x10x10=1000 cubits.
Revelation 21:16.	The Holiest of All in the foursquare city of God, as the Tabernacle of Moses and Solomon's Temple.
Revelation 21:10-21.	The 12 stones in the breastplate of the high priest having the 12 names of Israel in them.
Revelation 22:4.	The name of God in the forehead of the redeemed.

The order listed above basically follows the approach of the Tabernacle and lists the articles or furnishings found respectively in the Holy Place, the Most Holy Place, the Outer Court as well as things that pertained to the priesthood and sanctuary services.

2. The Tabernacle of David

A further distinctive portion of truth is that which is found in the Tabernacle of David and the order of worship established there, and from there incorporated into the Temple order. This also has its particular references in the Book of Revelation. That which is applicable concerning the Tabernacle of Moses is also true of the Tabernacle of David.

In Revelation Chapters 4-5 we see the Davidic order of worship before the throne. There is One in the throne (the Father God), and the Lamb before the throne and then the seven Spirits of God as seven lamps around the throne. The 24 elders, along with the four living creatures are there. The elders have harps and bowls of incense, symbolic of praise and prayer. These articles are from the Tabernacle of Moses (incense), and the Tabernacle of David (harps). The harps of the 144,000 singing "a new song" with the Lamb on Mt Zion all point to the Davidic order of worship in David's tabernacle (Revelation 14:1-4). The 24 elders represent the 24 courses of priestly ministry which David established in Zion's worship (1 Chronicles Chapters 15-16). (The student is referred to the text-book by the author, entitled, **"The Tabernacle of David"**.

3. The Temple of Solomon

Solomon's Temple was also a shadow of the heavenly temple. Solomon's Temple shadowed forth corporate truth, embodying in one structure the previous God-ordained structures of the Tabernacle of Moses and the Tabernacle of David. All the truths that were symbolized in the external forms, the truths that were fragmentary therein, all have found their fulness in the Temple of Solomon.

A consideration of the list of furnishings and articles above show their relationship to the Temple of Solomon. The New Testament shows that the church is presently God's temple in earth. Here His Spirit and glory reside and here His people are the worshipping priesthood (1 Corinthians 3:16; Ephesians 2:20-22). The New Testament also shows the true, the spiritual and the eternal temple in heaven (Revelation 15:1-8). All temples on earth pointed to the true and heavenly temple. The Lord Jesus Christ, in His earthly ministry, was also the temple of God and in Him God's name and glory were manifested (John 2:19-21). The Old Testament temple revelation was given to David and it was his son, Solomon, that built all according to the Divine and heavenly pattern, the details of which are found in 2 Chronicles chapters 1-8.

The Temple of Solomon is another "key" to the understanding of the Book of Revelation.

4. The Priesthood

In Exodus Chapters 28-29 we have the major details about the ministry of the Aaronic and Levitical priesthood. The Book of Leviticus gives much fuller detail.

Revelation has a number of references to that which pertains to the sanctuary and priesthood ministry. The garments of glory and beauty on the high priest, Aaron, point to the glory and beauty of the risen Christ (Revelation Chapter 1). The white linen garments on Aaron's sons and the Levitical priesthood point to the white garments of the righteousness of the saints under Christ. The difference in the New Testament order is that the Christian is a member of the order of Melchisedek, not the order of Aaron or Levi. The Levites were but priests; the Christians are kings and priests unto God. This is the order of Melchisedek, the order of Christ and His church (Psalm 110; Hebrews 7).

The ultimate fulfilment of this royal priesthood is found in the Book of Revelation, in Christ (the head), and the church (the body). Read 1 Peter 2:1-10; Revelation 1:6; 5:1-10; 20:6.

5. The Sacrifices of the Lord

In Leviticus Chapters 1-7 we have the laws concerning the sacrifices and offerings on the altar of God. All such sacrifices were fulfilled and abolished in Christ's perfect and once-for-all sinless sacrifice offered at Calvary (Hebrews chapters 8-9).

The New Testament takes these five Levitical offerings and the language of such is now applied to Christ and His church (Ephesians 5:1-2; Romans 12:1-2; 1 Peter 2:1-10). This is also evidenced in the language of Revelation in certain passages. Sacrificial offerings and blood atonement were the only Divine means of grace of averting Divine wrath. No atonement meant that every sinner was exposed to Divine wrath and the plagues of Divine judgment (Exodus 30:11-16; Numbers 16).

In Revelation, grace and mercy, law and judgment are seen in contradistinction. In Revelation 6:9-11 we see those saints who have made the supreme sacrifice in martyrdom, and there their blood-life is poured out at the base of the altar of sacrifice.

In Revelation Chapters 15-16, the wrath of God is poured out in the last seven plagues on unrepentant mankind who have taken the mark of the beast. No one is able to enter into the heavenly temple to make atonement, or "stand between the living and the dead", as did Aaron in Korah's rebellion (Numbers 16). When grace and mercy are despised, there remains only law and judgment. These are the two grounds upon which God deals with mankind — Law and Grace! If man falls from grace, he falls to the ground of law. Grace is mercy, Law is judgment! Man can accept and respond to which ever he wills. But God will deal accordingly to man on the ground he chooses to stand (Romans 1:16-19; 2:1-11; 4:15; Hebrews 8).

The understanding of the Temple of Solomon is another "key" in the understanding and interpretation of the Book of Revelation. The student is referred to the text-book of the author, entitled, **"The Temple of Solomon"**.

6. The Feasts of the Lord

In Leviticus Chapter 23 we have the laws of the Lord pertaining to the three major festival seasons in Israel's history. These three feasts are Passover, Pentecost, and the feast of Tabernacles. These feasts took place in the first, third and seventh months, respectively. These shadowed forth the ministry of the Godhead in relation to heaven and earth, and more especially the church, the redeemed people of God, whether in Old Testament or New Testament times.

The four Gospels reveal that the feast of Passover was wholly fulfilled in Christ. The book of Acts and the Epistles reveal that the fulfilment of the feast of Pentecost was fulfilled in the church, the body of Christ. There yet remains the fulfilment of the final feast, the feast of Tabernacles. As Passover and Pentecost find fulfilment, both historically in the earth, and spiritually in the church, so the feast of Tabernacles must find the same kind of fulfilment.

The Book of Hebrews shows the fulfilment of Tabernacles in Christ and His ministry, especially as it pertains to the great Day of Atonement. What has been fulfilled in the Lord Jesus Christ flows on in its outworking in the church.

The Book of Revelation shows things that pertain to the feast of Tabernacles as being fulfilled in the church. Tabernacles was the feast of the seventh month. Revelation is a book of sevens. The harvest was reaped in Tabernacles, after the blowing of trumpets and the Day of Atonement in Israel's history. In Revelation we see the trumpets blowing, the harvest ingathered, the palms of rejoicing in the hands of the redeemed.

All of this language is language of this final feast, the feast of Tabernacles. A general knowledge of the feasts of the Lord will also be another great key in the understanding and interpretation of the Book of Revelation.

The student is also referred to the author's text-book on **"The Feasts of Israel"**.

7. The City of Jerusalem

The city of Jerusalem was the centre of God's dealings with Israel as a nation in Old Testament times. The temple of God was in that city. The Lord said Jerusalem was the only place and only city on earth where He had recorded

His name. Jerusalem was the place where His name dwelt. This was upon the ark of the covenant in the temple, in the city of God .

The whole purpose for the Tabernacle of Moses, the Tabernacle of David, the Temple of Solomon and the city of Jerusalem was for God to have a place on the earth where His name could dwell. His name spoke of His nature, His being, His glory and presence. These Scriptures all attest to the truth of these things (Exodus 25:8; 20:24; Deuteronomy 12:5,11,21;16:1-16; Jeremiah 7:1-16,30; 1 Chronicles 13:6; 2 Samuel 6:2; 1 Kings 8:43; 9:7; Daniel 9:16-19).

The ultimate is found in Revelation Chapters 21-22, in the heavenly, foursquare city of God, New Jerusalem. It is the holy city, the city that Abraham, Isaac and Jacob were looking for. It is the city whose builder and maker is God. It is the city for which all believers look, for here we have no continuing city, but seek one to come (Hebrews 11:10-16; 12:22-24; 13:14). Nothing will ever defile this city, and nothing defiled or defiling can enter its gates. In contrast to the Old Testament, this is a city without a temple, for, the Lord God and the Lamb are the temple thereof (Revelation 21-22).

The city of Jerusalem is another "key" to the understanding of the Revelation. However, the earthly Jerusalem, where our Lord was crucifed, is "spiritually Sodom and Egypt", and both these places were destroyed by fire and brimstone and the plagues of Divine judgment (Revelation 11:8). Such will be the end of the earthly city of Jerusalem, which is likened to Hagar and Ishmael and is in bondage with her children (Galatians 4:21-31).

The New Jerusalem, which is from above, will remain eternally. Christians have their eyes on the heavenly Jerusalem, the eternal and holy city of God and not the earthly city which is to pass away, having served its purpose on earth.

As we have considered these seven major things, it will be seen that all typical persons, offices, events and institutions find their ultimate fulfilment in the Book of Revelation. One cannot interpret this book without some understanding of the things pertaining to these seven major things. Revelation uses much of the language of the type.

These many references listed in this chapter clearly show that, while there are no types found in Revelation, Revelation uses Old Testament typical language. Therefore a master-key to understanding Revelation is to understand the truths hidden in the Old Testament symbolic/typical structures, offices, persons, events and institutions.

The student will need to properly use the Typical Principle by doing extended analogies and then properly applying such in the interpretation of the Book of Revelation.

CHAPTER TWENTY-SIX

KEYS OF SIGNIFICANCE IN THE REVELATION

Revelation abounds with great significances when we consider some of its most important key words and key phrases. Apart from any specializing in the eschatology of Revelation, the key words and key phrases in Revelation provide interesting thematic studies in themselves. For the diligent student, these key words and key phrases, as in this chapter, provide much preaching and teaching material. The approach is in a Bible Study format and such can be developed fully by a consideration of the Scripture references given, especially as in the Book of Revelation itself.

The contents of this chapter fall into two classifications: Key Words and Key Phrases.

A. Key Words

1. Angels

The word "angel" is used as least 76 times in the Book of Revelation. As seen previously in Chapter 9 (**The Theology of The Revelation**), the Greek word for "angel" is "messenger". As noted in that section, the student needs to check the language, the context and function of the "angel" to see whether it speaks of heavenly angelic spirit beings, fallen angelic beings, human beings or the Lord Jesus as the Jehovah Angel-Messenger.

There seems to be one reference translated "an angel" which is better translated "solitary eagle" (Revelation 8:13. So Today's English Version, Living Bible, Amplified New Testament, New International, Phillips, Jerusalem Bible, Revised Standard and the New English Bible confirm, as well as most translations).

The student is referred to Chapter 9, for every reference to angelic ministry is there and classified into their respective groupings.

2. Beasts

There are three Greek words used in Revelation for "beast" or "beasts". The two major words provide interesting thought.

(a) "Ktenos" (Strong's 2934)

This words speaks of "domestic animals", and is found in Revelation 18:13.

(b) "Zoon" (Strong's 2226)

This word speaks of "a live thing, an animal" and is used of "the four beasts", or "the four living creatures". It is worthy to note that, though the lion and the eagle are not domestic animals, as is the calf (ox), they are classified simply as "live animals", and not placed in the "wild beast" catergory as in the next Greek word. The references to the beasts, or, better translated, "the four living creatures", are found in Revelation 4:6,8,9; 5:6,8,14; 6:1,6; 7:11; 14:3; 15:7; 19:4 along with Revelation 4:7,7,7,7; 6:3,5,7, in all there being twenty references to the living creatures. These living creatures are each related to the throne of God and His eternal purposes in creation and redemption.

(c) "Therion" (Strong's 2342)

This Greek word speaks of "a dangerous animal, a wild beast", and this word is used at least thirty-eight times in Revelation. It refers to the wild beasts of the earth (6:8), but especially to the Antichristal Beast, most commonly called "The Beast". Following are the references to this "wild beast" who devours the earth and causes all to receive his mark, his number and his name, or be killed. Following are the references to this awesome beast.

Revelation 11:7;
13:1,2,3,4,4,4,11,12,12,14,14,15,15,15,17,18;
14:9,11;
15:2;
16:2,10,13;
17:3,7,8,8,11,12,13,16,17,19,20,20;
20:4,10.

A full study of these references unveil the evil character and function of this Antichristal Beast in the last days, through to the second coming of Christ, by whom he is overcome and cast into the eternal lake of fire.

3. Book

The word "book" or "books" is used at least thirty times in Revelation. The following Bible study outline provides material for a worthy challenge. All mankind will be judged out of the books and everyone's destiny is determined eternally according to whether their name is in the Lamb's book of life or not. The references to books in Revelation fall into one of the following categories as a proper study reveals.

(a) The Book of Revelation

1:11; 22:7,9,10,18,18,19,19. Most often spoken of as "this book".

(b) The Book of Life

3:5; 13:8; 17:8; 20:12,12,15; 21:17; 22:19.

(c) The Seven-Sealed Book

5:1,2,3,4,5,7,8,9. Only the Lamb is worthy to open the book and break the seven seals thereof. It is the book of redemption pertaining to the earth, the inheritance which was lost in the first Adam.

(d) The Little Open Book

10:2,8,9,10. The student is referred to the Book of Daniel. By use of the Comparative Mention Principle, a comparison of Daniel 12 with Revelation 10 shows this book to be "the little open book" which Daniel had been told was "shut up and sealed to the time of the end".

(e) The Books of Works

20:12,12. Every person who has ever lived on earth has a book of their life-story. All will be judged according to their works, their lifestyle, as recorded in the book of works. Only those whose names are in the book of life will enter the city of God, the heavenly, holy and New Jerusalem.

4. Church

The word "church" or "churches" is used a total of twenty times in Revelation. In Matthew 16:15-20 Jesus promised to build His church. In the Book of Acts and on through the Epistles we see the Lord doing that. The Pauline Epistles provide for us the full revelation of God's purpose for the church in the earth.

When we come to Revelation, we have the final words of the Lord Jesus speaking to His church through the various local churches in Asia. The Book of Revelation is actually sent to the seven churches in Asia. Each of the seven is given a distinctive message from the risen Lord who stands in their midst.

Most expositors see these seven local churches in Asia as "example" churches, having a message, not only to their times but for all times, right through to the coming of the Lord Jesus the second time. Truth is truth in every generation, and without doubt, the messages to the seven churches are appropriate words for each and every generation.

Each letter is addressed to "the angel (messenger) of the church of ..." their particular city. The Lord speaks to the ministry of the church first. He always comes to the leaders first, then to the congregations. The references to the churches are listed here.

(a) The Angel of the Church

2:1,8,12,18; 3:1,7,14. He speaks to the messenger of the church first.

(b) The Churches

1:4,11,20,20; 2:7,11,17,23,29; 3:6,13,22 . The messengers speak to the churches, to their congregations. It is significant that the word "church" (es), is used nineteen times in chapters 1-2-3. The final mention of "the churches" in found in chapter 22:16, at the conclusion of the book. From chapter 4 through to chapter 21 the word "church" is not specifically mentioned, as God's judgments break forth on the earth.

5. Elders

The word "elders" is used twelve times in Revelation. The elders are associated with the four living creatures. They are seen in relation to the throne of God and the Lamb. They are especially involved in worship. They undoubtedly represent the redeemed out of every kindred, tongue, tribe and nation. They have harps and incense, symbolic of their function as kings and priests, after the order of Melchisedek.

It is a worthy study to follow each reference to elders and see their relationship to God the Father, and to the Son, the Lamb, and then their ministry of leading the worship of heaven. The references are to be found in the following.

4:4,10, 5:5,6,8,11,14; 7:11,13; 11:16; 14:3; 19:4. This study provides many lessons for those who are called to be elders in New Testament churches.

6. Great

The word "great" is used at least seventy-four times in Revelation. The references are too many to list out here. The student should check through Strong's Concordance for the many references. Every thing in Revelation is "great". There is great praise, great worship, great signs and wonders, and all closes with the great white throne judgment and the great and eternal city of God, the New Jerusalem.

7. Hear

The words "hear", "heareth", or "heard" are used at least forty-six times. One of the requirements of a true witness is that he must have "heard" that which he testifies about. In Revelation, John uses the expression "I heard" many times. See these references.

1:10; 4:1; 5:11,13; 6:1,3,5,6,7; 7:4; 8:13; 9:13,16; 10:4,8; 12:10; 14:2,2,13; 16:1,5,7; 18:4; 19:1,6; 21:3; 22:8,8.

The word "heard " is found in these references also: 3:3; 11:12; 18:22,22,23.

The word "hear" is found in 9:20; 22:17,18; as well as the expression "hear what the Spirit says to the churches" in 1:3; 2:7,11,17,29; 3:6,13,20,22; 13:9.

The student is referred to special notes on the expression, "he that hath an ear, let him hear what the Spirit is saying to the churches", under **Key Phrases**.

8. Kings/Kingdom

The words here are used at least thirty times in Revelation and provide a study worthy of consideration. The world is divided into two kingdoms: the kingdom of God and light, and the kingdom of Satan and darkness. All creatures, angelic or humankind, find their place in one of these kingdoms. There comes a time when the kingdoms of this world become the kingdoms of our God and His Christ, and He shall reign for ever and ever. (Revelation 11:15)

The kingdoms of this world, under the direction of Satan, will one day fall. For the believer, there is an eternal kingdom, the kingdom of God. The kings of this earth rise and fall with their kingdoms. There is a King of Kings and Lord of Lords who will sit eternally in the throne of His Father. When the kingdoms of this world are being shaken, the believer needs to know he is part of an everlasting and unshakeable kingdom. This is the truth of the Book of Revelation. Following are the references to kings or kingdoms.

1:5. Jesus is Prince of the kings of the earth.

1:6. Believers are kings and priests unto God.

5:9-10. The twenty-four elders are kings and priests unto God after the order of Melchisedek.

17:14; 19:16. Jesus is King of Kings and Lord of Lords.

15:3. Jesus is also king of saints.

Under the reign of the Antichrist there are ten horns which are ten kings (6:15; 10:11; 16:12,14; 17:19,12,12,18; 18:3,9; 19:18,19; 21:24). These ten kings give their kingdom to the beastly Antichrist (16:10; 17:12,17).

John was "in the kingdom and patience of God" when he wrote these things to strengthen the local churches (1:9).

9. Lamb

The theme of Revelation centres around the precious Lamb of God, the Lord Jesus Christ. The expression "the lamb" is used at least twenty-eight times in this book. John, the beloved apostle, was there when John the Baptist introduced the Lamb of God who would take away the sin of the world (John 1:29,36). This was in the Gospel of John. Philip, the evangelist, spoke to the eunuch about the Lamb of God in Isaiah (Acts 8:32). Peter, the apostle, speaks of the Lamb without spot and blemish, slain from the foundation of the world (1 Peter 1:18-20).

The Book of Revelation provides the final and eternal revelation of the Saviour, the Lord Jesus Christ, as the Lamb of God. Even in the marriage of Christ to His church in Revelation 19:1-6, it is "the marriage of THE LAMB".

Following are the references to the Lamb of God in Revelation.

5:6,8,12,13;	6:1,16;	7:9,10,14,17;	12:11;
13:8;	14:1,4,18;	15:3;	17:14,14;
19:7,9;	21:9,14,22,23,27;	22:1,3.	

We have but one reference to the counterfeit lamb, the Satanic lamb, who is the false prophet (13:11). The false prophet will be cast into the lake of fire with the beast when the King of Kings returns the second time (19:20).

10. Name

"Name" or "Names" is mentioned at least thirty-six times in the Book of Revelation. A study of this theme in Revelation shows that all the world is destined to receive a name upon them. It is the name of the Lord Jesus Christ, or the name, number and mark of the beast, the antichrist. The references to "the name" fall into two major catergories; those that speak of the name of the Lord, the true Christ, and those that speak of the name of the false Christ, the beast.

The churches are encouraged to "hold fast His name", and the overcomers are promised to have "a new name" placed upon them . Note these references to His name in the letters to the seven churches (Revelation 2:3,13,17; 3:1,4,5,5,8,12,12,12).

The godless, Christ-rejecting world takes the mark, number and name of the beast (Revelation 13:7,17; 14:11; 15:2).

They also blaspheme the name of God and those who dwell in heaven (Revelation 13:1,6,8; 16:9; 17:3,8).

The great harlot is named with the name of Mystery Babylon, the Great, Mother of Harlots and Abominations ofthe earth (Revelation 17:5)

Judgments on mankind have death-like names on them (Revelation 6:8; 8:11; 9:11).

Finally Jesus comes and He has a name written on Him that no man knew but He Himself. His name is called The Word of God (Revelation 19:12,13,16). The redeemed enter into the gates of the city of God and His name will be in their foreheads. The city itself has the names of the twelve apostles in her foundation, and the names of the twelve tribes of the Israel of God on her gates. The redeemed of all ages walk through the gates into the eternal presence of God and the Lamb (Revelation 21:12, 12, 14).

"The name" in Scripture always speaks of the nature and character of the person. So the redeemed will have the nature and character of the Lord Jesus Christ impressed on them and glorify that name eternally (Revelation 22:4; 15:4). The unredeemed have the nature and character of Satan upon them for all eternity.

11. Saints

There are at least thirteen mentions of "saints" in Revelation. The world is simply divided into two camps; the camp of the saints, or the camp of the sinners. All are either saved or lost, redeemed or unredeemed.

See what these references tell of the saints in the Book of Revelation (5:8; 8:3,4; 11:18; 13:7,10; 14:12; 15:3; 16:6; 17:6; 18:24; 19:8; 20:9). Jesus is King of saints.

12. See/Seen

The words "see", "seen" (saw), are used some sixty-five times in this book. As noted under the mention of the word "heard", in order for any one to be a true witness, they must have "seen and heard" the things of which they testify. A witness must see with his eyes, and hear with his ears, before he could testify with his mouth (Matthew 13:17; Luke 7:22; 10:24; John 3:32; Acts 4:20; 22:15 with 1John 1:1-5 and Deuteronomy 17:6; 19:15-21). Over and over again, John says, "I saw ..." and "I heard ...", and thus was a true witness of what he wrote in Revelation, as the following references show.

1:1,4,7,11,12,17,20,20;	2:1,12;	3:1,7,14;
4:1,4,6;	5:1,1,6,11;	6:1,2,3,5,6,7,9;
7:1,2,9,13;	8:1,2,7;	9:1,7,13,17,20;
10:1,5,8;	11:1,4,9,11,15;	12:1,7,13;
13:1,2,3,5,11;	14:1,6,14;	15:1,2,5;
16:1,8,13,15,17;	17:1,3,6,8,12,15,15,16,18;	18:1,9,11,18,21;
19:1,9,11,17,19;	20:1,4,4,7,11,12;	21:1,2,9,15,22;
22:1.6.8.16.		

To the church of Laodicea, Jesus exhorts them to buy from Him "eyesalve" that they might see their condition and need before His eyes (Revelation 3:18). For the church to be a true witness, we must also have seen and heard the Divine things and then proclaim such to a lost world.

13. Seven

The number "seven" (or seventh) is used at least fifty-nine times in the Book of Revelation. The full list of this number has been done in Chapter 24 (**"The Numerical Principle"**), to which the student is referred.

The number seven is the number of completeness, fulness and perfection in that which is temporary. Seven is the number of the Book of Revelation.

Perhaps one of the most significant things about the sevens in Revelation is seeing how the "sevenths" seem to end alike, bringing one to the close of this present age and on into the beginning of eternal things, as the following shows.

As the seventh seal is opened, and at the completion of the half-hour silence, and after the fire-filled censer is cast into the earth, there follows "voices, and thunderings, and lightnings and an earthquake" (Revelation 8:5).

As the seventh trumpet finishes sounding, and the temple of God is opened in heaven, there follows "lightnings, and voices, and thunderings, and an earthquake and great hail" (Revelation 11:15-19).

As the seventh vial is poured out, there follows "voices, and thunders, and lightnings, and there was a great earthquake" (Revelation 16:17).

Thus the **seventh seal, seventh trumpet and seventh vial** all end alike with these voices, thunderings, lightnings and an earthquake. These things point to God coming into activity in the earth. Undoubtedly, the fact that each of these "sevenths" end alike point to the fact that all of the "sevens" in Revelation reach their consummation at the coming of the Lord Jesus Christ. (Refer to Key Phrases also).

One other significance, relative to the number seven, is in the fact, that, with all the number sevens mentioned in Revelation, there is no mention of any period of time such as "seven years". For the Schools of Interpretation that teach "the seven-year Great Tribulation period" this puts such to the test to find proper Scriptural foundation for such a period of time this length. As seen in the chapter dealing with Chronology, there is a period of three and one-half years, but never seven! A study of the complete use of this number in Revelation yields much spiritual food for thought.

14. Sign

The Greek word which is translated "sign" is used eight times in this book also. The Greek word (SC 4591-2, "Semeion"), is translated by the English words, "signified", "wonder" and "sign" in the the following references (Revelation 12:1,3; 13:13; 15:1).

It is translated "miracles" in Revelation 13:14; 16:14; 19:20. The same root Greek word is translated "signified" in Revelation 1:1.

The thought is that God sent and "signified" to His servant John the things that are in the Book of Revelation. God spoke to him by signs. This is exemplified in the many signs, symbols and wonders in this book. The truth of this is explained in the chapter dealing with the symbols in Revelation.

15. Songs

Revelation is a book that abounds with songs, singing and praise to God and the Lamb. Throughout the judgments of God in the earth, there breaks forth the songs of praise, the songs of worship, the songs of redemption and the songs of creation. God is a God of song, of praise, of worship and is to be adored, not only for what He has done but also for who He is! A worthy study in Revelation is to consider the various songs that are sung and the word-content in each. Such should be the songs of the redeemed on earth, songs that are sung in heaven.

* The song of the living creatures to a thrice-holy God (Revelation 4:8)

* The song of the twenty-four elders, the song of creation (Revelation 4:10-11).

* The song of the living creatures and the elders; the new song of redemption (Revelation 5:8-11).

* The song of the angels, the living creatures, and the elders; the sevenfold doxology of praise to God (Revelation 5:11-12).

* The song of all creation; the fourfold doxology of praise to God (Revelation 5:13).

* The saying of the great multitude, saying praise to God and the Lamb (Revelation 7:10).

* The praise of the angels; a sevenfold praise to God the Father (Revelation 7:11-12).

* The saying of praise from great voices in heaven at the sounding of the seventh and last trumpet (Revelation 11:15).

* The saying of praise by the twenty-four elders as the seventh trumpet finishes sounding (Revelation 11:16-18).

* The new song of the 144,000 with the Lamb on Mt Zion. No one could learn this song but those redeemed from the earth (Revelation 14:2-3).

* The song of Moses and the Lamb by those who have gained the victory over the Antichrist and his image, number, name and mark (Revelation 15:3-4).

* The saying of the angel which commends the righteous judgments of God (Revelation 16:5-6).

* The saying of another angel commending God's righteous judgments (Revelation 16:7).

* The voice of the great multitude in heaven, saying, Alleluia; Salvation, and glory, and honour and power unto the Lord our God (Revelation 19:1).

* The saying repeated again – Alleluia (Revelation 19:3).

* The saying of the twenty-four elders and the four living creatures, as they say, Amen and Alleluia in worship to God on the throne (Revelation 19:4).

* The voice out of the throne, calling all God's servants, small and great, to worship and praise our God (Revelation 19:5).

* The voice of the great multitude, sounding as many waters, mighty thunderings, all saying, Alleluia, for the Lord God omnipotent reigns (Revelation 19:6).

The Revelation, in spite of the ongoing judgments of God and the Lamb, is a book of songs. There are songs of creation, songs of redemption, songs and sayings of praise and thanksgiving to God and the Lamb for all that is done and for who God is. God is great in both creation and redemption. The language of the songs are full of content, meaning and words of significance. These songs set a standard for what the songs of the redeemed should be even here on earth. Paul says to the churches of Ephesus and Colosse to "let the Word of Christ dwell in you richly; teaching and admonishing one another in Psalms, Hymns and Spiritual Songs, singing and making melody in your hearts to the Lord" (Colossians 3:16; Ephesians 5:18-19). The songs in Revelation are filled with Word-content! Songs and sayings of praise abound in the book.

16. Throne(s)

The word "throne" or "thrones" is used some fortysix times in Revelation. The same Greek word is sometimes translated "seats". The references in Revelation are catergorized here as to which throne is being spoken of.

(a) The Throne of God

The seven Spirits before the throne of God	1:4.
The seven Spirits are as seven lamps of fire burning before the throne	4:5.
The overcomer can sit in the Father's throne with the Son	3:21,21
The throne is set in heaven and One sits on that throne	4:2,2.
There is a rainbow around the throne	4:3.
The twenty-four elders are round that throne on seats (thrones)	4:4,4.
Out of the throne proceeds voices, lightnings and thunders	4:5.
There is a sea of glass before the throne	4:6.
In the midst and round about the throne were the living creatures, full of eyes both before and behind	4:6.
The twenty-four elders and four living creatures round the throne fell down in worship before the One on the throne	4:9,10.

The One in the throne holds a book sealed with seven seals,
and when the Lamb takes the book out of the Father's hand,
all in heaven and earth worship the Father God in the throne 5:1,6,7,11,13.

The kings and rulers of the earth fear Him who sits on the throne   6:16.

There is great praise from the great multitude out of tribulation
to Him who is in the throne seen in these verses   7:9-17.

The golden altar of incense is before the throne   8:3.

The man-child is snatched up to God and His throne at birth   12:5.

The 144,000 sing their song to God in Mt Zion before the throne   14:3,5.

A great voice comes out of the throne as the vials are poured out   16:7.

God in the throne is worshipped by all His own creatures   19:4,5.

It is a great white throne of judgment   20:11.

God the Father sits eternally in that throne   21:5.

(b) The Throne of God And The Lamb

In Revelation 22:1-3 we see that this is the throne of God and the Lamb. The Father and the Son are one in the plan and purposes of redemption. Those who overcome are granted to sit with Him in His Father's throne. This is the throne of God, the Father (Creation) and of the Son, the Lamb (Redemption).

(c) The Throne of the Elders

The twenty-four elders are seated on seats around the throne. The Greek word for "seats" is the same Greek word for "thrones". The elders are enthroned in their relationship and function to the throne of God and the Lamb. The elders are vitally interested in the work of the Lamb and His purposes in the earth. They represent the redeemed of earth, out of every kindred, tongue, tribe and nation. They also sing the new song of redemption through the blood of the Lamb. They have harps of praise, and bowls of incense and prayer. They shall reign on the earth in the glory of the kingdom of the Lord and His Christ (Revelation 4:4; 11:16; 5:9-10).

(d) The Throne of the Saints

In Revelation 20:4 we see the saints who are in the first resurrection and these are raised to sit on thrones also. They rule with the Christ of God who redeemed them.

(e) The Throne of Satan

Revelation also speaks of "Satan's seat" (Grk. "thronos"), and this throne of Satanic power is given to the Antichrist who causes the world to worship the dragon by means of receiving the mark, number and name of Satan in their hands or foreheads (Revelation 2:13; 13:2; 16:19).

The message of Revelation is that the thrones of earth will rise and fall, but there is a throne above all – the throne of God and the Lamb – and this throne shall never fall. It is eternal in the heavens. John saw throughout the Revelation, that all of God's dealings proceed from this throne. What comfort and assurance this was to John and to the churches in Asia, and to the church of all ages.

* It is a throne of glory (Matthew 25:31).

* It is a throne of grace (Hebrews 4:16).

* It is a throne of righteousness (Psalm 97:2).

* It is a throne of holiness (Psalm 47:8).

* It is a throne of judgment (Psalm 9:7; 89:14).

* It is a heavenly throne (Psalm 11:4; 103:10).

* It is an eternal throne (Psalm 45:6).

* It is the throne of God and the Lamb (Revelation 22:1,3).

17. Twelve/Twenty-Four

The numbers "twelve" and "twentyfour" are used some twentytwo and eight times respectively. Twentyfour is twice twelve, so repeats the truth of the number twelve. The student is referred to the chapter dealing with the Numerical Principle for the list of references to these numbers.

The number twelve, or its multiples, speak of the number of government, apostolic ministry, power and authority. The number twentyfour speaks of priestly order and ministry. Throughout the total Bible we see the numbers twelve or twentyfour.

In the Tabernacle of Moses, the number twelve is impressed on Israel's life. The twelve sons of Jacob were the fathers of the twelve tribes of Israel. In the Tabernacle of David, the number twenty-four is impressed on Israel's life. This was in the realm of worship. There were twenty-four priests in their twentyfour courses, and they worshipped the Lord in their appointed courses twentyfour hours a day. The student is referred to the textbooks which deal with these Tabernacles for fuller study on these things.

God's government will subdue Satan's rebel government, and the fallen, sinful and cruel governments of earth. Eternity will see the government and kingdom of God over all, and the redeemed will take their places in the order of worship before God and the Lamb.

18. White

The student is referred to the chapter dealing with the Symbolic Principle in Revelation.

The word "white" is used at least nineteen times in this book. It is significant to note that "white" always speaks of God, of Christ, or of the angels, or of the saints in the Book of Revelation. It is not once used of Antichrist or his followers or of Satan.

White is pure, holy, untainted and speaks of righteousness and holiness whether pertaining to God or His people. Although this has been dealt with in **The Symbolic Principle**, because of its importance, we list the references out here for further study.

*	His hair was white as snow, white as wool	1:14,14.
*	The overcomer receives a white stone	2:17.
*	The overcomer shall walk with Him in white	3:4,5,18.
*	The elders are clothed in white raiment	4:4.
*	The first seal was a white horse and rider	6:2.
*	The martyred saints are given white robes	6:11.
*	The tribulation saints are clothed in white robes	7:9,13.
*	Their robes are white through the blood of the Lamb	7:14.
*	The Son of Man sat on a white cloud	14:14.
*	The angels were clothed in white linen	15:6.
*	The garments of the bride are white linen righteousness	19:8
*	Jesus comes riding on a white horse	19:11.
*	The armies with Jesus ride on white horses also	19:14.
*	Their garments are white line, white (bright) and clean	19:14.
*	All mankind will be judged before a great white throne	20:11.

A study of every reference to white in the New Testament shows that this is God's colour, the colour of His angels, His saints, and speaks of the righteousness of the saints. It is not used of Antichrist or any time ever of Satan and his followers.

19. Worship

The word "worship" (or "worshipped", "worshipping") is used twentyfour times in the Book of Revelation. A consideration of this word reveals that all the world will either worship God and the Lamb or Satan and the Antichrist. Satan fell in heaven because he wanted the worship due only to God. He climaxes the end of this age with receiving such worship from sinful and apostate mankind. He seeks to rob God and the Lamb of the worship due to each.

(a) Worship Of God And The Lamb

Revelation 4:10; 5:14; 7:11; 11:16; 14:7; 15:4; 19:4,10; 22:9. God and the Lamb alone are to be worshipped.

(b) Worship Of Satan And The Antichrist

Revelation 13:4,4,8,12,15; 14:9,11; 16:2; 19:20; 20:4. The severest punishments are measured out on those who worship the beast and receive his mark, number and name. The beast-worshippers will be tormented with fire and brimstone in the presence of God and the angels for all eternity. Mankind finds himself worshipping devils at the close of this age. Satanist churches abound in our day (Revelation 9:20)

(c) Not To Worship Angels

John was forbidden to worship the messenger (angel) that brought the Revelation to him. He was told to worship God (Revelation 19:10; 22:8). True messengers of God refuse to accept worship of men but direct all worship to God, to whom alone it belongs. Jesus will make those who persecute the church bow in submission to them for their arrogance and pride (Revelation 3:9), but true worship belongs to God (John 4:20-24). True worshippers worship Him in spirit and in truth.

In one vision John is given a measuring rod, and he is told to "measure the worshippers" (Revelation 11:1). It is a challenge to all believers to seek that their worship should measure up to the Divine standard as laid down in the Word of God. Eternity will include all that God has planned for the redeemed, and all will have a spirit and attitude of eternal praise and worship to God and the Lamb.

B. Key Phrases

1. As It Were

This phrase is used at least twelve times. It is simply an expression of something that is seen or takes place that is inadequate to describe It is "something like", "hard to describe, but like this".

The references to this phrase are found in the following Scriptures in Revelation.

4:1	6:1	8:8	8:10
9:7	9:9	10:1	13:3
14:3	15:2	19:6	21:21.

2. After These Things

"After this" or "After these things" is also used several times, the references in Revelation being 4:1; 7:1,9; 18:12; 19:1. In studying Revelation, the student needs to see what John refers to, and what events have taken place before there is a change of scene, which generally begins with this phrase, "After these things".

3. Blessed Are They

In Revelation there are seven major blessings on overcomers. These may be spoken of as the "Seven Beatitudes of Revelation". They provide a study in themselves for the diligent student. Revelation is the only book that pronounces a special blessing upon all those who read it, hear it and obey it. The Book of Revelation opens with a blessing but closes with a curse on those who would tamper with the contents therein.

* Blessed is he that reads, hears and keeps the words of this prophecy –1:4.

* Blessed are the dead which die henceforth in the Lord –   14:13.

* Blessed is he who watches and keeps his garments – 16:15.
* Blessed are they which are called to the marriage supper of the Lamb –19:9.
* Blessed and holy is he that has part in the first resurrection – 20:6.
* Blessed is he that keeps the sayings of the prophecy of this book – 22:7.
* Blessed are they that do His commandments; they have right to the tree of life – 22:14.

4. God Almighty

"God Almighty" or "The Almighty" is used nine times in Revelation. It speaks of the One who is the master and controller of everything. It speaks of the All-powerful, or God Omnipotent.

The references are found in these Scriptures in Revelation. Revelation 1:8; 4:8; 11:17; 15:3; 16:7,14; 19:6,15; 21:22. It is of great assurance to know that everything is under His control. Satan and his hosts are mighty, but God is Almighty. He alone is omnipotent.

5. He That Has An Ear To Hear

There is much significance in this phrase as used in the Book of Revelation and the Gospels. This expression was first used expressly by Jesus, as the Son of Man, while on the earth. In the New Testament it is used sixteen times on occasions through the Gospels and Revelation.

Jesus used this in His earthly ministry – Read Matthew 11:15; 13:9,43; Mark 4:9,23; 7:16; Luke 8:8; 14:35. He speaks here as THE WORD made flesh (John 1:1-3,14-18).

Jesus used this expression in His heavenly ministry – Read Revelation 2:7,11,17,29; 3:6,13,20,22. However, we have two additional phrases linked with this in Revelation. That is, "He that hath an ear to hear, let him hear, **what the Spirit says, to the churches.**"

It is also worthy to note here that Jesus is now speaking by THE SPIRIT in His heavenly ministry as head of the church.

The final reference to this first phrase is found in Revelation 13:9. "He that hath an ear to hear, let him hear." What is missing from this verse? (1) The Spirit, and (2) The Churches! Neither of these are mentioned. This shows some significance with relation to the ministry of the Holy Spirit in this period of time, and the function of the church in this time.

One other great significance relative to this phrase is this. In the Gospels the word spoken is always in the plural, "He that has **ears** to hear, let him hear." In Revelation the word spoken is always in the singular, "He that has an **ear** to hear, let him hear."

In Revelation it takes a finer listening in order to hear what the Lord Jesus is saying to the church by His Spirit than when He was here on earth, walking in the flesh.

The prophet Amos foretold a day coming when there would be "a famine of **hearing** of the Word of the Lord" (Amos 8:11-12). And Jesus told His disciples to "take heed **how** they hear", and also to "take heed **what** they hear" (Mark 4:23-25; Luke 8:18). Believers are called to make sure they do not have eyes that do not see, nor ears that do not hear, nor a heart that fails to perceive (Matthew 13:15-16; Acts 28:27).

6. He That Overcomes

In Revelation there are altogether eight promises to those believers who are overcomers. Such provides another worthy study and challenge both in John's day and in the day in which we live. The Lord calls His people to be overcomers, not to be overcome. In Revelation, all are either overcome or overcomers.

The word "overcome" is used more especially in John's writings, at least twenty times in his Gospel, Epistles and Revelation. Read John 16:33; 1 John 2:13,14; 4:4; 5:4,5.

The Antichrist makes war with the saints and overcomes them (Revelation 11:7; 13:7). But the Lamb makes war and overcomes the Antichrist and his ten kings at His advent (Revelation 17:14).

The promises to the overcomers are found in these Scriptures in Revelation.

* He that overcomes shall eat of the tree of life in God's Paradise –   2:7.

* He that overcomes is not to be hurt of the second death –   2:1 1.

* He that overcomes receives the hidden manna, and a new name
    in a stone –   2:17.

* He that overcomes receives the morning star, and the rod of
    power over nations –   2:26.

* He that overcomes walks in white and his name is confessed
    before heaven –   3:5.

* He that overcomes will be a pillar in God's temple with
    a new name on it –   3:12.

* He that overcomes shall sit with Jesus in the Father's throne –   3:21.

* He that overcomes shall inherit all things, and God will be his God –   21:7.

The Lord has provided everything by which believers may be overcomers in this life. He has given us His word (1 John 2:13-14), His blood (Revelation 12:11), His faith (1 John 5:4-5), and He Himself, who is THE overcomer lives in our hearts (1 John 4:4; Colossians 1:27-29).

7. I Know Your Works

This phrase is used eight times, and especially as the Lord speaks to the seven churches in Asia. Read Revelation 2:2,9,13,19,23; 3:1,8,15.

The New Testament shows that believers are not saved by works, but we are saved unto good works. Works before salvation are "dead works", which need to be repented of (Hebrews 6:1-2; 9:14). But after salvation, Jesus told His disciples to let their light shine before men, so that others would see their good works and glorify their Father which is in heaven (Matthew 5:16). Paul also tells the believers to maintain good works (2 Timothy 3:17; Titus 2:7,14).

At the judgment seat of Christ, all our works will be tried by the fire and believers will be rewarded accordingly, whether their works be wood, hay, stubble, or gold, silver and precious stones (1 Corinthians 3:12-13).

Ultimately, all mankind will be judged out of the books according to their works (Revelation 20:12-15).

So churches are to maintain good works, works of the Spirit, works according to the Word of God, and works done out of a pure heart of love – only these will stand the test in "that day".

8. The Holy Spirit

The student is referred to the chapter dealing with "**The Theology of The Revelation**", as the ministry of the Holy Spirit was dealt with in Chapter Nine. However, there are several additional significant things concerning the ministry of the Holy Spirit in Revelation that provide challenging meditation.

References to the Holy Spirit are found in Revelation in these verses, and the Spirit is mentioned at least twentytwo times in this book.

Revelation 1:4,10; 2:7,11,17,29; 3:1,6,13,22; 4:2,5; 5:6; 11:11; 14:13; 16:13,14; 17:3; 18:2; 19:10; 21:10; 22:17.

In Revelation 1:4; 3:1; 4:5; 5:6 John sees the "seven spirits of God" before the throne, and then on the Lord Jesus Christ Himself. Most expositors see the sevenfold Spirit on the Lord Jesus as prophesied in Isaiah 11:1-4. There "the spirit of wisdom, knowledge, understanding, counsel, might, fear of the Lord, and the Spirit of Jehovah" rest upon Him Who is the stem of Jesse, and the Son of David.

Another significant expression relative to the Holy Spirit is "in the Spirit", used four times in Revelation, at significant visions given to John.

It is not that John is "in the flesh" or "in the Spirit" as Paul tells the believers in Romans 8:9. It speaks of John being " in the Spirit" as to eternal and spiritual realities. Note these references for they provide another significant Bible Study Outline.

* "In the Spirit" to see the conditions of the seven churches (Revelation 1:10). There was the sound of a great voice.

* "In the Spirit" to see heaven opened and the seven-sealed book (Revelation 4:2). There was the sound of a great voice.

* "In the Spirit" to see the harlot church riding the seven-headed beast (Revelation 17:3). There was the sound of the voice of one of the seven angels.

* "In the Spirit" to see the bride-city, the New Jersualem (Revelation 21:10).There was the voice of one of the seven angels.

Then there is evidence of Satanic and evils spirits at work also in Revelation. Wherever and whenever the Holy Spirit is at work, then Satan and his evil spirits seek to counterfeit and hinder the work of the Spirit (Revelation 16:13,14). All will eventually be cast into the lake of fire for eternity.

9. Lightnings, Thunders, Earthquakes, Voices

Another significant phrase is that which pertains to "lightnings, thunderings, earthquakes and voices". This expression is used four significant times in Revelation. The use of this in Scripture shows that it always speaks of God coming into activity in relation to His dealings with mankind, as a whole, or with His people.

In Egypt God sent lightnings, thunders and voices in the plagues of judgment (Exodus 9:22-35).

On Mt Sinai, God sent lightnings, thunderings and voices as He spoke to Israel in the ten commandments (Exodus 19:16-28).

Read these references to:

* Lightnings (Luke 10:18; Isaiah 26:9,20-21; 29:6);

* Thunderings (John 12:27-32; 1 Samuel 7:10;12:18);

* Voices (Exodus 9:22-35; Psalm 29:3-5);

* Earthquakes (Exodus 19:18; 1 Kings 19:11; Matthew 27:51-54).

Everything is to be shaken that can be shaken so that God may establish His unshakeable kingdom.

In Revelation we have "thunders" (Revelation 6:1; 10:3,4,4; 14:2; 16:18; 19:6). And again, in Revelation we have "earthquakes" (Revelation 6:12; 8:5; 11:13,15,19; 16:17-21).

The significant things about the four major references to "lightnings, thunderings, earthquakes and voices" is that all end alike at their particular sevenths.

* At the opening of the seven-sealed book, there are lightnings, thunderings, earthquake and voices (Revelation 4:5).

* At the opening of the seventh seal, there are lightnings, thunderings, earthquake and voices at the golden altar, as the censer is turned upside down into the earth. (Revelation 8:5).

* At the sounding of the seventh trumpet, and the opening of the temple of God in heaven, there are lightnings, thunderings, and earthquake and voices (Revelation 11:15-19).

* At the pouring out of the seventh vial of the wrath of God there are voices, thunders, lightnings and a mighty earthquake (Revelation 16:17-21).

The fact that the seventh seal, the seventh trumpet and the seventh vial all end alike with "lightings, thunderings, an earthquake and voices", points to the fact that all these things consummate at the second coming of the Lord Jesus Christ in judgment.

For the diligent student, these Key Words and Key Phrases, in some outline format, provide a rich field of study. Enough frame-work has been given upon which to build some serious studies in the Book of Revelation.

CHAPTER TWENTY-SEVEN
A STUDY OUTLINE OF THE REVELATION

All Bible students should recognize the importance of outlining when it comes to the ministry of the Word, whether preaching, teaching or exposition of the Scriptures. Outlining requires good skill and creativity. Whatever method of Bible study is undertaken, outlining is important.

There are various methods of outlining which may be used successfully. The following approach is a general one in this area. The key to successful outlining is the ability to organize properly the data that has been acquired. No one wants to be stranded with an endless pile of facts and without any proper method of presentation. For this reason, a thorough understanding of proper outlining techniques is most beneficial and time-saving.

An outline is the simplest means of showing the plan of study or presentation. It is merely a means of grouping similar facts. It should not be a struggle to create, but rather should serve to aid the writer or speaker. Like a builder's blueprint, an outline may be changed as the need arises or it may be expanded to include new ideas.

1. Outlining helps in the understanding of Scripture.
2. Outlining helps in the study of Scripture.
3. Outlining helps in the memorization of Scripture.
4. Outlining helps in the presentation of Scripture.

The following outline of Revelation is basic and presents a simple approach for a study of the Book of Revelation. The whole book is outlined in a framework of "sevens", and, the writer believes, without forcing anything extreme on the structure of the book. The student should find this outline simple to follow in any study or exposition of the book. The book is divided into twelve sections with their appropriate sevens and parenthetical visions.

SECTIONIZED OUTLINE PLAN OF THE REVELATION

SECTION ONE

THE SEVENFOLD INTRODUCTION
1.	Title and Blessing	Revelation 1:1-5
2.	The Salutation	Revelation 1:4-6
3.	The Declaration	Revelation 1:7
4.	The Witness of the Almighty	Revelation 1:8
5.	The Trumpet Call to the Writer John	Revelation 1:9-10
6.	The Vision of the Seven Golden Candlesticks	Revelation 1:10-13,20
7.	The Vision of the Son of Man	Revelation 1:12-20

SECTION TWO

THE SEVEN CHURCHES
1.	The Church of Ephesus	Revelation 2:1-7
2.	The Church of Symrna	Revelation 2:8-11
3.	The Church of Pergamos	Revelation 2:12-17
4.	The Church of Thyatira	Revelation 2:18-29
5.	The Church of Sardis	Revelation 3:1-6
6.	The Church of Philadelphia	Revelation 3:7-13
7.	The Church of Laodicea	Revelation 3:14-22

SECTION SEVEN

THE SEVEN PERSONAGES – HEAVEN AND EARTH

1.	The Lamb and the 144,000	Revelation 14:1-5
2.	The Angel with the Everlasting Gospel	Revelation 14:6-7
3.	Another Angel	Revelation 14:8
4.	Another Angel	Revelation 14:9-11

Parenthetical – Between Fourth and Fifth Visions
(a) Exhortation to the Saints	Revelation 14:12-13
(b) Vision – The Harvest of the Son of Man	Revelation 14:14,16

5	Another Angel	Revelation 14:15
6.	Another Angel	Revelation 14:17,19-20
7.	Another Angel	Revelation 14:18

SECTION EIGHT

THE SEVENFOLD SANCTUARY SCENE

1.	The Seven Angels	Revelation 15:1
2.	The Seven Last Plagues	Revelation 15:1
3.	The Sea of Glass	Revelation 15:2
4.	The Victor's Song	Revelation 15:2-4
5.	The Open Temple in Heaven	Revelation 15:5
6.	The Seven Vials of Wrath	Revelation 15:6-7
7.	The Smoke of the Glory of God	Revelation 15:8

SECTION NINE

THE SEVEN VIALS OF WRATH

1.	The First Vial – Boils	Revelation 16:1-2
2.	The Second Vial – Blood in the Seas	Revelation 16:3
3.	The Third Vial – Blood in the Rivers	Revelation 16:4

Parenthetical – Between Third and Fourth Vials
(a) Cry of the Angel of theWaters	Revelation 16:5-7

4.	The Fourth Vial – Sun Heat	Revelation 16:8-9
5.	The FifthVial – Great Darkness	Revelation 16:10-12
6.	The Sixth Vial – River Euphrates	Revelation 16:12

Parenthetical – Between Sixth and Seventh Vials
(b) Three Frog-like Unclean Spirits	
– Preparation – Armageddon	Revelation 16:13-16

7.	The Seventh Vial - Great Hail	Revelation 16:17-21

SECTION TEN

THE SEVEN JUDGMENTS

1.	Religious/Ecclesiastical Babylon	Revelation 17:1-18
2.	Political/Commercial Babylon	Revelation 18:1-24

Parenthetical
(a) The Hallelujah Chorus	Revelation 19:1-7
(b) The Marriage of the Lamb	Revelation 19:8-10

3.	Armageddon – Kings and All Nations	Revelation 19:11-21
4.	The Antichrist Beast and False Prophet	Revelation 19:20
5.	The Devil bound – jailed for 1000 years	Revelation 20:1-6
6.	First Resurrection, Saints judged, Reign for 1000 years	Revelation 20:4-6
7.	Gog and Magog, Second Resurrection, Great White Throne Judgment, Death and Hades, the Lake of Fire	Revelation 20:7-15

SECTION ELEVEN

THE SEVEN NEW THINGS

I.	The New Heaven	Revelation 21:1
2.	The New Earth	Revelation 21:2-8
3.	The New City Jerusalem	Revelation 21:9-23
4.	The New Nations	Revelation 21:24-27
5.	The New River	Revelation 22:1
6.	The New Tree of Life	Revelation 22:2
7.	The New Throne	Revelation 22:3-5

SECTION TWELVE

THE SEVENFOLD CONCLUSION

1.	The Angel Messenger	Revelation 22:6,8,9,16
2.	The Coming Quickly	Revelation 22:7,10,12,20
3.	The Prophecy and the Prophets	Revelation 22 :6,7,9,20,28,29
4.	The Unsealed Book	Revelation 22:7,9,10,18,19
5.	The Final Call and Blessing	Revelation 22 11-17
6.	The Final Plague Warnings	Revelation 22: 18-19
7.	The Benediction	Revelation 22:21

There are many varied outlines of Revelation, and these are generally according to the particular view that is held. This outline is the writer's view of the Book of Revelation and it has been found to be a good framework upon which to build an exposition of Revelation.

AMEN and AMEN

CHAPTER TWENTY-EIGHT

SUPPLEMENTAL – SELF-STUDY GUIDE ASSIGNMENTS

This chapter sets out some Self-Study Guide Assignments. These assignments are based on the chapters that deal specifically with the principles of interpreting the Book of Revelation, Chapters 11 through to 25, making fifteen assignments in all.

It is a principle of nature that "you lose what do not use". If one fails to use their limbs, then in due time one loses the use of their limbs. This is applicable to every area of life. Another principle of nature is that "you learn to do everything by doing it". One learns to sing by singing, one learns to speak by speaking, one learns to play an instrument by playing, and so forth. The same is true of Bible study. You learn to study by studying, and you learn to use principles of interpreting the Word by using these principles. These assignments are designed to help the earnest student to use the principles that have been set out in this text. The book **teaches** the principles; the student **applies** the principles. This is the purpose of the assignments in this chapter. It is recommended that before the student uses the principles that each specific chapter be read again to help in the assignments.

1. The Context Principle – Chapter 11

Re-read Chapter 11 on the Context Principle, especially noting the example given out of Revelation Chapter 1 on the golden lampstand, where the Context Principle is applied. Using the Context Principle for your assignment here, read Revelation 8:1-5 concerning the golden altar of incense. Then draw a diagram having seven concentric circles and place the appropriate Scriptures or words in the appropriate circle. These then become the base for a proper exposition of this passage. The word placed in the first circle is the word "incense", as this is the heart of the passage under consideration.

You should have the following in these circles when your assignment is completed:

1. The Word – "Incense" (8:3)
2. The Verse Context –
3. The Passage Context –
4. The Chapter Context –
5. The Book Context –
6. The Testament Context –
7. The Bible Context.

2. The First Mention Principle – Chapter 12

The first mention of the "Seven Beatitudes" in the Book of Revelation is found in Revelation 1:3.

Using a three-part outline, write a message (minimum 150 words) on this first beatitude, expounding the verse on the three things required for one to qualify for "the blessing". Supply additional Scriptures on your three-point message.

3. The Comparative Mention Principle – Chapter 13

Using the Comparative Mention Principle, do a study of Daniel Chapter 12 and also Revelation Chapter 10. Then set out the parts of each of these chapters that can be compared. There should be at least seven important comparisons. Then see if it is possible that the **"sealed book"** of Daniel 12 is the **"little open book"** in Revelation 10. Give sound reasons to your conclusions whether this is so or not so.

4. The Progressive Mention Principle – Chapter 14

Using the Progressive Mention Principle, trace the references in Revelation concerning the phrase, **"the seven Spirits"**. Then write a paper (minimum 150 words) on what Revelation tells you about the seven spirits.

Follow these three steps of:

1. Observation – What does Revelation say about the seven spirits?
2. Interpretation – What does Revelation mean about the seven spirits?
3. Application – How can this be applied practically to one's life? Use other Scripture references to help you on this assignment.

5. The Complete Mention Principle – Chapter 15

Using the Complete Mention Principle (only through the Book of Revelation), trace the theme of **"The Lamb"**, using every reference, from the first mention to the final mention and develop a Bible study about **"The Lamb"**; Who He is, What He does and What He says, in Revelation.

6. The Election Principle – Chapter 16

Write a paper on Revelation 17:14, especially on the ones that are with the Lamb, those that are called, chosen and faithful (minimum 150 words). Using the Election Principle, provide from Strong's Concordance the Greek definitions of these three qualifications and how such can be a challenge to our generation.

7. The Covenantal Principle – Chapter 17

Using the Covenantal Principle, write a paper (minimum 150 words), which explains which covenant and its elements are being dealt with in Revelation 2:7; 22:2,14. Give clear arguments for your reasons in your answer.

8. The Ethnic-Division Principle – Chapter 18

Using the Ethnic-Division Principle, try and discover what two companies of people are found in Revelation 7:1-8 and 7:9-17. Re-read Chapter 18 in the text to help you in your research. Make sure you give valid Scriptural reasons for your conclusions as to who these companies of people are.

9. The Chronometrical Principle – Chapter 19

Re-read Chapter 19 on the Chronometrical Principle. There we see that one of the controversial periods of time mentioned in Revelation is the period of time designated as "time, times, and half a time", or "forty-two months", or "1260 days" (Revelation 11:2,3; 12:6,14; 13:5).

Some Schools of Interpretation say:

* This period is symbolic of the church era and covers the time from Christ's first coming to His second coming.

* This period is the "last half" of the seventieth week of Daniel's prophecy, the period of the Great Tribulation, after Antichrist breaks the covenant with the Jews "in the midst of the (70th) week".

* This period totals ten and a half years of trouble.

* This period is simply another three and a half years of trouble, and is nothing to do with seventy weeks of Daniel's prophecy, as that period of 490 years was finished about the time of Stephen's death.

* This period is the final half of the seventy week prophecy as the first half was completed in Christ's three and one-half years ministry.

Read
"More Than Conquers" (W.Hendriksen),
"The Seventy Weeks Prophecy & The Great Tribulation" (P. Mauro),
"Rightly Dividing The Word of Truth" (C.I. Scofield), and,
"The Seventy Weeks Prophecy" (K.J. Conner).

After studying and research on these differing views, write a paper on what your conclusions are and what you understand this period of time is referring to. Give sound reasons for your answer.

10. The Breach Principle – Chapter 20

Using the Breach Principle, explain how this principle can be applied by a consideration of man's state in Genesis Chapters 1-2 **before the Fall**, and man's state in the Book of Revelation, **after redemption** is completed! (minimum 150 words).

11. The Christo-Centric Principle – Chapter 21

Using the Christo-Centric Principle, follow the Outline Study format as provided here setting out the majesty of Christ in His second coming as in Revelation 19:11-21. From the passage, supply the appropriate phrases and verses (specified or implied) as in example #1.

* His Mount – A white horse (verse 11)   (Example #1)
* His Titles –
* His Warfare –
* His Eyes –
* His Head –
* His Name –
* His Clothing –

* His Followers –
* His Mouth –
* His Rule –
* His Feet –
* His Majesty's Name –

12. The Moral Principle – Chapter 22

In Revelation 11:1-2, John is given a vision of the temple, the altar, the worshippers and the outer court of the temple. Using the Moral Principle, discover what the major moral and spiritual lesson is in this vision. Write a paper (minimum 100 words) explaining the moral of the vision and how such may be applied to our lives.

13. The Symbolic Principle – Chapter 23

Using the Symbolic Principle, take the Scriptures in Revelation concerning **"the four beasts" (or "the four living creatures")**, and do an extended analogy on each, showing how they, in these references, symbolize Christ and/or the saints. Supply additional Scriptures from the Bible that support your conclusions.

14. The Numerical Principle – Chapter 24

Using the Numerical Principle, read Revelation Chapters 21-22 and make a full list of all the **"twelve's"** in these chapters, whether specified or implied. Write a full summary paragraph on the meaning and significance of the number twelve in the eternal city of God, New Jersualem.

15. The Typical Principle – Chapter 25

Even though Revelation itself does not have types in it, yet it refers to numerous types in the Old Testament. In the Old Testament, the typical/symbolic structures of the Tabernacle of Moses and Temple of Solomon are accounted for in many chapters. These were shadows on earth, in earthly habitations of God, of what the true and heavenly Tabernacle and Temple are (Revelation 15:5). Using the Typical Principle, draw an outline diagram of the three sections of the Tabernacle of Moses, then go through the Book of Revelation and discover what articles of furniture from the Tabernacle of Moses are referred to. Once you discover them, place them in their appropriate positions on your diagram. Then place with each article of furniture the specific Scripture references from the Book of Revelation that you discovered. It would be appropriate to re-read Chapter 25 to help you in your assignment.

Conclusion:– If the student will constantly use and apply these principles of interpretation, then the result can be a sound exposition of the Book of Revelation.

AMEN & AMEN

BIBLIOGRAPHY

Bullinger, Ethelbert W., *Number in Scripture*, Kregel Publications.

Conner, Kevin J/Malmin Ken., *The Covenants*, Portland, Oregon, Bible Temple Publishing, 1976.

Conner, Kevin J., *New Covenant Realities*, Blackburn, Australia, Acacia Press, 1990.

Conner, Kevin J., *The Tabernacle of Moses*, Portland, Oregon, Center Press, 1974.

Conner, Kevin J., *The Tabernacle of David*, Blackburn, Victoria, Acacia Press, 1976.

Conner, Kevin J., *The Temple of Solomon*, Blackburn, Victoria, Acacia Press, 1988.

Conner, Kevin J./Malmin, Ken, *Interpreting the Scriptures*, Portland, Oregon, Bible Temple Publishing, 1976.

Conner, Kevin J., *The Seventy Weeks Prophecy*, Blackburn,Victoria, Acacia Press, 1983.

Conner, Kevin J., *Interpreting the Symbols & Types*, Portland, Oregon, Bible Temple, 1980.

Conner, Kevin J., *The Feasts of Israel*, Portland, Oregon, Bible Temple, 1980.

Conner, Kevin J., *The Foundations of Christian Doctrine*, Portland, Oregon, Bible Temple, 1980.

Conner, Kevin J./Malmin, Ken., *Interpreting the Scriptures*, Portland, Oregon, Bible Temple, 1976.

Jensen, Irving J., *Revelation, A Self-Study Guide*, Chicago, Moody Bible Institute, 1971.

Payne, F.C., Hunkin, Ellis & King, *The Seal of God in Creation and the World*, Adelaide, Australia.

Terry, Milton S., *Biblical Hermeneutics*. Grand Rapids, Michigan, Zondervan Publishing, 1974.

Tenney, Merrill C., *Interpreting Revelation*, Grand Rapids, Michigan, Wm.B. Eerdmans Publishing Company, 1957.

Lee, Paul Tan., *The Interpretation of Prophecy*, Indiana, BMH Books, Inc., 1974.

Ramm, Bernard L., and others, *Hermeneutics*, Grand Rapids, Michigan, Baker Book House, 1972.

Vallowe, Ed. F., *Keys to Scripture Numerics*, 528 Pine Ridge Drive, Forest Park, Georgia 30050.

SCHOOLS OF INTERPRETATION
Historic Pre-Millennialism

Alford, Henry., *London, Longmans, Green & Co*, 1894.

Frost, Henry W., *The Second Coming of Christ*, Grand Rapids, Michigan, Wm.B. Eerdmans, 1934.

Guinness, H. Grattan., *The Approaching End of the Age*, Hodder & Stoughton, 1880.

Ladd, George E., *The Blessed Hope*, Grand Rapids, Michigan, Wm.B. Eerdmans, 1956.

Ladd, George L., *A Commentary on Revelation*, Grand Rapids, Michigan, Wm.B. Eerdmans, 1972.

Ladd, George L., *The Presence of the Future*, Grand Rapids, Michigan, Wm.B. Eerdmans, 1974.

West, Nathaniel, *Studies in Eschatology; The Thousand Years in Both Testaments*, New York, Fleming H. Revell, 1889.

Post-Millennialism

Boettner, Loraine., *The Millennium*, Philadelphia, Presbyterian & Reformed Publishing Co., 1957.

Campbell, Roderick., *Israel & The New Covenant*, Philadelphia, Presbyterian & Reformed Publishing Co., 1954.

Hodge, Charles., *Systematic Theology*, New York, Scribner's, 1871.

Kik, J. Marcellus., *An Eschatology of Victory*, Nutley, New Jersey, Presbyterian & Reformed Publishing Co., 1974.

Shedd, W.G.T., *Dogmatic Theology*, New York, Scribner's Sons, 1888.

Strong, Augustus H., *Systematic Theology*, Philadelphia, Griffith & Roland Press, 1907.

Warfield, B.B., *Biblical Doctrines*, New York, Oxford University Press, 1929.

A-Millennialism

Allis, Oswald T., *Prophecy & The Church*, Philadelphia, Presbyterian & Reformed Publishing Co., 1945.

Berkhof, Louis., *Systematic Theology*, Grand Rapids, Michigan, Wm.B. Eerdmans, 1941.

Berkhof, Louis., *The Second Coming of Christ*, Grand Rapids, Michigan, Wm.B. Eerdmans, 1953.

Cox, William E., *Amillennialism Today*, Philadelphia, Presbyterian & Reformed Publishing Co., l972.

Cox, William E., *An Examination of Dispensationalism*, Philadelphia, Presbyterian & Reformed Publishing Co., 1971.

Cox, William E., *Biblical Studies in Final Things*, Philadelphia, Presbyterian & Reformed Publishing Co., 1967.

Farrar, Dean., *The Early Days of Christianity.*

Hendriksen, William., *More Than Conquerors*, Grand Rapids, Michigan, Baker Book House, 1939

Hendriksen, William., *Three Lectures on the Book of Revelation.*

Hughes, Archibald., *A New Heavens & A New Earth*, Philadelphia, Presbyterian & Reformed Publishing Co., 1958.

Kuyper, Abraham., *Chiliasm, or the Doctrine of Premillennialism*, Grand Rapids, Michigan, Zondervan Publishing House, 1934.

Mauro, Philip., *The Seventy Weeks Prophecy & The Great Tribulation*, Swengel, Pennsylvania, Bible Truth Depot, 1944.

Mauro, Philip., *Things Which Soon Must Come To Pass*, Sterling, Virginia, G.A.M. Publications, 1990.

Murray, George L., *Millennial Studies*, Grand Rapids, Michigan, Baker Book House, 1948.

Pieters, Albertus., *Studies in the Revelation of St. John*, Grand Rapids, Michigan, Zondervan Publishing House, 1937.

Swete, H.B., *The Apocalypse of St. John.*

Dispensational Pre-Millennialism

Anderson, Robert., *The Coming Prince*, Grand Rapids, Michigan, Kregel Publications, 1969.

Blackstone, William E., *Jesus is Coming*, New York, Fleming H.Revell, 1908.

Chafer, Lewis Sperry., *Dispensationalism*, Dallas Seminary Press, 1936.

Chafer, Lewis Sperry., *Systematic Theology*, Dallas Seminary Press, 1947-48, Vol 4.

Darby, John N., *Synopsis of the Books of the Bible*, New York, Loizeaux Brothers, 1950.

Gaebelein, Arno C., *The Hope of the Ages*, New York, Publication Office, 1938.

Haldeman, I.M., *The Coming of Christ, Both Premillennial & Imminent*, New York, Charles C.Cook, 1906.

Ironside, H.A., *The Lamb of Prophecy*, Grand Rapids, Michigan, Zondervan, 1940.

Larkin, Clarence., *Dispensational Truth*, Philadelphia, USA, 1918.

Larkin, Clarence., *The Book of Revelation*, Philadelphia, USA, 1919.

Lindsay, Hal., *The Terminal Generation*, Old Tappan, New Jersey, Fleming H.Revell, 1976.

Lindsay, Hal., *The Late Great Planet Earth*, Grand Rapids, Michigan, Zondervan, 1970.

Newell, William R., *The Book of The Revelation*, Chicago, Moody Press, 1935.

Pentecost, J. Dwight., *Prophecy for Today*, Grand Rapids, Michigan, Zondervan, 1971.

Pentecost, J. Dwight., *Things to Come*, Findlay, Ohio, Dunham, 1959.

Peters, George N.H., *The Theocratic Kingdom of our Lord Jesus, the Christ*, 3 Vols., Grand Rapids, Michigan, Baker Book House, 1957.

Ryrie, Charles C., *Dispensationalism Today*, Chicago, Moody Press, 1965.

Sauer, Erich., *From Eternity to Eternity*, Grand Rapids, Michigan, Wm.B. Eerdmans, 1954.

Seiss. J.A., *The Apocalypse*, Grand Rapids, Michigan, Zondervan, 1800(?).

Scofield, C.l., *Rightly Dividing the Word of Truth*, New York, Fleming H. Revell, 1907.

Scott, Walter., *Exposition of The Revelation of Jesus Christ*, Pickering & Inglis, London.

Walvoord, John F., *The Millennial Kingdom*, Findlay, Ohio, Dunham, 1959.

Footnote:

The above four classifications of books on eschatology basically fall into the various Schools of Interpretation dealt with in Chapter Two – **"Schools of Interpretation of The Revelation"**. For helpful convenience, they may be reasonably grouped as follows:

1. **Historic Premillennialism**
   The Historicist School of Interpretation – Time Continuous.

2. **Postmillennialism**
   The Postmillenial School of Interpretation – Time Unfolding.

3. **A-Millennialism**
   The A-Millennial School of Interpretation – Time Past, Time Unfolding

4. **Dispensational Premillennialism**
   The Futurist School of Interpretation – Time Present.

(There are variations within the above, but these would be a reasonable grouping of the different Schools of Interpretation).